Charting an
American Republic

ALSO BY JUDE M. PFISTER

*America Writes Its History, 1650–1850:
The Formation of a National Narrative*
(McFarland, 2014)

Charting an American Republic

The Origins and Writing of the Federalist Papers

JUDE M. PFISTER

McFarland & Company, Inc., Publishers
Jefferson, North Carolina

LIBRARY OF CONGRESS CATALOGUING-IN-PUBLICATION DATA

Names: Pfister, Jude M., author.
Title: Charting an American Republic : the origins and writing of the federalist papers / Jude M. Pfister.
Description: Jefferson, North Carolina : McFarland & Company, Inc., Publishers, 2016. | Includes bibliographical references and index.
Identifiers: LCCN 2016036637 | ISBN 9781476662312 (softcover : acid free paper) ∞
Subjects: LCSH: Federalist. | Constitutional history—United States. | United States—Politics and government—History.
Classification: LCC KF4515 .P45 2016 | DDC 342.7302/4—dc23
LC record available at https://lccn.loc.gov/2016036637

BRITISH LIBRARY CATALOGUING DATA ARE AVAILABLE

ISBN (print) 978-1-4766-6231-2
ISBN (ebook) 978-1-4766-2740-3

© 2016 Jude M. Pfister. All rights reserved

No part of this book may be reproduced or transmitted in any form or by any means, electronic or mechanical, including photocopying or recording, or by any information storage and retrieval system, without permission in writing from the publisher.

Front cover illustration © 2016 iStock

Printed in the United States of America

McFarland & Company, Inc., Publishers
  Box 611, Jefferson, North Carolina 28640
    www.mcfarlandpub.com

To my wife,
Miriam

Acknowledgments

This book was the result of a propitious confluence of events too long to enumerate. However, the author acknowledges the role chance plays in any such events and is extremely grateful that those events saw fit to shine on him. That said, there are real-world debts to repay, however inadequately. First, as always, thanks to my colleagues Joni Rowe and Sarah Minegar at Morristown National Historical Park. They are two of the hardest working and most devoted preservationists I know. Thanks are due to the 2015 Morristown NHP summer intern Allison Alecci, who assisted with images. The park's fantastic Lloyd W. Smith archival collection is truly a gem and I benefitted greatly from the original sources found there. Thanks to Tom Ross, superintendent of Morristown NHP. Thanks are due to the Washington Association of New Jersey for its trailblazing efforts in historic preservation over a century ago, and especially to former board member, the late Alan Shaw, whose encouragement was greatly appreciated.

I wish to thank Kelly Cobble, Adams National Historical Park, for her assistance with several images. Thanks also to Doug Mayo at the Rockefeller Library at Colonial Williamsburg. Special thanks to Rebecca Romney at Bauman Rare Books. I would also like to thank Jonathan Connolly, David Riggs, and Michael Byrd at Colonial National Historical Park. David Cowen at the American Museum of Finance is a true colleague and scholar. Thanks to my National Park Service colleagues at Independence National Historical Park, Karie Diethorn and Andrea Ashby. A great thank you is due to Debbie Van Buren.

While many had a hand in this project, only one is ultimately responsible for the final product. As such, I take full responsibility for any errors within.

Table of Contents

Acknowledgments vi

Preface 1

Part I. America: Getting Started 5

1. 1781—Mutiny, Government, Yorktown and Paris 7
2. The First Continental Congress 38
3. The Articles of Confederation 66

Part II. The Failure of the National Government 85

4. Annapolis and Alexandria 87
5. Shays' Rebellion 106
6. The Constitutional Convention of 1787 124

Part III. Success 155

7. The Cast 157
   James Madison 157
   John Jay 164
   Alexander Hamilton 177
8. *The Federalist* Papers 183
9. The Foundation of *The Federalist* Papers and the Philosophy of the American Founding 211

Conclusion 220

Appendix 1. Closing Communication of the Annapolis Convention, September 1786 223

Appendix 2. The Continentalist Number I, July 1781 by
   Alexander Hamilton 225
Appendix 3. Putting Pen to Paper: How *The Federalist*
   Papers Physically Came to Be Written 228

Chapter Notes 235

Bibliography 251

Index 257

Preface

One aspect that is often overlooked or lost in the general understanding of the American Revolution is the fact that the Revolution was much more than the military action that occurred over the course of eight years (1775–1783). The social, political, and economic transformations that transpired were just as significant, and perhaps more so, than the military aspect of the eight years of fighting. This understanding is not unknown and generally acknowledged by historians in the academic world; however, it is much less known or acknowledged by the general public. Historians first started writing about the Founding Era over two hundred years ago, yet from the outset the effort to understand the ideas that drove the military action has been difficult to trace.

John Jay, serving in Paris at the Peace negotiations in 1783 to end the American Revolution, hit upon the idea of trying to understand the thinking that occurred en route to independence when he wrote a letter to the secretary of the Congress Charles Thomson on July 19 of that year. Jay described his desire to see a history of the Revolution from the standpoint of the political or non-military aspect. Jay wrote, "it need not be burdened with minute accounts of battles, sieges, retreats, evacuations & etc.—leave those matters to the voluminous historians."[1] Jay had encouraged Thomson to write the history, as he had the best working knowledge, having been secretary of the Continental Congress since it first met in 1774. Jay, writing this letter in 1783, as the Paris Peace negotiations that formally ended the War for Independence were concluding, sensed a noteworthy moment in history was passing and it needed to be recorded. Unfortunately, Thomson did not take up the challenge (others encouraged him too, and he did make notes and drafts but destroyed them before his death). This book, however, will take some inspiration from Jay (as he is a main figure, having been a co-author of *The Federalist* papers) and focus on the governing, political side of the equation of the Revolutionary era. The military story has been told so many times and in so much detail there is little more that need be said. In 1895, historian Herbert Friedenwald wrote an article for the Pennsylvania Magazine of History and Biography. He lamented this lack of Congressional history when he wrote:

> The popular, and to a great degree the scientific mind has always been much attracted by the opportunities afforded for recounting the story of successful deeds at arms and of the display of heroism in adversity. In consequence, the purely military features of the Revolution have received such adequate treatment, from nearly every point of view, that only here and there does an obscure point yet await elucidation.[2]

Stories of military exploits got assistance from countless veterans, before they died, recounting their tales over the decades after the War. Their stories were in turn handed down to new generations and so on and so on. The Continental Congress, by comparison, could hardly compete. It is hard to imagine former members gathering the children and grandchildren around the dining table or fireplace to regale them with the great deeds that father or grandfather performed while in the Continental Congress.

However, as every story must have a beginning, this book will begin in chapter 1 with the military story rippling through the critical year 1781, which began with a mutiny and culminated with the victory at Yorktown.

Yet, it is this complexity that allows us to fully appreciate and recognize the genius of people from the past. More importantly and specifically for this study, it allows us to understand the creation of *The Federalist* papers in their context and situational environment. That environment was multifaceted and constantly shifting and some of that fluidity will, hopefully, come across as one reads this book. Members of the Continental Congress (the main characters of this book) came and went while attitudes and understandings wavered. Finding the common ground was difficult when the ground was sometimes not even there. Finding common ground was nearly impossible when some of your Congressional colleagues did not even bother to show up for sessions of Congress.

Heroes

The heroes of this book are the thinkers—and their ideas—of the colonial, Revolutionary, and the Early National Period, of American history. This period covers about ten years, from 1780 to 1790. This is a somewhat arbitrary date range, but it nonetheless provides a timeline as framework for placing this story within. It has long been settled that the soldiers, fighters, and especially George Washington, are the heroes of this time period and of the American Founding. Without the contest of arms, the pronouncements of thinkers would have little effect; as was the case in the period this study will look at, combat is a much more effective persuasion than mere words, especially during a revolt. Yet, revolt was what faced American thinkers from 1775 to 1783, when the resort to military measures was employed. Still, the first thing the colonial thinkers did was form a congress, not an army. The Continental Army was officially formed on June 14, 1775, while the Continental Congress met for the first official time on September 5, 1774.

Could the Continental Congress have survived the War without the military? Probably not. Without the Continental Congress, could the military have survived the War? Many would instinctively say yes; in reality though, probably not. One of the premises of the Revolution was civilian control of the military—an idea which would surface in the Constitution and in *The Federalist* papers (number eight) and be echoed in the Bill of Rights' amendment three against quartering troops in private homes (which was also connected to the British Quartering Act of 1765).

At best, it can be said the Continental Congress and the military were necessary foils for one another. The debate will probably never be settled—it is hard not to glorify a soldier, and easy to disregard a politician. Still, without those who thought—and fought—for the Revolution and its aftermath, America, had it survived, would have been a far different place.

The Federalist *Papers*

Unabashedly, this book celebrates the United States Constitution. The 1787 Constitution has put astronauts on the moon, fought world wars, permitted slavery, racism, and imperialism. Within the Constitution were (and are) the abilities to adapt to a world constantly in flux. The Constitution, in other words, is flexible. It would be impossible for us to live today with certain aspects of the 1787 Constitution as written.

Where did the *The Federalist* papers come from, and why? What was their relationship to the Constitution? The papers, one of the first sustained attempts at political lobbying in the United States, did not happen in a vacuum. This book will survey the lineal ascent of the story from 1781 to 1788, when the Constitution was fully ratified, to see how *The Federalist* papers fit into the overall equation.

There are many excellent publications about *The Federalist* papers, but they require much of the reader, as most were written by academics, for other academics. Many also draw seemingly endless comparisons to contemporary topics and politics. The study of *The Federalist* papers is important in its own right, and in its own time and context; it needs no reference to today for understanding.

John Jay is often relegated to a less than minor role in most studies of *The Federalist* papers. While true that he was ill most of the time and produced only a handful of the essays, his influence was nonetheless significant in contributing to the production of the essays. Alexander Hamilton actually considered Jay a great catch for the project, as Jay was by far the most notable of the three writers in 1787. This study will reintroduce Jay and bring him into the story, where he belongs, once again.

The present work will allow the actors to speak for themselves, will keep the story in their time period, and will allow readers to understand a development that was recognized at the time by Thomas Jefferson as "the best commentary on the principles of the government which ever was written."[3] The Revolution and the peace that followed were human in making, in scope, and in ending. The actors were real people with hopes and imaginations every bit as big as ours today for the future.

Definitions

There are many plausible arguments as to when the colonies should be referred to as states. A date that is often referenced is the Articles of Confederation period. While not formally ratified until March of 1781, the Articles (they will be covered in chapter 3) were in draft for a number of years prior. In the Articles, the colonies are referred to as states. To make it easy, and since this book deals primarily with the period post-dating 1777 when the draft Articles were submitted to Congress, "states" will be the preferred term and used throughout.

Similarly, the phrase/title *The Federalist* papers can be seen or employed in a number of fashions. As with "states," in an effort to standardize usage, this book will put *The Federalist* in italics (while leaving papers in roman type) indicating the combined collection of essays written in 1787–1788. Finally, quotations from eighteenth-century manuscripts will be generally updated with modern spelling and grammar. Arcane spelling or grammar can distract from the overall content, and for this study, it is more important what was meant than precisely how it was written.

PART I

America: Getting Started

The ending of the American Revolution was only the beginning of the story of the American fight for independence. After the actual contest of arms (after the British departed, arms were still resorted to internally, such as Shays' Rebellion) was over, the contest of ideas and debate began in earnest. Social, economic, and cultural aspects now would take center stage as Americans fought one another in a battle of wills over the shape and scope of the new government. The governing infrastructure for the colonies produced during the War, the Articles of Confederation, limped through the country's first few years of existence. Before those first few years though, the nasty business of mutiny, government, and war, had to come to an end in the pivotal year of 1781.

CHAPTER 1

1781—Mutiny, Government, Yorktown and Paris

Mutiny

January 1, 1781, started like most days. In Morristown, New Jersey, site of a small winter encampment, the troops seemingly went about their business. The predictable, repetitious patterns of camp life however, were about to change; and change quickly.

After the debilitating winter at Morristown in 1779–1780, George Washington was, as his wife Martha phrased it in a letter, "so unhappy that it distressed me exceedingly."[1] Washington himself rode the emotional roller coaster during the eight years of war, and no one was more aware of this than his wife, and, in all ways, his partner. One problem that continually challenged his army was enlistment. The difficulty was to have enough soldiers to maintain the Continental Army at a reasonable fighting level. The disjointed arrangements in the Continental Congress, with each state jealously guarding its own prerogatives, led to extremes of manpower constantly being exhibited.

One example occurred in Morristown, in December 1779, at the time that Washington was arriving at the Theodosia Ford mansion, where he made his headquarters that winter. At the same time that the Continental Army soldiers were filing into the Morristown area for their encampment, state militias were being de-mobilized and sent home. One famous occurrence of this was a young captain named John Marshall of the Eleventh Virginia Continental Regiment Culpeper, Virginia, militia. The future Supreme Court Chief Justice, declared "excess" manpower by his militia, was released and walked back home to Virginia in one of the worst winters in recorded history to assault the east coast. Marshall went on in 1780 to study law at the College of William and Mary with George Wythe before returning to the military later that year. The real significance of this is that as the Continental Army was desperate for enlistments, some militias were releasing soldiers as excess. A unified, national congress could have been more pro-active in such situations. However, that was not the case. The arrangement that existed in 1780 was the one Washington had to work with, and he did. It was against this backdrop that he wrote one of his many requests for new enlistments directly to the state governors, as directed by Congress, in October of 1780, exactly one year before Yorktown and a little over two months before the mutiny.

Writing from his headquarters near Passaic Falls (New Jersey) on October 18, 1780, Washington, in a circular to the states, wrote:

> In obedience to the orders of Congress, I have the honor to transmit you the present state of the troops of your line, by which you will perceive how few men you will have left after the 1st of January next. While I inform you also that the Regiments of the other lines will be in general as much reduced as yours, you will be able to judge how exceedingly weak the Army will be at that period, and how essential it is the states should make the most vigorous exertions to replace the discharged men as early as possible.[2]

Washington continued by sounding his favorite theme—ensuring enlistments for the duration of the War. Many leaders agreed with Washington concerning the enlistment issue. Individual states could be more exacting with their own militia, but the Continental Congress could not be as exacting with the Continental Army. Washington wrote "Had we in the commencement raised an army for the War, … we should not have suffered those military checks which have so frequently shaken our cause."[3] He continued in the same letter, "The intervals between the dismission of one army and the collection of another have more than once threatened us with ruin, which humanly speaking nothing but the supineness or folly of the enemy could have saved us from."[4] Again, Washington lamented the lack of a central, national, coordinated congress, with the ability to raise, equip, keep, and maintain a national army. He also hinted at another central theme in this letter—the Americans (and French) did not so much win the War as much as the British lost it. In fact, the 2014 winner of the George Washington Book Prize was titled *The Men Who Lost America: British Leadership, the American Revolution, and the Fate of Empire*, by Andrew O'Shaughnessy.[5]

Not only was an effectual Congress a constant worry to Washington, but the constant threat of mutiny was as well. Slightly over two months after sending his circular letter to the states, a mutiny occurred among the Pennsylvania Line encamped at Morristown, New Jersey. Strikingly, the mutineers, all enlisted men, found the source of their grievances in the same source that vexed their commander: Congress. Washington famously kept a separate military status as general and dealt with strictly military matters, as opposed to Congressmen who handed the political affairs during the War. He had always advocated a strict separation of the military and their civilian leaders and therefore refrained from overt suggestions on how to do their job; even if it led to a mutiny.

The letter books of Enos Reeves contain a thorough account of the events staged by the disaffected men. According to Reeves, the mutineers stated that their troubles were not within the powers of their officers to handle; "their business was not with the officers, but with Congress and the Governor and Council of State."[6] Regardless of the intentions, Washington, in a fit of revenge, ordered Robert Howe, whom he sent to deal with the mutiny, to execute "a few of the most active and most incendiary leaders."[7] Washington knew the soldiers had legitimate concerns, and knew they directed it towards the proper recipient—Congress—yet he felt compelled to make a "living" example out of "a few" of those bold enough to state their case. Washington wrote to Philip Schulyer, father-in-law of Alexander Hamilton, that "the event, which I have long dreaded would be the consequence of keeping the Army without pay, clothing, and (frequently without) provisions, has at length come to pass ... declaring it to be their intention to go to Congress, and demand a redress of their grievances."[8] Knowing the anguish of his men, he still felt the need to sacrifice "a few."[9]

Some members of Congress saw the mutiny for what it was—a desperate measure by desperate men who had fulfilled their obligations. John Witherspoon, the Enlightenment influenced leader of the College of New Jersey at Princeton, in writing to the President of Congress, reported that "It appears from all accounts that they [the soldiers] have behaved with surprising regularity in all respects (their revolt excepted) and seem disappointed that Mr. Reed [President of Pennsylvania] did not proceed and trust himself to them [at a meeting in Princeton between the mutineers and the leaders of Congress and Pennsylvania]."[10]

The mutiny had a positive impact overall as the troops did receive a list of agreements to address their grievances. Joseph Reed, President of Pennsylvania, and General James Potter, of the Council of Pennsylvania, carried out negotiations within a week of the actual start of the mutiny. Instead of heading to Philadelphia to confront Congress as planned, the mutineers agreed to stop at Princeton and held negotiations there. The Journals of the Continental Congress on January 24, 1781, record:

> The Committee of Congress and of the Council [of Pennsylvania] agreed upon the measures to be pursued by them in conjunction and in particular, that not only

everything justly due to the soldiers of the Pennsylvania line should be granted, but that a construction favorable to them should be put upon the form of enlistment....

The Committee received undoubted information, that the soldiers during their march had observed very strict order, and had done very little damage to the inhabitants in passing through the Country....[11]

It was not just Americans who saw Congress as inept, petty, weak, and out of touch. At the end of January 1781, a month after the mutiny began, and with Lord Cornwallis wreaking havoc on the Southern States, a mocking bit of doggerel meant to represent a Last Will and Testament was published by a Loyalist in New York.[12] It ran in the *Royal Gazette* and rather than invoking God, as most wills of the time did, it invoked the Devil. The point of the piece was to yet again defame Congress. In less than one month, at the beginning of 1781, a year that would end with Britain defeated, Congress had been castigated for its weakness and inability to govern by mutineers, Washington, and now the Loyalists. The Articles of Confederation still were in draft and would not be ratified until March 1. Ironically, the day before the piece appeared in the *Royal Gazette*, Maryland agreed to join the Confederation of States, thus assuring the passage of the Articles of Confederation and the signing of them into effect creating America's first national government. Thus, in fact, Congress revived itself, on paper anyway.

Congress seemingly had nowhere to turn for support or sympathy. It had created its own ineffectualness by imposing such narrow parameters on its power. Jealous of their own prerogatives, and fearful of creating another national power too closely similar to the one they hoped to be independent from, the colonists set the stage for a near breakdown of civil authority. Not that anarchy threatened, but a loss of a national voice loomed. The members of the Congress were certainly aware of the feelings that people had towards them.

James Duane, a member of Congress from upstate New York, commented on the motivations of the mutineers, which, whatever their actions, were still patriots:

The insurrection of the Pennsylvania line, however deeply to be regretted, was accompanied by circumstance which afford some consolation. The enemy at New York on receiving the information were elated beyond all bounds, and gave way to the most extravagant expectations: [yet quite quickly] they were sunk into dejection; and sullen silence succeeded their short lived triumph![13]

The British clearly thought the mutineers were willing to desert, but that was certainly not the case. General Henry Clinton, the British commander in New York, was initially thrilled when he heard of the mutiny. In fact, he sent a spy with a guide to try and negotiate a mass desertion. The two British agents, when they arrived at the mutineer's camp, were instead taken into custody and turned over to General Anthony Wayne, commander of the Pennsylvania Line who was with his troops throughout the mutiny (although he was not among those taking part and yet not a prisoner either). Wayne hastily tried the two, and had them executed without delay.

Connecticut Congressman Jesse Root wrote to Governor Jonathan Trumbull on January 8, 1781, less than a week after the mutiny began. He was very succinct as to the need for a more powerful, national government:

> Congress must exercise the proper powers and establish all the necessary executive boards and offices; and as the wealth of a nation is the aggregate wealth of its citizens, the spring of industry, and economy the prospect of advantages, which prospect will be more or less operative according to the opinion the people have of the justice of the government under which they live....[14]

James Duane (and by extension Congress itself) was certainly not unaware that their fractious operations had taken a toll after its nearly seven years of existence. Duane, in his letter to Washington quoted above, added:

> The day is at length arrived when dangers and distresses have opened the eyes of the people and they perceive the want of a common head to draw forth in some just proportion the resources of the several branches of the federal union. They perceive that the deliberate power exercised by states individually over the Acts of Congress must terminate in the common ruin; and the legislature, however reluctantly, must resign a portion of their authority to the national representative, or cease to be legislatures.[15]

No doubt other members of Congress disagreed with Duane's assessment of the situation as he described it in this letter to Washington. Still, it is fair to say, opinion was in Duane's favor; even today, the consensus in ranking the effectiveness of the Continental Congress is reflective of this line of thought which saw, and sees, the role of a national Congress during the War as having been greatly constricted by the demands of the states.

One of the best brief contemporary accounts of the mutiny was by Congressman John Sullivan to the minister of France, the Chevalier de la Luzerne, written on January 13, 1781, just after an agreement to conclude the affair. Sullivan wrote:

> Many of the men were held by enlistments which expressed the time of service to be for three years or during the war. As the three years began to expire about the first of January they inquired of their officers whether they were to expect their discharges at the end of that period. The officers in general supposed the term of enlistment was not to expire but with the war. This construction gave them much uneasiness which was increased by some arrearages of pay which they were to have received from the state....
>
> The affair was conducted with so much secrecy that the officers had not the most distant suspicion of it till the evening of the first of January.... The soldiers showed no

disposition to injure their officers, though some who were intoxicated with liquor discharged their muskets, killed one officer and wounded three or four.... The inhabitants say that on their march they never suffered the soldiers to enter their houses, even for water; nor was any article taken from them during their march.... They said they were only seeking a redress of grievances, which when obtained they would cheerfully return to their duty.... The committee of Congress have appointed Commissioners to determine respecting their enlistments, to discharge such as are entitled thereto and to give them the necessary certificates....[16]

Further Unrest

Enlisted soldiers were not the only military members to mutiny; they were, however, the only ones who faced death for doing so. Two years after the Pennsylvania Line mutiny, on January 1, 1783, Gouverneur Morris wrote to John Jay about another army disturbance. Morris, serving in the Continental Congress, in a mixture of cipher and traditional wording, informed Jay that numerous officers from several state units were "now here with a petition to Congress from the Army for pay."[17] This was not the revolt of the Pennsylvania Line, but it was for all intents and purposes demanding what the enlisted soldiers demanded—pay. Morris certainly knew this and wanted to avoid a repeat of what transpired two years earlier. The big difference from January 1, 1781, and January 1, 1783, was that the fighting was over (however, the Paris Peace Treaty would not be signed until November 1783). Morris lamented in cipher to Jay that, "It is, however, a most melancholy consideration that a people should require so much of experience before they will be wise."[18] To Morris, he was perplexed as to why, having already experienced one mutiny over pay, the United States had not put in place legislation to ensure funds were available to ensure the military was paid. This lack of funding, and the means to raise it, were much larger issues plaguing the United States during and after the war and directly factored into the Constitution.

A few weeks later on January 28, 1783, during debates in Congress, James Madison made the following entry in his personal notes on congressional discussion:

> It ought to be carefully remembered that this subject [military back pay] was brought before Congress by a very solemn appeal from the army to the justice and gratitude of their country.... The patience of the army has been equal to their bravery, but that patience must have its limits; and the result of despair cannot be foreseen, nor ought it to be risked.[19]

All told, 1781, prior to Yorktown, was a year full of unmet expectations, high hopes, and low accomplishments. Two major events proved significant for the topic of this study though. The Pennsylvania Line mutiny and the formal approval of the Articles of Confederation both pointed towards a future with a much stronger central, national, government. If the united states were to survive, the way forward was clearly through a stronger union of the states. The united states must become the United States. However, in the summer of 1781, that concern, while much more pressing, was still in the future. The fall campaign was shaping up as the hot months rolled by and Yorktown seemed ever more likely to be factoring into the immediate battle plans of Generals Washington and Rochambeau.

Yorktown

The big gun made a deafening BOOM! Fire and smoke belched from the cannon tube as George Washington righted himself after turning away and ducking after personally placing a portfire on the touch hole, igniting the powder. The cannonball itself, after exiting the tube at around 500 miles per hour, is believed to have caused some slight damage after landing behind enemy lines.[20] The shot's real significance, though, like a fiery messenger, was what the ball, and the sound, meant; there could be little doubt what that message was. The ball and the boom had made their point. The battle, and whatever fate allowed following, was to commence.

When George Washington ceremoniously began the battle of Yorktown in 1781 by firing the first American cannon, signaling the beginning of the bombardment that would culminate in Cornwallis' surrender, little did he know that he was also signaling the beginning of a process that would see the independent colonies move from a confederation to a republic—from the united states to the United States. Washington's action, symbolic though it was, ignited more than the black powder needed to propel a fourteen-pound ball with lethal force across a battlefield. He had ignited as well the passions, the fears, the hopes, and the commitments that would play out over the next almost ten years as the new states struggled to craft a government to replace the one they had overthrown—the only one they had ever known. It would be well that the man who ignited this fury would ultimately someday lead the new government. The process to get to that point would be long and difficult. He would have many fellow travelers. However, at the time Washington fired that cannon, there was little to offer that the end was near. He certainly was not planning or thinking about a new government.

George Washington was probably not conscious of the fact that his cannon shot signaling the end of British control of North America could likely be heard in nearby Jamestown, Virginia, across the peninsula from Yorktown. Jamestown, of course, was the site of the first permanent English (Virginia Company) settlement (1607) and the first representative government in North America (1619). Now, in 1781, the British world in North America would come to an end just twenty miles from where it began. Their world would end as violently as it began one hundred and seventy-four years earlier (which included cannibalism, as recent archaeologic studies have discovered).[21] The seat of England's greatest colony sat front row for Britain's greatest defeat. Indeed, it was not known immediately after Yorktown that this was the end. News of the defeat did not reach London until November 25, and it was not until February 27, 1782, that the House of Commons voted to end hostilities. The new Prime Minister (a former Prime Minister, serving from 1765 to 1766), Lord Rockingham, was committed to a peace settlement with the Americans, although it may not have been exactly what the Americans had envisioned.

For now, October of 1781, George Washington had his hands full dealing with the British and coordinating with the French. The opening cannon shot on October 9 would lead ultimately to the British surrender under Cornwallis on October 19, 1781, and the effective end of the American War for Independence. Cornwallis surrendered his army, but the War formally dragged on almost another two years until the Treaty of Paris was officially signed on September 3, 1783. For the two years of quasi-war after Yorktown, the new states could still hide behind the ineffectual Articles of Confederation as their outline of government.

Washington had no reason to think about the future much beyond the battle. He certainly knew he had the numerical advantage and the naval advantage with the French Admiral de Grasse in control of the Chesapeake Bay. Lord Cornwallis, having spent the summer imparting damage on the states (the colonies started to refer to themselves as states by 1777) of North and South Carolina and Virginia, and trying to figure out if he should be attacking Philadelphia or Rhode Island next, had turned his army toward Yorktown and the coast for resupply and regrouping after its successful campaign. Washington, with his Army outside New York in April 1781, had little reason to think the end of the war was near.

There is little to show that Washington saw Yorktown as anything except another battle; momentous, given its potential size, but only a battle. He certainly knew he possessed some great advantages this time around. His troop strength was one of the best overall during the entire war thanks

1. 1781—Mutiny, Government, Yorktown and Paris 15

to the French contingents. While these proved opportune for him, they were no guarantee.

For Washington, Yorktown represented something akin to the alignment of the planets astrologers point to, indicating an expedient omen. The French Army and Navy were at his disposal, and more importantly, the British high command in North America was in disarray. British Generals Clinton and Cornwallis were not communicating well. When they did communicate, it was still confused and full of misunderstandings. Finally, British Admirals Hood and Graves were no match for the French Admiral de Grasse and his fleet.

Cornwallis

While mutiny and political turmoil raged in the Northern states in 1781, the British were laying waste to several Southern States, inflicting terrible damage to property and life. Georgia, Florida, Virginia, and North and South Carolina all experienced the War firsthand. With the War at a standstill in the north, the British saw their best chance was to step up the offense where they could. The British strategy overall was scattered and hampered by poor communications among the commanding generals. By July 1781, they were already looking to Yorktown, Virginia, as a possible staging and re-supply site due to the deep-water ports available for the large British ships. Situated inland from the Chesapeake Bay, it seemed an ideal spot for resupply and recouping after an arduous, though successful, summer.

In retrospect, the summer of 1781 provided an overview of how the War would lead inevitably to Yorktown in the fall. Benedict Arnold, now serving with the British, began the year raiding in Virginia. Cornwallis advanced in North Carolina, while the Americans won a victory at Cowpens in South Carolina. Finally, Cornwallis retreated to Wilmington, North Carolina, on the coast, after his costly victory at Guilford Courthouse. By the end of April 1781, Cornwallis had arrived in Virginia in an attempt to disrupt American supply routes into the south—he would not leave Virginia until October 1781, after Yorktown, and no longer a commanding general.

With Cornwallis in Virginia, now combined with Arnold's forces, they envisioned a massive wedge forming to split America asunder between north and south. In May Washington and the French general Rochambeau met in Connecticut to organize operations against the British under their

Commander-in-Chief General Henry Clinton in New York. Clinton ultimately ordered Cornwallis to establish a base near an opening to the Chesapeake Bay, and on August 2, 1781, he chose Yorktown as his headquarters. Things were beginning to fall into place for the Americans, as there began a series of propitious events which would prove unstoppable, and Cornwallis, as yet, was none the wiser. Washington, learning of a French fleet under de Grasse sailing from the West Indies to the Chesapeake, ordered the combined American and French armies to head south to Virginia. On July 12, 1781, James Roberston—civil governor of New York for the British—wrote to William Knox about intercepted correspondence indicating Washington had plans to move his army to Virginia:

> It has been known for some weeks by intercepted letters and otherwise that Washington is forming a plan for the campaign with the French general's proposal to relieve Virginia by a direct move to the Chesapeake, with, all the French land and naval forces, that Rochambeau opposed this, because he judged the French sea forces inferior to ours, and the season destructive to any troops that attempt to operate in Virginia in the hot months.[22]

Congress too was worried about the Southern theater during the spring of 1781. In fact, as early as February 1781, Congress had ordered "that all the Continental Troops, from Pennsylvania to Georgia inclusive, are to compose the southern Army."[23] In this letter, the President of Congress Samuel Huntington, in writing to Washington, continued, "Congress deemed themselves under a necessity of adopting the measure of ordering the Pennsylvania Line [the one that mutinied in January] to the southward without consulting your Excellency, from the late intelligence received from that quarter."[24]

By September 1, nearly all was in place in Yorktown for the Americans—save Washington and Rochambeau. General Lafayette and Admiral de Grasse were within striking distance. French soldiers were in Jamestown across the peninsula from Yorktown awaiting orders to advance. In fact, Lafayette at the time had more troops under him than did Cornwallis, and Washington and Rochambeau had yet to arrive. It was clear the French could have had Cornwallis before Washington ever arrived. However, it was his war, and his country. So, they waited. The noose tightened when the French fleet defeated the British on September 5, severing their supply lines and leaving Cornwallis few, if any, options. After six years of bloodshed, events truly seemed to be coalescing in Washington's favor. Yet, the British were not about to let this occur without trying to upset events.

Cornwallis Arrives at Yorktown

Cornwallis arrived at Yorktown on August 1, 1781. Lafayette had been shadowing Cornwallis for some weeks and realized probably sooner than Washington that if Cornwallis remained at Yorktown, and Admiral de Grasse could control the Chesapeake, Cornwallis had few alternatives once Washington and Rochambeau arrived. Lafayette, as ever, was the enthusiastic leader Washington relied upon to keep his spirits up—and in this evolving scenario, Lafayette did not let him down.

Cornwallis had settled on Yorktown as a headquarters due to the availability of the deep harbors in the region south along the York River. This would allow easy resupply to his troops and also a place of refuge for the larger warships operating against the Americans and French. Cornwallis, according to Lafayette's spies, seemed secure in his strength, position, and certainty. Historian Burke Davis, in a book devoted to the Yorktown campaign, wrote:

> The Earl's [Cornwallis] moves were unhurried, almost languid, as if he were a victim of the heat, until the third week of August when he brought the last of his troops to Yorktown. He explained to New York [General Henry Clinton, Cornwallis' commander] that he was fortifying not because he expected an attack but only to hold open a port [for] the fleet....[25]

At the end of August Cornwallis had the first indication that the waters of the Chesapeake might not be as British as he had imagined. The British ship *Guadeloupe* undertook a reconnoitering upon reports of unidentified ships at the mouth of the York River. Their reports back to Cornwallis caused alarm—the ships in the Bay were French. On August 31, Cornwallis wrote to General Clinton in New York that the French were in the Chesapeake. Cornwallis, in what has become one of the greatest "what ifs" of the War, choose not to attack the smaller ground forces coming ashore from the French fleet. Even General Clinton in New York could not understand Cornwallis' timidity in not removing this growing threat. Lafayette, naturally, was elated at the news his spies were relaying to him. The entire Yorktown peninsula was nearly overrun with British, German (the Hessian mercenaries in the employment of George III), American, and French forces, each anticipating the others' moves.

Through the first week of September, Cornwallis continued to seem in denial regarding his mounting predicament. He attempted to rally his troops by encouraging them not to believe everything they were hearing, and seeing, about the French. Adding to the discomfort of the rumors, the intense heat of late summer also claimed its share of the bounty—the Germans seemed particularly susceptible to fever and what we today would recognize as heat stroke. Cornwallis even continued his positive (in light of the situation facing him) reports to Clinton in New York, not mentioning the toll the heat was taking. Alternating between concern and false bravado, Clinton found it difficult to understand the true dimensions of what was rapidly unfolding on the Yorktown peninsula in September of 1781.

By mid–September however, Cornwallis began to acknowledge that he might have overplayed his confidence. He knew the Washington and Rochambeau armies were in route to strengthen Lafayette and he knew the chances of Clinton sending a powerful enough British fleet were slim. Cornwallis always considered the British Navy to be his lifeline should the situation on land get out of hand. Yet even as late as September 23, he believed the York River offered an escape route if necessary. Even with the French in the Bay, Cornwallis thought the river might somehow save him. He even briefly entertained an attack on Williamsburg to hasten a retreat out of Yorktown, but this plan never materialized in part due to news of the arrival of Washington.

Congress was reporting to Thomas Nelson, the Governor of Virginia, much the same news. On September 4, the Virginia Delegates to Congress wrote to Nelson:

> We have the pleasure to inform you that General Washington with a part of the American Army, and the Count de Rochambeau with the whole of the French are thus far on their way to Virginia. The American troops passed through the town on Sunday, the first division of the French yesterday and the second will follow them tomorrow. The fine appearance they make as men, the perfection of their discipline as soldiers, and the zealous attachment they manifest to the Allies of their Sovereign authorize the highest expectations from their services in the field.[26]

Other delegates wrote to their respective states as well commenting on the French and American troops heading through Front and Chestnut streets in Philadelphia on their way south.[27]

Congress continued to prognosticate about the Virginia campaign. In a September 4, 1781, letter, Congressman William Sharpe, writing to Nathanael Greene, discussed the arrival of John Laurens (American statesman who facilitated supplies for the Continental Congress with France) and the consequences of his mission to France:

> Colonel Laurens has arrived from France and brought to Boston sixteen thousand eight hundred stand of arms, materials for near ten thousand suits of clothes, a considerable quantity of military stoves, medicines, etc. He has also obtained and brought from the coffers of our ally a considerable sum of solid coin.... If the naval operations of our ally should prove successful this campaign we have everything to hope and nothing to fear. I wish the several states could be impressed with the necessity of preparing

Chestnut Street in front of the Pennsylvania State House (Historic American Buildings Survey).

> for a vigorous prosecution of the war for a number of campaigns yet to come as the most effectual way to obtain a speedy and honorable peace.[28]

This letter identified clearly that some were unclear what was brewing on the Yorktown peninsula and even with the Articles in effect (and thus a formal government), some states were not contributing to the war effort.

The Unfolding of Events

There are seemingly endless contemporary accounts or interpretations of the battle of Yorktown. Private accounts from observers, political accounts from Congress, and of course military accounts; all had varying perspectives. During the course of the weeks-long battle (siege really) one American in particular would achieve the military glory he so long coveted—Alexander Hamilton. This highly ambitious young man, already with several anonymous political essays to his credit, will factor in later chapters as one of the co-authors of *The Federalist* papers. For now, at Yorktown, he wanted action, and he wanted it soon. His wait would not be long as he would distinguish himself by leading the attack which captured redoubt number nine.

Yorktown was not so much a battle as a series of battles interspersed with the elements of a siege. It was a difficult, protracted affair which in some sense lingered while both sides tried to comprehend what was happening to them. Lafayette had arrived in Williamsburg on September 4, and set out at once to secure the former capital of Virginia. Many of his 7,000-man strong army was ill, including Lafayette himself. He was, however, well enough to greet Washington when he arrived at Williamsburg ten days later on September 14 with his army not far behind. Among those soldiers in Williamsburg upon Washington's arrival were the Pennsylvanians, whose mutiny at the start of the year momentarily gave pause, and a reality check, to nearly everyone involved in the American effort.

Washington and Lafayette quickly established their headquarters to allow them to finalize their plans without delay. Washington commandeered the handsome brick home of George Wythe near the Governor's Palace for his headquarters. Wythe, a signer of the Declaration of Independence, was in 1781 serving as the first professor of law at the College of William and Mary—whose campus and building were a hospital during the battle and siege of Yorktown. Lafayette established his headquarters in the Peyton Randolph home. Randolph, the first president of the First Continental Congress, had died in 1775 and his widow ran the plantation. Now, the stately wood frame house would shelter one of the highest ranking representatives of America's greatest ally.

Amidst all the well-wishing and celebratory dinners he attended upon arrival, Washington had one great concern. The fate of Admiral de Grasse was still unknown after his encounter with the British fleet. Washington knew without de Grasse's naval support, cornering Cornwallis would prove nearly impossible. News from de Grasse soon arrived though, much to Washington's relief, that he was victorious against the British and that he now controlled the Chesapeake at the York River. Following on Admiral de Grasse's news, Washington also received happy news that Admiral de Barras had arrived from Rhode Island with much needed supplies and artillery for the Americans and their allies. For once during the War, Washington finally had an army, numerical superiority over the British, naval superiority, and abundant supplies. Whether a sense of excitement animated Congress and the Army overall is hard to say with any degree of certainty. Yet, after six years of warfare without an effective national government, the

1. 1781—Mutiny, Government, Yorktown and Paris

Top: George Wythe house, Williamsburg, Virginia (Historic American Buildings Survey). *Bottom:* Wren building, College of William and Mary (Historic American Buildings Survey).

states finally came through and passed and formally ratified the Articles of Confederation. Whatever their shortcomings (and there were many), it was nonetheless a national government. Over the summer as Congress exerted what power it had, Washington too could take some measure of solace from the enhanced capabilities of his forces by the addition of French soldiers and naval power. The summer of 1781, aside from the perditions of Cornwallis' southern campaign, offered the first real sense of potential ready for the taking should anyone have chosen to accept it.

On September 15, with Washington strengthening the enclosure around Cornwallis, he no doubt was starting to sense that something big could actually happen, however cautious he may have chosen to be. The Americans wanted something, which might actually mean the end, finally, of the War. Washington wrote to his second in command General Lincoln to make all possible haste to take up his positions just outside of Williamsburg. Washington also requested a meeting with Admiral de Grasse to impress upon him the need to stay in the Chesapeake until the Yorktown campaign was over, preferably with Cornwallis' defeat. Without the French navy, Washington knew victory could not be had.

The meeting with de Grasse occurred aboard de Grasse's flagship the *Ville de Paris*. Washington and his entourage were treated to the highest standards of French military hospitality. Washington received the assurances he wanted and left satisfied that victory was nearer at hand. Washington's trip back to his Williamsburg headquarters would take nearly three days in the rough weather upon the York River. Concerned that events may have quickened while he was with de Grasse, he was pleased to find that Cornwallis had been very quiet and had not made any offensive movements.

As September moved on, events in Yorktown rapidly advanced to the point that any correspondence became outdated the moment it was sealed for the post. In one example from September 25 the Virginia delegation wrote to Virginia Governor Thomas Nelson lamenting "that no authentic intelligence has come from them to Congress for ten days past, although we are informed from every quarter that there has been an action of some consequence at sea."[29] Communications during the eighteenth century obviously were not what we enjoy today. Messages often took several days to travel between Virginia and New York during the buildup to the Yorktown campaign. This only exacerbated the tensions and stress both commanders felt. To add insult to this problem, most messages had to be encoded and multiple copies created. This was an arduous undertaking when everything was written by hand without the benefit of mechanical reproduction.

As if Washington was not under enough pressure to produce a victory in Yorktown (or any victory for that matter) President of Congress Thomas McKean wrote in a confidential letter on September 26 to inform Washington that larger geopolitical concerns were weighing on American independence:

> We are plainly told, *that we cannot have any more forces from France, by sea or land, after this campaign,* nor are we to *rely* on any further pecuniary assistance: The situation of affairs in Europe will demand their utmost exertions there, and they expect to render as much real service to the common cause in other places, as they could possibly do in America [emphasis in original].[30]

On September 27, with a final clarification from de Grasse after some tense letters which seemed to indicate he (de Grasse) was leaving, Washington drew up his final plan of battle. His September 25, 1781, letter to de Grasse was filled with pleadings for de Grasse to stay in place and with his entire force. Washington wrote:

> I most earnestly entreat Your Excellency farther to consider that if the present opportunity should be missed; that if you should withdraw your maritime force from the position agreed upon, that no future day can restore us a similar occasion for striking a decisive blow; that the British will be indefatigable in strengthening their most important maritime points, and that the epoch of an honorable peace will be more remote than ever.[31]

The Quiet Before the Storm

Near the end of September, the allies were ready for some initial sorties. On September 28, the combined American and French forces started on their way to Yorktown from their respective, scattered, positions on the peninsula, toward the waiting British forces. As the allies moved closer to the British lines, the fighting began to increase, but no large battles had occurred. Raiding parties, reconnaissance patrols, and chance encounters (which happened quite frequently in close quarters) were the extent of the conflict as both sides sought the best advantage. Cornwallis continued to wander between belief and disbelief over Clinton in New York and his enveloping predicament in Yorktown. After a week of this back and forth, Washington felt ready to launch his first major strike. The weather seemed to go in Washington's favor too—going from blistering heat to autumn coolness almost overnight. When the allies had finished surveying Cornwallis' defenses, they could determine it "consisted of eight redoubts, defensive works surrounded by trenches, palisades (rows of wooden stakes), frasies (sharpened poles facing outward towards the enemy) and abates (wooden stakes)."[32] The Yorktown campaign was one of the war's great engineering feats as well as great military planning on the part of Washington and the French. The British fortifications and allied advances were all planned based on the mathematical calculation of the capability of artillery. On October 9, the shelling by the allies began.

The Conclusion

There exist numerous first-hand accounts of the siege of Yorktown and the military end of the British control of her thirteen colonies. A brief look at some of those accounts of what occurred provide a unique window on the events of October 1781.

One of the more famous accounts came from Ebenezer Denny, an ensign in the Pennsylvania Continental regiment (the regimental line that mutinied in January 1781 in Morristown) who went on to become the mayor of Pittsburgh in the nineteenth century.

On September 1, Denny recorded that the army was "in high spirits."[33] He and his comrades were encamped behind the main building of the College of William and Mary (known today as the Wren building), which was being used as a hospital as mentioned before. Denny was quite impressed with Williamsburg and the active pace of military preparations under Baron von Steuben, "our great military oracle."[34]

On October 15, Denny reported:

> Heavy fire from our batteries all day. A shell from one of the French mortars set fire to a British frigate, she burnt to the water's edge and blew up—made the earth shake. Shot and shell raked the town in every direction. Bomb-proofs the only place of safety.[35]

Denny described the scene when the British asked for negotiations on October 17:

> In the morning, before relief came, had the pleasure of seeing a drummer mount the enemy's parapet, and beat a parley, and immediately an officer, holding up a white handkerchief, made his appearance outside their works; the drummer accompanied him, beating. Our batteries ceased. An officer from our lines ran and met the other, and tied the handkerchief over his eyes. The drummer sent back, and the British officer conducted to a home in rear of our lines. Firing ceased totally.[36]

The carnage of the campaign became visible after the actual surrender on October 19.[37] Again, Denny, who seems to have been at the right place constantly, reports, "Glad to be relieved from this disagreeable station. Negroes lie about, sick and dying, in every stage of the small pox. Never was in so filthy a place—some handsome houses, but prodigiously shattered. Vast heaps of shot and shells lying about in every quarter...."[38]

Admitting It's Over

Cornwallis had the difficult job of breaking the news to his superior General Henry Clinton in New York that one-quarter of all British forces in America were now prisoners. In a letter dated October 20, Cornwallis wrote, "Sir, I have the mortification to inform your Excellency that I have been forced to give up the posts of York and Gloucester, and to surrender the troops under my command, by capitulation of the 19th instant as prisoners of war to the combined forces of America and France."[39]

In Congress, the news was received with great relief. Every member it seemed wanted to write to someone with the news. Elias Boudinot of New Jersey wrote to his brother Elisha, "I take the first opportunity that offers of congratulating you on the glorious success of allied arms, in the capture of Lord Cornwallis and his whole army ... a day famous in the annals of American History."[40] Virginia delegate Edmond Randolph wrote to his colleague Theodorick Bland, "since your departure not a syllable of foreign intelligence has occurred. Nor indeed have we heard anything domestic, except the surrender of Cornwallis...."[41]

Cornwallis had spent much of 1781 decimating the Southern States; his inhumane treatment of runaway slaves was commented on by Ebenezer Denny as seen earlier. Other acts (murder, property destruction) that went beyond military necessity were also questioned. As such, there were quite a number of calls for Cornwallis to be captured and tried as a war criminal. The North Carolina delegation to Congress, writing to the North Carolina Governor Alexander Martin a mere three days after the surrender, stated:

> Congress have been zealously pressed to confirm the exchange of Lord Cornwallis for Mr. [Henry] Laurens [prisoner in the Tower of London]. This proposition is the more extraordinary as the enemy at first pretended to liberate Mr. Laurens unconditionally.... Such an officer is rated at 1,200 men, which is too large a gift to be made to a nation that never wishes to give us anything except hard measures.... We confess that in this debate we have thought it our particular duty to give Lord Cornwallis credit for the numberless murders he has committed in the Carolinas and Georgia.[42]

Actually, Cornwallis the prisoner was treated quite well, especially by the French, who held dinners in his honor. There were many who thought

Washington was far too lenient. In fact, a committee was formed to look into the surrender and the charge that Washington was too easy on Cornwallis. Tench Tilgham, a long time confident of Washington's, wrote to him on October 27:

> A committee, consisting of Mr. Randolph and Mr. Boudinot, were appointed to inquire of me the several matters of a particular kind which were not included in your dispatches. They not only went into these, but into the motives which led to the several Articles of the Capitulation, and I have the pleasure to inform you, that they were perfectly satisfied with the propriety and expediency of every step which was taken—and so indeed were the whole Body of Congress, except the South Carolinians, whose animosities carry them to that length, that they think no treatment could have been too severe for the Garrison, the officers and Lord Cornwallis in particular.[43]

All in all, Yorktown was a fine performance by the victorious General Washington. He had every reason to be proud, satisfied, and vindicated. Yet, what had happened? The year after Yorktown is fascinating in that neither side quite knew what to do next. Was the War over? If so, who won? Presumably the American's did, but while Yorktown was a staggering defeat, the British were hardly left destitute. (Clinton actually had a relief fleet ready to leave New York before he learned of the defeat and surrender.) Still, after six years of war, what more could be done? Events in Europe necessitated both Britain and France moving their forces out of America as soon as possible. America itself was near the verge of collapse on several fronts. The economy was in tatters, public support for war was floundering, and the national structure of government, while formally approved, was wholly inadequate. Yet, the British situation was not that solid either. James Madison, one of the most astute observers in Congress, wrote to Edmund Pendleton on October 30:

> With what hope or with what view can they [the British] try the fortune of another campaign? Unless they can draw succor from compassion or jealousy of other powers of which it does not yet appear that they have any well-founded expectation, it seems scarcely possible for them much longer to shut their ears against the voice of peace.[44]

A decision would have to be made. Were peace negotiations the next step? No one person or group on either side made this momentous decision. It was certainly fraught with an untold number of troubles. Still, what did Yorktown mean for the overall American cause? There were more questions than answers.

Victory?

Setting aside the question of American victory without French assistance, where was America to go after the smoke cleared? Just as interesting

1. 1781—Mutiny, Government, Yorktown and Paris

Victory monument, Yorktown Battlefield (Colonial National Historical Park).

is whether or not Yorktown was viewed as *the* victory, or just *a* victory. The expectations that go along with a win were certainly varied. Some wanted a win, any win, to help with recruitment—for the army and Congress; some wanted a win to show European allies that America was worth the investment; some wanted a final, disabling blow to force Britain into peace talks.[45]

As it would turn out, Yorktown provided something for everyone, including the British, many of whom looked eagerly for a way out of the stalemate of the American War for Independence. One enormously ironic aspect of the surrender which Cornwallis left out (he may not have realized it early on) was something only the vagaries and chaos of a war could produce. Andrew O'Shaughnessy recounts the tale in his prize-winning book:

> Cornwallis was taken into custody by John Laurens, who had drawn up the article of capitulation and who was the son of Henry Laurens, a former president of Congress. His father had been captured by the British on his way to negotiate a treaty with the Dutch and had become a prisoner in the Tower of London, whose absentee governor was Cornwallis, now the prisoner of John Laurens.[46]

Treaty of Paris, 1783

News of the Yorktown defeat reached London on November 25, 1781. The Prime Minister, Lord North, was distraught over the reports. George III seemed to be more sanguine. Both however sensed the rebellion was over—in the colonists' favor. The British public at large wanted an end to the American conflict. It should be remembered that although Yorktown was the biggest loss for Britain leading to American independence, other elements in the Empire fell at the end of 1781 as well. "The weeks that followed [Yorktown] tolled one disaster after another: the fall of St. Eustatius to the French, followed by St. Christopher, Nevis, and Montserrat, the recapture by the French of posts in Dutch Guiana earlier lost to the British, the loss of Minorca to Spain."[47] The grand total of British losses as of the end of 1781 was thirteen colonies and eight islands. Some of the British losses were not territory but military engagements, such as occurred in Ceylon.[48] (The British fought several naval engagements with the French throughout 1782 in the Indian Ocean near Ceylon—the British lost.) This tally further illustrates the global reach of the American War for Independence.[49]

It was February 1782 when the political situation in Britain really forced the King's hand. With the collapse of the North government George III had no choice in forming a new government of Whigs (the opposition party) and moving forward with peace negotiations. The failure of the North ministry to obtain victory in the American rebellion ensured American peace and independence was achieved. The North ministry failed to garner the support to carry the American War decisively over eight years of conflict. The political will to wage war in America had collapsed. Not deterred, North and his government made hopeless efforts before they left office to end the fighting with something less than full independence and by offering concessions to America's allies. This initiative failed, but it was yet another example of the global nature of the conflict, with proposed British concessions ranging from the West Indies to India.

The transition to the Paris peace negotiations in 1783 played out rather quickly, given how long the actual warfare took. Even though Britain was exhausted in America, her forces were still fighting in spots literally all over the globe (such as Ceylon mentioned above). The Prime Minister, Lord North, felt Yorktown was the end. King George III however, was not as convinced, he could repeatedly switch between acknowledgment and rejection of the loss.[50] By 1782, the Parliament Tories loyal to George were defecting. More and more, members wanted to end the American War. The Prime Minister resigned, along with his government, on March 20, 1782. George III was faced with few options regarding the American War. He could not form a new government with enough pro-war Tories and George III had to face political realities and allow his new government (under former Prime Minister Rockingham) to enter peace negotiations with the Americans. Before negotiations though, British military leadership in America had to be changed to reflect the new realities in Parliament. Sir Guy Carleton was sent to New York to replace Clinton as commander-in-chief. "He was instructed to avoid offensive measures and to capitulate rather than to defend himself against major attack."[51] The combat appeared over. At the same time, Richard Oswald was sent to Paris to begin peace negotiations with Benjamin Franklin, America's minister to France, and who suggested Oswald be sent to talk as a negotiator. The political turmoil allowed Franklin, in Paris, to write his old friend Lord Shelburn, now part of the new Rockingham government, and suggest to him that Richard Oswald would be a good person to send to start the negotiations for peace.

Franklin was really the first American with the opportunity to do something about actual peace to make the first move. Britain was ready to talk, America was probably ready overall, and someone had to start the process. Fortunately, Franklin, due to his years of successful service in Britain, could write directly to the top of the government to suggest starting the process. Over the summer of 1782 Oswald and Franklin, soon to be joined by John Adams and John Jay (Henry Laurens arrived a year later in the fall of 1783), worked on a draft treaty after much discussion. The inevitability of independence was all but accepted at this point, the difficulty was getting it on paper and everyone concerned to agree to the terms.

When Franklin began negotiations with Richard Oswald of Britain in Paris, he was working with instructions from the Continental Congress that had been prepared in June 1781, which required the Americans to cede to the French Court control of the negotiations. This directive would cause some moments of angst for the American delegates. These instructions were prepared four months before Yorktown when things looked much different for the Americans. Without question though, the one non-negotiable item was British recognition of American independence. While this seemed like it was beyond discussion, it actually was not.

The unique aspect of the talks which produced the draft treaty was the lack of specific instructions from Congress to the negotiators. As mentioned, the instructions they had were a year old and not really useful. Of course this was mainly the result of the time it took for communication, but also the timidity of Congress to deal singly with Britain as opposed to letting France take the lead.[52] Representative of the attitude in Congress during the summer of 1782 was a letter by Congressman William Few of Georgia to fellow Georgian General James Jackson. Few hits all the "high notes" about the activities occurring in Paris and London, which Congress simply must wait to hear about. Few wrote:

> ... Britain has changed her Ministry [Rockingham for North] and they it seems are disposed to change the system of the War in America [Tarleton for Clinton], but see no reason to believe that it is their intention to yield us our independence or cease to exercise every means in their power to injure and destroy us. Finding they cannot by force accomplish their diabolical designs they are now about trying the effect of artifice and intrigue.[53]

With communication so slow, and France, Britain, Spain, and Holland all trying to squeeze concessions out of the peace talks with American independence—in their limited view—a secondary byproduct, America seemed to stand little chance of being heard. Congress again through its weakness almost allowed the benefits won during six years of destruction to be lost under the pressure of European politics. Had the American negotiators completely followed their instructions and allowed France to lead, and the Americans follow, the treaty would have been much different. America would probably still have obtained independence, but other issues such as trade, boundaries, and foreign representation, could have been much less in the Americans favor. In fact, America could have ended up as some type of French suzerainty, thus exchanging one monarchy for another. One of the negotiators, John Jay, thought France (and Spain) would likely prolong the war to obtain non–American concessions beyond independence.[54]

Contentious topics such as good faith, boundaries, and formal recognition all hampered the talks well into 1782. Boundaries, and land ownership, were long-standing issues among the states themselves. In fact, it was one of the main reasons the Articles of Confederation took so long to be ratified. The former colonies, some relying on their colonial charter grants claiming territory from sea to sea felt obliged to keep these pledges. However, the 1763 Treaty ending the French and Indian War appeared to consolidate western land under the Crown, rather than individual colonies.

Therefore, upon declaring independence, smaller states not boarding the west felt the land should be communal United States land, not the individual bordering states' land. Maryland was the lone holdout after Rhode Island and Delaware gave up their objections to the definition in the Articles. Even as Congress feared to enter the debate over boundaries, "Congress wisely refrained from any assertion of jurisdiction, and only urgently recommended that states having claims to western lands should cede them in order that an obstacle to the final ratification of the Articles of Confederation might be removed."[55]

John Jay, minister to Spain, was directed to Paris to assist and arrived on June 23, 1782. John Adams, minister at The Hague, did not arrive until October 26, 1782. Henry Laurens, the final American negotiator, after Jefferson declined the role due to the death of his wife, arrived last. Laurens was away from most of the work due to personal issues (his son was killed in battle and he himself was physically and emotionally injured by his imprisonment in the Tower), but actively participated enough near the end to find a spot in the famous unfinished painting by Benjamin West.[56] For decades, if not longer, it was fashionable to portray the Americans in Paris—Benjamin Franklin, John Jay, John Adams, and Henry Laurens—as some version or variation of country bumpkins. They were often portrayed as men out of their league against the seasoned and devious diplomats of Europe. This interpretation served many purposes: America the underdog, America the humble but resolute foe, America the land where the average "Joe" could go toe-to-toe with Europe's best. These are all comforting stories and stories which many of us cherish from our school days. Fortunately, Congress sent as ministers some of the most capable, talented, and determined men available for foreign posting to Europe (actually they were all already in Europe serving in other posts). Indeed, Franklin had spent much of his adult life in England representing various American interests. As Congressman John Witherspoon stated in a speech before Congress in June 1781, "The first appearances we make upon the public state, are of consequence" and we had to get it right the first time.[57] While America as a whole may have signed on to the notion that "all men are created equal," Congress had enough foresight to recognize that not just anyone could deal with European diplomats.

The colonies from the very beginning of organized resistance in 1774 had always at least made an attempt to operate with a unified voice. This pretense barely survived the War, and it limped through the peace process with Jay, Franklin, Adams, and Laurens, taking matters into their own hands on many occasions. As late as October 1782, Congress was still trying

Unfinished portrait of the signing of the Paris Peace Treaty, 1783. Copy by unknown artist, after Benjamin West (Adams National Historical Park).

to calm the concerns of the Chevalier de la Luzerne, the French minister to America, by telling him the negotiators would not make any deals without consulting the French first. However, "unbeknownst to Congress, the commissioners defied their principals and went on to sign their preliminaries without consulting the French."[58] The American ministers were well aware of the Congressional directives they were disregarding and even enjoyed some dark humor at the expense of their rule-breaking.[59]

When the draft November 1782 treaty arrived in Congress on March 12, 1783, the biggest debate occurring was between the pro–French forces in Congress who were concerned that the American commissioners were not working with the lead of the French. In fact, Jay was indeed moving forward with talks without the guidance of France. Oddly, Hamilton and Madison, both congressmen, were quite critical of the commissioners overall, especially Jay, for their reluctance to engage with the French. (Yet, five years later Jay would partner with both Hamilton and Madison on *The Federalist* papers.)

Proviſional Articles,

Signed at *Paris*, the 30th of *November*, 1782,

BY THE

Commiſſioner of His BRITANNIC MAJESTY,

AND THE

Commiſſioners of the UNITED STATES of AMERICA.

Publiſhed by Authority.

LONDON:

Printed by T. HARRISON and S. BROOKE, in *Warwick-Lane*.

MDCCLXXXIII.

Provisional Peace Treaty with Great Britain, November, 1782 (Morristown National Historical Park).

Even between Franklin, Laurens, Adams, and Jay, there was disagreement on how to proceed. Adams and Jay were much more willing to deal directly with Britain while Franklin and Laurens were more willing to let France take the lead. Whatever transpired over the course of the roughly eighteen months of negotiations and communicating, it seems clear the Americans got a better deal (of course it can never be known for certain) by working without French input which would have no doubt included French demands as well as American. Many pro–French Americans saw the proposed treaty as being pro–British in that while Britain gave up much—especially their colonies—the treaty none-the-less split American and French interests, which many saw to be in Britain's favor. Congress did eventually conduct a mini-investigation into the conduct of the Peace Commissioners and their dealings. Nothing of significance was discovered. Indeed, in the peace negotiations can be found the seed of a certain American isolationism which flourished through much of America's early national period.

Prime Minister Rockingham died suddenly on July 1, 1782, making The Earl of Shelburne Prime Minister. Unfortunately, Shelburne entertained some prospect of America and Britain coming together and refused to recognize full independence. His obstinacy nearly derailed the talks. Amid all of the endless changes of government in Britain, John Adams, in Holland, wrote to John Jay on July 8, 1782: "As to peace, no Party in England seems to have influence enough to dare to make, one real Advance towards it. The present ministry is really to be pitied. They have not power to do anything."[60]

The main British negotiator Richard Oswald habitually referred to the states as colonies at first—naturally that did not seem useful to the Americans. In October, Oswald received a new commission granting him authority to negotiate with the thirteen united states. Some see this date, October 1782, as when America gained independence, essentially upon recognition from Britain. Negotiations continued to move forward, with external issues like boundaries, trade and fisheries, the status of Loyalist reparations, and Britain's geo-political concerns—especially with France and Spain—entering the discussion. By November 1782, a draft treaty was essentially ready and sent to Congress and Parliament. An open letter to both Houses of Parliament on the proposed peace appeared near the end of 1782. It started:

> America has obtained her end, she must be independent. The object of France is in a great measure achieved. She has torn away from England her valuable territories in the West, diminished her military character, outshone her in the arts of humanity, sunk her

1. 1781—Mutiny, Government, Yorktown and Paris

consequence among the nations, loaded her with near one hundred millions of additional debt, severed from her the noblest continent that ever formed an appendage of empire, and all with a rapidness unprecedented in the annals of events....[61]

Perhaps most importantly for the negotiations, the Americans felt a sense of justice about contractual debt obligated prior to the start of the War. The Peace Commissioners wrote to the Secretary for Foreign Affairs Robert R. Livingston on December 14, 1782:

> In our opinion no Acts of Government could dissolve the Obligations of Good Faith, resulting from lawful contracts between individuals of the two countries, prior to the War. We knew that some of the British creditors were making common cause with the refugees, and other adversaries of our independence: besides sacrificing private justice to reasons of state and political convenience, is always an odious measure, and purity of our reputation in this respect in all foreign commercial countries, is of infinitely more importance to us, than all the sums in question. It may also be remarked, that American and British creditors, are placed on an equal footing.[62]

This acknowledgment was one of the most salient features of the Treaty. It clearly put the United States in the realm of a world power by its support of a basic element in law—this reliance on law would become a hallmark of the American identity. This clause would be a regular feature of cases in the new Supreme Court ten years hence, when John Jay was the first Chief Justice, as many states sought to enact laws on their own which contradicted the Treaty's express definition of the sanctity of contracts.

Besides boundaries and trade, the other issue which concerned the negotiators in Paris was debt accrued by Colonial Americans and the plight of the Loyalists who numbered at least equal to the non–Loyalists. To illustrate their point, an anonymous New York Loyalist expressed his (or her) concerns in the summer of 1783:

> The rebels breathe the most rancorous and malignant spirit everywhere. Committees and Associations are formal in every Colony and resolves passed that no refugees shall return nor have their estates restored. The Congress and Assemblies look on tamely and want either the will or the power to check those proceedings. In short, the mob now reigns as fully and uncontrolled as in the beginnings of our troubles and America is as hostile to Great Britain at this hour as she was at any period during the war.[63]

The Loyalist issue was even more contentious than the debt issue. British negotiator Richard Oswald wrote to the American Commissioners on November 4, 1782:

> You may remember, that from the very beginning of our negotiations for settling a peace between Great Britain and America, I insisted that you should positively stipulate for a restoration of the property of all those persons, under the denomination of Loyalists or Refugees, who have taken part with Great Britain in the present War.[64]

The American Commissioners replied, claiming the weakness of the national government to impose certain legal restrictions upon the states:

> In answer to the letter you did us the honor to write on the 4th instant we beg leave to repeat what we often said in conversation, viz. that the restoration of such of the estates of Refugees, as have been confiscated, is impracticable; because they were confiscated by laws of particular states, and in many instances, have passed by legal titles through several hands—Besides, Sir, as this is a matter evidently appertaining to the internal polity of the separate states, the Congress, by the nature of our Constitution, have no authority to interfere with it.[65]

On January 20, 1783, Britain entered into a general armistice with the United States and also an agreement with France and Spain.[66] In Britain, political machinations among the Whigs saw Prime Minister Shelburne overthrown by the combined forces of Charles James Fox and former Prime Minister Lord North, who still hoped some closer alliance could be reached with the United States than full independence. These initiatives went nowhere over the summer of 1783 and the final treaty (the original draft with no changes) was signed on September 3, 1783, a date, which oddly, virtually no American knows.

Yet, it was from that date forward that allowed for the massive migration westward that so characterizes the nineteenth century and conjures so many romantic versions of American history. Prior to 1783, with land title clarity disputed, few Americans ventured far beyond the Mississippi River. The Treaty helped clear the way for this settlement:

> ... so long as the title to that territory was in doubt no considerable body of people would move into it, and it was not until the Treaty of Peace in 1783 determined that the western country as far as the Mississippi River was to belong to the United States that the dammed-up population broke over the mountains in a veritable flood.[67]

As divided as the states were politically, it is remarkable that the war and the peace were conducted under the aegis of the Congress as the supreme voice of the country. However impractical, or even impossible, that seemed, it did happen. The summer of 1782 often saw Congress lamenting the lack of information on the progress of peace negotiations. Congressman Jesse Root wrote to the Governor of Connecticut Jonathan Trumbull, "We have received no information respecting the negotiations for peace, said to be carrying on in Paris, but through the channel of British papers. Great tumults have taken place in New York among the Tory and refugees in consequence of the advices from England and the measures taken by Sir Guy Carlton in respect to them."[68]

One member, John Taylor Gilman, appeared to be so out of tune with what was going on he completely missed the news. On December 17, 1782, while the preliminary Treaty was making its way to American, Gilman wrote to Meshech Weare, President of New Hampshire, that "….by the latest accounts from Europe, it appears probable that negotiations for peace will be seriously entered upon soon…."[69]

Yet, on August 13, 1782, James Madison, in a letter to Congressman Edmund Randolph, mentioned for the first time that Britain was planning on recognizing American independence. Madison wrote, "I transmitted to you a few days ago by express the contents of a letter … announcing the purpose of the British Court to acknowledge the independence of the 13 Provinces."[70]

Congress officially declared an end to hostilities on April 15, 1783.[71] On November 22, 1783, the Definitive Treaty of Peace reached Congress and as per usual, not enough delegates were available to ratify (or reject) it. President of Congress Thomas Mifflin, urgently requested to governors to send delegates so Congress could conduct its business and consider the Treaty. The Treaty had a six-month window before it would expire and need to be redone in Paris. Time was indeed of the essence. As it seemed with just about everything Congress did, an element of drama was necessary. States did not seem compelled to send their delegates for this final act of the nearly ten-year long war. Connecticut and South Carolina were the last two states whose delegates arrived in Annapolis (where Congress was meeting) to consider the Treaty. This occurred on January 13, 1784, which left very little time to get the ratified treaty back to Paris. Yet again, time was indeed of the essence. Three separate copies raced to Europe; weather, poor navigation, and assorted delays conspired to get the copies to their destination late. Still, the parties took no notice of this and formally exchanged the signed copies on May 12, 1784, thus officially, finally, ending the American War for Independence in America's favor.

Chapter 2

The First Continental Congress

The Continental Congress was the glue, or the thread, which held the colonies together. The Continental Congress was without question a major element in American history. Even more so than the Continental Army, the Continental Congress was America. Whatever its faults (and it had plenty), it truly represented all of the colonies. Many studies of the Continental Army often subtitle their books saying the Army was where America survived, or America survived as long as the Army did. To the extent that this is true, it is even more manifestly true that Congress kept the idea of America viable. Without Congress, America the concept did not exist. It is simply too easy to dismiss politicians (somehow forgetting that somebody actually had to vote them into office), that is the biggest problem the historical image of the Continental Congress must contend with. Max Farrand has written:

> Congress became the butt of many jokes, but men could not hide the chagrin they felt that their government was so weak. The feeling deepened into shame when the helplessness of Congress was displayed before the world. Weeks and even months passed before a quorum could be obtained to ratify the treaty recognizing the independence of the United States and establishing peace. Even after the treaty was supposed to be in force the states disregarded its provisions and Congress could do nothing more than utter ineffective protests.[1]

Congress, therefore, is often overlooked because of reasons which already have been, and will continue to be, discussed. However, this work has made it a point to study the Congress within its world and environment without the baggage of two centuries to weigh it down. Chapter 1 has already covered the salient feature of the middle period of the Congress' fifteen-year life—the surrender at Yorktown and the subsequent peace—and that leaves the formation of the Congress for the current chapter, and

Congress' one attempt at creating a true national government—the Articles of Confederation—for chapter 3. One item to recall at the outset is that there were two Continental Congresses (although some count three, calling the Continental Congress after formal passage of the Articles of Confederation the Confederation Congress—this study will stick with two Congresses), the first lasting from September through October of 1774, and the second from May of 1775 to March of 1789. Collectively they are generally referred to as the Continental Congress as though there was no difference between them. The biggest difference between them was in the two-month-long First Congress, there were no hostilities to deal with. By May 1775, when they reconvened as the Second Congress, hostilities had already begun. The years of the Congress covering the Constitutional Convention and the era of *The Federalist* papers are examined in chapters 6 and 8.

A congress (a word dating from the sixteenth century, meaning coming together) was an idea whose time had come by 1774. Yet, what was this congress to mean; what was it to do exactly; how was it to conduct itself? As with so much else in Colonial America during this time, there are far more questions than answers—if answers are even to be had. With great uncertainty as to what would happen, the individual colonies agreed, some reluctantly, to a colony-wide congress to meet in Philadelphia in September 1774, a date now almost completely forgotten.

The First

There are no shortages of claims as to being the first representative, deliberative, body in the colonies. No doubt one could argue the Pilgrims contemplating the Mayflower Compact aboard the *Mayflower* in 1620 could get the credit.[2] Then again, the Jamestown settlement of 1607 must have had those wise members who could be counted on to debate serious matters of state—such as the "state" was on that swampy spit of land off the James River. In fact, the Virginia House of Burgesses, established in 1619 (still a year before the Mayflower Compact) as an advisory council to the Governor, is generally considered the first European-style elected body to deliberate in America. Throughout the seventeenth and well into the eighteenth century, a gathering of some type, composed of elected members, became ingrained in the American attitude toward governing. Especially after the beginning of troubles with Britain, Americans saw their best bet at first was to form a committee. Of course, at the time this was truly a select club, those who could vote and those who could serve. They were rarely democratic in the larger sense and certainly not representative in the way we see that term today. Acknowledging those limitations existed leaves us with the reality that those who voted and those who served were not really that far removed from each other. There was certainly a sense of inbreeding when it came to the ruling class in Colonial America.

This attitude towards a committee gathering reached a crescendo during the crisis that erupted after the French and Indian War ended in 1763. From the moment Britain realized the costs of that war, and the financial burden it placed on the country, it attempted to extract some of the funds necessary to pay down the debt from those who benefitted most from a geographical perspective—this meant the American colonies, where much of the French and Indian War occurred. It can easily be argued that the empire as a whole benefitted from that war, through trade, expansion, and prestige. Still, for those who lived on the front lines in America, some of those benefits were not easily calculable.

Nearly ten years removed from the first attempt by Britain to impose a tax of some sort on the American colonists to help defray the costs of military protection, the delegates to the First Continental Congress in 1774 no doubt wondered about the efficacy of an all-colony gathering. There was much anticipation, but much apprehension as well. At the absolute foundation of the dispute with Britain was taxation.[3] The accurate observer will note that this is not an anti-tax slogan, rather, merely a slogan which says taxes will not be imposed without someone who represents another being part of the debate to impose the tax. This phrase took on an intense meaning by 1774, when the delegates (or more appropriately given the individualist views of the colonies diplomats from their respective colonies) met in Philadelphia. The idea of no-representation was anathema to the colonial leaders, with peer pressure mounting, these men (they were only men at this point) gradually saw fit to claim a larger share of government than provided by the King and Parliament. In fact, many, if not most, saw this as their constitutional right as Englishmen. (England did not, and does not, have a written constitution under the common law system.)

The idea of the delegates being diplomats, representing separate colonies rather than a unified country, bears some legitimacy. While the most ardent radicals (Patrick Henry, Samuel Adams) were no doubt for independence by this point, they had no idea what would come after independence. They probably just thought the individual states would survive alone in the world, cherishing their separate independence and liberty, whatever that meant.

What Was Liberty?

Liberty, or the concept of it, was a fluid notion during the Revolutionary Era. No two people were likely to answer the same way if asked about its meaning. Saying liberty meant freedom, or freedom from tyranny (in the form of George III or Parliament) was a great slogan and could get soldiers to fight and die, but it could not govern a country. Too often, the liberty question got encumbered in religious language which only further helped to obscure its meaning. In a wonderful essay, historian Robert Ferguson tackles this topic. He writes, "These arguments [about liberty], endlessly repeated in a variety of forms, served the Revolution well, but they raised substantial problems in the peace that followed."[4] This was a serious problem and could have posed significant impediments for the fledging United States. Liberty from Britain was one thing, liberty from a national government, when one is being called into being, was quite another. In *Federalist* twenty-six Hamilton speaks of "liberty more ardent than enlightened" and Ferguson highlights the writings of Theophilus Parsons from Massachusetts, who had given the topic much thought. Ferguson quotes Parsons, who wrote "The artful demagogue, who to gratify his ambition or avarice, shall, with the gloss of false patriotism, mislead his countrymen."[5] Ferguson continues, "A 'false patriotism' had grown from inflated conceptions of liberty, and the combination was preventing a proper legal balance from emerging in the new order."[6] The liberty question would impact the legal aspects of creating the new government and will be covered in greater detail in later chapters. For now, it is enough to know that the law was ever present in government and those who sought to govern by it would have a difficult time indeed against those inclined to carry the liberty concept to unworkable levels.

There were probably thirteen separate notions of liberty and freedom and the rights of man, one for each colony. Conceivably, this was how independence from Britain would have looked had the King and Parliament decided the fight was not worth it and simply let the colonies go.

In 1780, Joseph Galloway, former Speaker of the Pennsylvania Assembly and one of the primary Tory conservatives at the First Congress, published a short work entitled *Historical and Political Reflections on the Rise and Progress of the American Rebellion*. Galloway had left America in 1778 when the situation became untenable for a Tory of his stature. In his book, Galloway wrote about this idea of the delegates (and, given the extra-legal status of the Congress, "delegates" was a polite term) being more diplomats:

HISTORICAL AND POLITICAL

REFLECTIONS

ON THE

RISE AND PROGRESS

OF THE

AMERICAN REBELLION.

IN WHICH

The Caufes of that Rebellion are pointed out, and the Policy and Neceffity of offering to the AMERICANS a Syftem of Government founded in the Principles of the Britifh Conftitution, are clearly demonftrated.

BY

The AUTHOR of LETTERS to a NOBLEMAN, on the Conduct of the AMERICAN WAR.

LONDON:
Printed for G. WILKIE, No. 71, St. Paul's Church-Yard. MDCCLXXX.

[Price 3 s.]

2. The First Continental Congress 43

In regard to the political state of the Colonies, you must know that they are so many inferior societies, disunited and unconnected in polity. That while they deny the authority of Parliament, they are, in respect to each other, in a perfect state of nature, destitute of any supreme direction or decision whatever, and incompetent to the grant of national aids, or any other general measure whatever, even to the settlement of differences among themselves. This they have repeatedly acknowledged, and particularly by their delegates in Congress in the beginning of the last war; and the aids granted by them since that period, for their own protection, are a proof of the truth of that acknowledgement.[7]

The list of what are commonly referred to as British abuses and usurpations of colonial rights began in earnest with the Stamp Act, which in fact produced its own American Congress as a way to express American displeasure. The Stamp Act Congress, the first organized gathering of the colonies, convened in New York on October 7, 1765. The young John Dickinson, of Delaware (or Pennsylvania), as President, gained the most attention. A moderate to conservative, Dickinson guided the Congress in attempting to work out differences with Great Britain rather than antagonize them. (Dickinson will be discussed at length in chapter 3.) Nine years later, his more radical colleagues would take charge in the First Continental Congress. After the Stamp Act Congress—which certainly created concern among the British, but little else—the colonies kept one another informed of issues touching on the growing problems with Britain through Committees of Correspondence rather than through a formal gathering such as a congress or assembly.

The Stamp Act was followed by the Quartering Act, the Declaratory Act, the

John Dickinson (Historic American Buildings Survey).

Opposite: **Title page of Joseph Galloway's history (Morristown National Historical Park).**

Townshend Acts, the Tea Act, and finally, the Intolerable (Coercive) Acts. This long series of legislative action essentially had as its goal the taxation of the American Colonies in some form or another. That was the purpose in the beginning under the Stamp Act and it was still the purpose by 1774. The idea that the Americans could somehow maintain a government without a viable taxing power would haunt them until the Constitutional Convention in 1787. Quite simply, without taxes, you could not have a government. The Acts quickly took on the quality of Britain trying to prove it could legislate for the colonies as they saw fit, and ultimately legislate them into submission. This process continued with the colonies taking a consistently more resistive stance until they haltingly hit upon an idea that would forever change their relationship with Britain.

Philadelphia—Carpenters Hall, 1774

Carpenters Hall, as the name implies, was associated with the association or guild of carpenters and builders in Philadelphia. More properly, it was styled the Carpenters Company of the City and County of Philadelphia. The organization was founded in 1724. The mission of the organization was "for the purpose of obtaining instruction in the science of architecture and assisting such of their members as should by accident be in need of support, or the widows and minor children of members."[8] Much of its early history is more tradition-based than evidentiary. It is safe to say that this particular organization was quite prosperous and well maintained. In the early years it was perhaps more of a contractor's guild than a trade union, although it was fluid in its focus.

Delegate John Adams of Massachusetts noted in his diary for September 5, 1774, that from the City Tavern (where many of the delegates lodged), Carpenter's Hall was but a short walk and there the arriving delegates "took a view of the room, and of the chamber where is an excellent library; there is also a long entry where gentlemen may walk, and a convenient chamber opposite the library."[9] The library Adams referred to was none other than the famous Philadelphia Library Company, founded upon an idea from the fertile mind of Benjamin Franklin. The Library Company occupied the second floor of the Hall, and no doubt would provide a peaceful refuge or excellent reference materials for the delegates as necessary.

In 1774, Philadelphia was the largest city in the colonies with about thirty thousand residents. Philadelphia was worldly. There were theaters, concert venues, salons, churches, and fine dining opportunities. Philadelphia

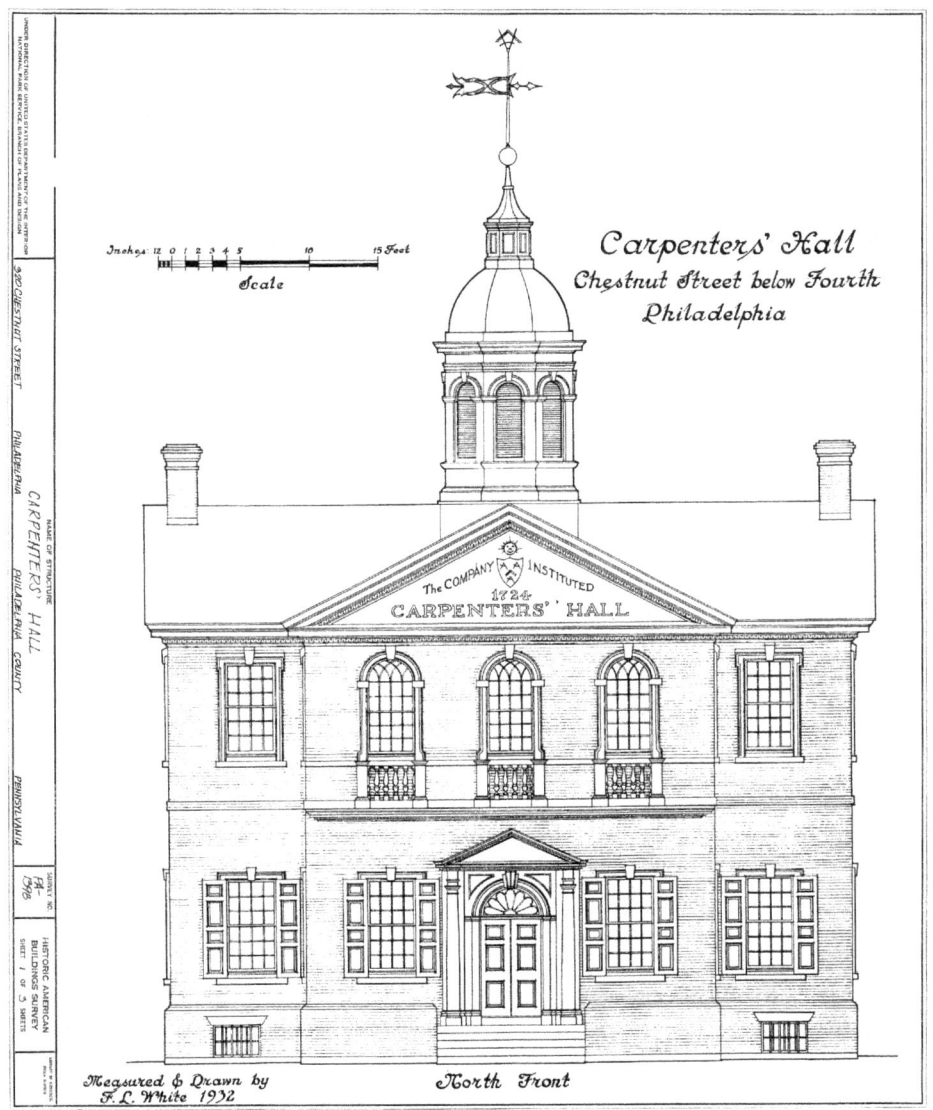

Carpenter's Hall, Philadelphia, meeting site of the First Continental Congress (Historic American Buildings Survey).

also had something many of the delegates had not seen, streets that intersected at right angles. The layout of Philadelphia, so regular and geometric, was met with great approval.

Using the already established Committees of Correspondence, the colonies, during the spring and summer of 1774, were able to arrange for the general Congress to be held in September. The choice of the Hall actually had political overtones. The Hall itself was a relatively new building, dating from ca. 1772. It had, as the name implies, a hall, a large meeting space; so too did the Pennsylvania State House. The issue, however, was the apparent political persuasions of each site. The State House was nominally controlled by the Speaker, Joseph Galloway, a committed conservative who would eventually emigrate to England. The Hall, by contrast, was nominally controlled by Charles Thomson, a committed radical who was already secretary to the radical elements in the Carpenters Company, which regularly met in the Hall to denounce Britain and plan protests. In fact, over the summer of 1774, rival elements met at the State House and the Hall in what amounted to a mini-preview of the events to occur in September and October of that year.

The Carpenters Company was needed by the radical (not yet rebel) leaders as they represented some of the financially lower strata in society, the working men whose support would no doubt be necessary should war break out:

> Resistance to Britain was being organized on a broad basis and those marshaling public sentiment were courting the favor and support of the tradespeople and mechanics.... The Philadelphia carpenters were considered to be the most influential and best organized of the industrial bodies and the choice of their Hall was an expression of the growing democratic outlook.[10]

Merrill Jensen has observed:

> The events of the years 1763 to 1774 served to fortify this type of thinking [that the working man was necessary for revolt], for in their dispute with the mother country the colonial ruling classes fatally but inescapably sought the support of the farmers and the 'mechanics.' When tax and trade laws could not be evaded by dutiful petitions, popular riots [Boston Tea Party] were encouraged by the aristocracy of the towns to give point to their constitutional theories about the right of self-government.[11]

Some of the delegates who attended the First Congress, horrified by the destruction of property by mobs, and the lawlessness of groups like the self-styled Sons of Liberty, did what they could against the radicals in the Congress, but to no avail. They knew as well as anyone that you could not overthrow a government nearly a millennium in the making and have nothing to replace it.

Coming Together

Of all the acts declared by the British government after the Stamp Act of 1765, the Coercive Acts (also known as the Intolerable Acts in America)

2. The First Continental Congress

compelled the separate colonies to come together and debate their future as a collection of colonies. On March 28, 1774, the British government passed the Coercive Acts in response to the continued destruction of British property by American mobs. Specifically, the Coercive Acts sought to reclaim the costs of the tea destroyed in Boston harbor in December 1773. The Acts included the Boston Port Act, which effectively sealed the harbor until restitution was made for the tea. It was this separate act, within the overall Acts, that created the most outrage among the colonists. (The other aspects of the Coercive Acts dealt with governing, liability of British officials acting in their appointed capacity, and an act allowing Catholics to fully worship in Canada—something largely Protestant Americans took a dim view towards. Yet ironically, the Americans would need the support of Europe's two most Catholic monarchies—France and Spain—to fight Britain.) While the bulk of these Acts directly impacted Boston and Massachusetts, the leaders there were quick to remind all of the colonies that the Boston-specific aspects of the Acts could easily happen to them, an argument that had been made before and an argument the Bostonians would not cease making at the First Congress. The Virginians, seen along with the Massachusetts men as leaders on a colonies-wide level, agreed that a unified response to the Acts was in order. Colony-wide embargoes were one thing, but a colony-wide gathering to debate and then petition the British government was something else. This was the genesis of the First Continental Congress. Throughout the summer of 1774, events rapidly moved towards some type of all-colony gathering to discuss what was happening and where to go from what seemed to be an impasse. Every colony came to agree that a congress was necessary as the next step. No one colony could act alone any longer. Still, Massachusetts led the way at this point, as it was the focus of the Intolerable Acts. Given all the protestations of being loyal subjects, it is hard to believe that most of the delegates could not sense that the First Continental Congress had an ominous air about it.

In the House of Burgesses in Williamsburg, a young, relatively unknown legislator named Thomas Jefferson called for a day of fasting and reflection for June 1, 1774, to show solidarity with Boston. After this, the Royal Governor of Virginia (the Scottish peer Lord Dunmore) dissolved the Burgesses for their impertinence and willingness to take their fellow colonist's side in the brewing argument. The Burgesses however unofficially reconvened in the Raleigh Tavern in Williamsburg and encouraged by sentiments from other colonies resolved to take a stronger stand.

The Bostonians, not wanting to handle their evolving revolt alone, proposed from the start of the First Congress that the "Colonies write in an agreement to stop importations and exportations from and to Great Britain."[12] This relieved pressure from the Bostonians and essentially spread their developing revolt throughout the colonies; not that the other colonies felt pressured into anything. They were just as ready for this move as Boston was—or at least those leading the charge against Britain—and naturally not every delegate followed. Rhode Island, New York, and Philadelphia all encouraged the calling of a general congress of the colonies.

1774

The events that transpired in 1774 that culminated in the First Congress filled many with equal measures of dread and excitement. The Massachusetts delegation had the most to lose by far, with the majority of the Intolerable Acts specifically targeting that colony. Their most notable delegate, John Adams, (his cousin Samuel was probably just as notable) was almost giddy upon arrival in Philadelphia, writing in his diary for Monday, August 29, 1774:

> A number of carriages and gentlemen came out of Philadelphia to meet us…. We were introduced to all these gentlemen, and most cordially welcomed to Philadelphia. We then rode into town, and dirty, dusty, and fatigued as we were, we could not resist the importunity to go to the tavern, the most genteel one in America … and after some time spent in conversation, a curtain was drawn, and in the other half of the chamber a supper appeared as elegant as ever laid upon a table.[13]

What a way to start a revolt. Adams would never forget this hospitality and he never wavered from his support of American causes after this, such was the impact of his arrival upon him. Adams also noted that night "there will be at the Congress about fifty-six members, twenty-two of them lawyers…."[14] Adams went on about the walks he took before Congress commenced on September 5, and of meeting all of the most notable gentlemen of the colonies. His descriptions of his colleagues are famous, and have been referenced countless times over the years in attempts to give an element of humanness to otherwise statuary-like figures from the past.

The manner in which many of the delegates departed for the First Congress from their homes fits into the overall theatrics common to the eighteenth century. The Massachusetts contingent, departing Boston, rode together in a fancy coach, with guards and attendants. "It was a cavalcade befitting an embassy en route to a diplomatic meeting of tremendous importance—an entourage designed to claim legitimacy and dignity."[15]

Legitimacy and dignity were also displayed through bearing, attention to grooming, and fashionable dress. The delegates often commented in letters about their colleagues' appearance—everything from height, weight, eyes and faces to clothing. Overall, they were an observant group but necessarily observant due to the stakes involved in the Congress. These "word portraits," as mentioned earlier, were used for decades to help humanize the delegates.

The wealthier delegates spared little expense in outfitting themselves for this event (the First Congress was just as much a time to see and be seen). Whether for those visiting or for the locals, finery was the dress code and method of operation. Lastly, "these provincial representatives would also have noticed the colleagues' etiquette, manners, and the way they carried themselves. Consciously adhering to a mutually understood code of genteel behaviors…"[16] This code, of course, was meaningful only to the very few in society who had a part in its establishment. "Visible wealth was more important at the Congress because members found themselves disassociated from the identity well established within their own provinces where people often knew intimately the history of a person and his family."[17] As the years moved on into the Second Continental Congress, this spectacle became much less noticeable or necessary.

Congressman Silas Deane of Connecticut wrote to his wife on August 29:

> The city is full of people from abroad and all the lodgings in town full, or engaged…. We spent this day visiting those [delegates] that are in town, and find them in high spirits, particularly the gentlemen from the Jerseys, and South Carolina. In the evening we met to the number of about thirty, drank a dish of coffee together, talked over a few preliminaries, and agreed to wait for the gentlemen not arrived…. This day, therefore, Friday, I mean to ramble over the city and make my observations.[18]

A week later, Deane wrote again to his wife, right after the first official meeting of the delegates, "I have never met, nor scarcely had an idea of meeting, with men of such firmness, sensibility, spirit, and thorough knowledge of the interests of America, as the gentlemen from the Southern provinces appear to be."[19]

John Adams too seemed to sense something special about the Southern delegates; he confided to his diary that "these gentlemen from Virginia appear to be the most spirited and consistent of any."[20] Adams took his seat along with the other delegates and began working officially on September 5, even though only twenty-five delegates had arrived. At this point, their work was mainly getting to know one another and indulging in comradeship.

Two weeks into the Congress, the work seemed to have become settled and a routine established. John Adams wrote to his wife Abigail on September 14 that "my time is totally filled from the moment I get out of bed until I return to it. Visits, ceremonies, company, business, newspapers, pamphlets, etc., etc., etc."[21] Two weeks later, on September 29, Adams again wrote to Abigail and she must have wondered what kind of fun her husband was having away from the family farm in Braintree; he wrote:

> ... I shall be killed with kindness in this place. We go to Congress at nine, and there we stay, most earnestly engaged in debates upon the most abstruse mysteries of state, until three in the afternoon; then we adjourn, and go to dine with some of the nobles of Pennsylvania at four o'clock, and feast upon ten thousand delicacies, and sit drinking Madeira, Claret, and Burgundy, till six or seven, and then go home fatigued to death with business, company, and care. Yet I hold it out surprisingly....[22]

It was not all hard work in Philadelphia for the delegates. There was "down-time" and many members used it wisely to take in the city of Philadelphia, the grand city of Colonial America. "For every hour that the deputies to the Congress spent debating inside Carpenter's Hall, they spent another socializing in the streets, taverns, coffeehouses, carriages, and homes of Philadelphia."[23] This time to unwind was more than simply having a good time. More than not, these activities allowed delegates to come to understand their colleagues in a way that being in Congress all day would not permit. "Regularly participating in the exclusive rituals of genteel dining in the homes of elite Philadelphians was also a key component of the delegates' efforts to claim for themselves, separately and collectively, political legitimacy."[24]

The delegates had much to be giddy about. They saw themselves, mostly, as being part of great events—events that had yet to occur but which everyone seemed to know would. As such, they saw themselves as the shaper of those events. This was an envious position to be in without question. Something big was in the air as Silas Deane wrote to his wife, "Inform my friends that we are in high spirits, if it is possible to be really so when the eyes of millions are upon us, and who consider themselves and their posterity interested in our conduct."[25] So, right from the beginning there was a sense of events having more meaning than just the immediate crisis.

It should be remembered, that the colonies at this point still had royal governors, such as William Franklin of New Jersey. Franklin was the son of Benjamin by a mistress and was anxious for news of what was occurring across the Delaware River from New Jersey in Philadelphia.

On September 3, 1774, Joseph Galloway, the influential Pennsylvania member of Congress later to become a Loyalist (and personal friend of William Franklin) wrote to the Governor Franklin:

> I am just returned from Philadelphia, where I have been to wait on, and endeavor to find out the temper of the delegates.... I have not had any great opportunity of sounding them. But so far as I have, I think they will behave with temper and moderation. The Boston Commissioners are warm, and I believe wish for a non-importation agreement, and hope that the colonies will advise and justify them in a refusal to pay for the tea until their grievances are redressed.[26]

A Brief Summary

Twelve colonies (Georgia was preoccupied with Native American issues and wanted British assistance with that endeavor and consequently did not attend, to avoid upsetting Britain) met in Philadelphia beginning on September 5, 1774, to organize the response to Britain and the Intolerable Acts. Their goal in this Congress, especially for Massachusetts, was to show that what affected one colony, affected all the colonies, and the time for unified action was long overdue. This was not a new idea, but it had been difficult to get colony-wide acceptance of this type of a unified undertaking. The Congress determined that they would allow open debate and all colonies (big or small) had an equal say, and one vote each. One of the major documents the delegates issued was a Declaration of Rights, whereby the delegates pledged their allegiance to the King and Britain. (This reinforced the notion that the argument the colonies had was with Parliament; "Parliament had had nothing to do with the creation of the American Colonies, the rights of the colonists were guaranteed by Crown grants of charters, which were, when accepted and acted upon, covenants between the Crown and colonists."[27]) This appears to have been a genuine pledge and no thought of independence was seriously publically entertained (except by the most radical elements); the Declaration represented the last stand of the moderates. The main point of this Declaration though was questioning Parliament's right to tax the colonies; again, not a new idea. Finally, the First Congress passed the Articles of Association, which called for an embargo of British goods commencing on December 1, 1774. (There was also an agreement not to export to Britain.) Finally, the Congress agreed that if Britain failed to address the colony's grievances, it would reconvene in May 1775. Feeling themselves satisfied, after nearly two months of debate and not being publically too conservative or too radical, but leaving the door open to a more radical approach, they disbanded. While only a few harbored serious thoughts of independence, the vast majority, who saw it as an awful alternative, nonetheless knew that it was the logical end of their grievances if Britain would not act or come to the negotiating table.

Declaration of Rights

Prior to the Declaration of Independence, James Duane, a moderate Congressman from New York, gathered support as the main inspiration behind the Congress' Declaration of Rights. It is a surprisingly mild and timid document, nowhere near the fire-breathing character of the other more famous declaration—the Declaration of Independence. Of course, the two declarations really cannot be compared too much as each one had very specific reasons for its creation. The Declaration of Rights is however consistently overlooked in favor of its more famous successor. This makes some sense, why study a document that was ignored by all concerned? It would seem though that some would want to see it remembered so as to be able to say that the American radicals were not that radical and that attempts were made to avoid an all-out breech leading to war. Still, the absence for the larger historical record of the Declaration of Rights is telling.

Part of the reason for this absence was that the report goes by several names. It was considered a memorial, a declaration, a resolution, and others—we will stick with Declaration of Rights. The essence of this declaration was to lay before the King the grievances of the colonies. The Congress saw Parliament as the source of their problems and thought an appeal directly to the King would be better received. The Declaration begins:

> Whereas, since the close of the last war [French and Indian], the British Parliament, claiming a power of right to bind the people of America, by statute in all cases whatsoever, hath in some acts expressly imposed taxes on them, and in others, under various pretenses, but in fact the purpose of raising revenue....
> And whereas, assemblies have been frequently dissolved, contrary to the rights of the people ... and reasonable petitions to the crown for redress have been repeatedly treated with contempt, by his majesty's ministers of state...
> That the inhabitants of the English colonies in North America, by the immutable laws of nature, the principles of the English constitution, and the several charters or compacts, have the following rights....[28]

Money. Money, revenue, taxes; the First Congress seemed to boil their opposition to the British down to the need for money to run the empire. From that central focus, all other matters of opposition flowed: quartering of troops, freedom of worship for Catholics in Quebec, dissolving of colonial assemblies, among others. It is interesting that this declaration references only the laws of nature whereas the 1776 declaration references Nature's God as well. Likewise, the 1774 declaration references statutes as being the cause of America's problems, not the English constitution, under which the delegates saw the statutes as being unconstitutional anyway. The 1774 declaration was actually similar to the Stamp Act Congress declaration nearly ten years previous. Declarations were the way Americans sought to make their feelings known.

The first dated entry in the Journals of the Continental Congress is September 5, 1774. It lists those delegates "chosen and appointed by the several Colonies and Provinces in North America to meet and hold a Congress at Philadelphia assembled at the Carpenter's Hall."[29] And with that, self-government (leading directly to independence) in Colonial North America, began. The second order of business was electing a president; to this position, the delegates unanimously elected the Virginian Peyton Randolph. Charles Thomson (the radical secretary of the Carpenter's Union) of Pennsylvania was selected as secretary, a post he would hold for the entire fifteen-year history of the Continental Congress.

By September 27, nearly three weeks into their meetings, Congress reported in their Journal that they were considering "the means most proper to be used for a restoration of American rights."[30] By this point, there was no question that American rights, in Congress' view, had been violated. Yet, individual members still sought ways to reconcile without taking such a harsh view of rights.

Joseph Galloway of Pennsylvania, good friend of Governor William Franklin and later a Loyalist who left for England in 1778 as mentioned, spoke on September 28 to the delegates:

> He [Galloway] told Congress that he came with instructions to propose some mode, by which the harmony between Great Britain and the Colonies might be restored on constitutional principles: that this appeared to be the genuine sense of all the instruction brought into Congress by the delegates of the several Colonies. He had long waited with great patience under an expectation of hearing some proposition which should tend to that salutary and important purpose; but, to his great mortification and distress, a month had been spent in fruitless debates on equivocal and indecisive propositions, which tended to inflame rather than reconcile—to produce war instead of peace between the two countries.[31]

Galloway gave a long speech imploring his colleagues to consider the ramifications of their language. He went so far as to say independence was all but already declared when the colonies rejected the Stamp Act ten years pervious, making already then the argument that Parliament could not tax them. Galloway called the Declaratory Acts (passed after Britain rescinded the Stamp Act) necessary "in order to save its [Britain's] ancient and incontrovertible right of supremacy over all the parts of the empire."[32] It was probably apparent to most by now that a battle for the future would lead through the past—history would factor greatly in the American argument. Both sides would invoke ancient history and rights to justify their course of action. And America's greatest historian would turn out to be Thomas Jefferson; his *Summary View of the Rights of British America* will be reviewed shortly.

Try as he might, Galloway, and a handful of others, simply could not contain their colleagues. The radicals would carry the day. As historian Edmund Burnett has observed, "The summoning of the congress had been engineered chiefly by the radical element, with only here and there the intervention of a moderating hand."[33] The impression we have of serious looking, graven men, on their knees, wringing their hands and profusely perspiring over their fate is probably not that accurate. Independence was very much in the air and the radicals were as pleased as could be, and less radical men like Galloway knew it. However, Congress did go so far as to prepare a moderate plan of a proposed union between Great Britain and the colonies. This would have been more like a confederation with a head appointed by the King and a council of the colonies chosen by them—this was the Plan of Union drafted by Galloway. This would have been something quite new within the imperial British government. It could perhaps be seen as addressing the defect which William Franklin saw in the British constitution with respect to the colonies.[34]

Galloway was more than a conservative, more than a Tory. He surprised many of his colleagues towards the end of September when he introduced a Plan of Union. There was genuine surprise when Galloway presented this, for two reasons. His radical colleagues were not aware anything like this was being contemplated, and they were in no way willing to endorse a plan that sought a union more strengthened and more formally codified than that which already existed. Galloway's plan struck a raw nerve precisely because it sought to elucidate, rather than obscure, the relationship between Britain and American. His plan sought to put words into an unwritten constitution whereby the relationship would be spelled out, and laid out, for all to see and judge. To the radicals, this must have been anathema. Clarity in the relationship was the last thing they wanted. Undefined murkiness suited their purpose quite well. The clearer the relationship, the less argument; these gentlemen needed mud, the thicker, the less clear, the better. Galloway wrote about this extensively after his return to England (in fact, it is his 1780 publication that preserves his Plan, as it was removed from the official record of the Congress). Galloway bitterly complained that the radicals had gained control of Congress and refused to allow genuine debate. He held they "had gained such complete control of Congress that the moderates could be pushed aside with but small consideration."[35] One of the arguments Galloway said his opponents raised against his plan was the delegates, by approving the plan, would usurp the rights of the individual legislatures; thus meaning that the delegates felt they had no power or authority to approve such a plan to be presented to Britain. This was an issue which would haunt America until the Constitutional Convention and would form the backbone of the arguments in *The Federalist* papers. Where does power reside? If with the states, then no country could really exist. What would exist would be a loose confederation of sovereign entities bound by some loose written law. The Constitution, and more importantly *The Federalist* papers, relieved America of the uncertainties of ineffectual government. Galloway's thinking raised the specter of law; but where did law reside? The delegates ranged over many possible foundations: the laws of nature (which Jefferson would rely on in the Declaration of Independence), the English common law, colonial Charters, colonial legislation? There existed a hodgepodge of legal sources, all with varying claims as the source and foundation of American law and guidance (especially given that the Congress was an extra-legal body to begin with). Depending on the perspective of the delegate, it could be one or a mixture of sources. Again, the muddle served the radicals well.

Concurrently, Congress was leaving little to chance. In Boston, local leaders were being advised not to let down their collective guard and to be vigilant about British activity. More and more the delegates spoke and wrote of the horrors of a possible civil war (knowing all too well it was coming). President Peyton Randolph, writing to British General Thomas Gage in Boston, sounded this theme:

> We entreat your excellency to consider what a tendency this conduct [Parliament's various Acts] must have to irritate and force a free people, however well-disposed to peaceable measure, into hostilities, which may prevent the endeavors of this Congress to restore a good understanding with our parent state, and may involve us in the horrors of a civil war.[36]

This is not surprising given that many of the delegates, nearly all students of history, looked to the English Civil Wars of the seventeenth century for encouragement and guidance.

The Congress set about immediately to appoint committees.[37] Two primary committees would look into the British infringement of American rights and the best method(s) for restoring them. The first would tackle the rights issues, and the second committee would look into American trade and industry and how best to bolster American commerce against the loss of British markets. Several members wasted no time in staking their claim to the current crisis. Patrick Henry of Virginia, as recorded by James Duane, "insisted that by the oppression of Parliament all government was dissolved, and that we were reduced to a state of Nature."[38] Some saw this as typical Henry hyperbole, others as something more ominous. Henry continued, according to Duane, "that there were no longer any such distinctions as colonies, that he conceived himself not a Virginian but an American."[39] Henry could always be counted on for a good show, and he did not disappoint. His theatrics were well received and did much to bolster enthusiasm among the delegates, and probably made the equally bombastic Samuel Adams a bit jealous.

Regardless of theatrics, government was necessary. A more reasoned voice, John Jay (future co-author of *The Federalist* papers) responded to Henry's performance, "could I suppose that we came to frame an American constitution, instead of endeavoring to correct the faults in an old one—I can't yet think that all government is at an end."[40] Thomas Lynch, Jr., of South Carolina, stated more succinctly a few weeks later that "the masses can't live without government, I think, one year."[41]

The main goal of the Massachusetts delegation, and just reward for Adams' hard work, was achieved by mid–September. In his diary for September 17, John Adams wrote, "This is one of the happiest days of my life. In Congress we had generous, noble sentiments, and manly eloquence. This day convinced me that America will support Massachusetts or perish with her."[42] Massachusetts, and Boston more precisely, would not have to stand alone against the Intolerable Acts and Britain. Resolve was now confirmed that the colonies, collectively united, were standing against Britain. Still, what did this mean? How did one stand against another if the other seems bent on using force? Surely the more astute delegates knew where things were headed. For all their protestations of fealty to Britain, the hardest among them knew it was a sham and only a matter of time before war arrived.

Joseph Galloway, the staunch Tory conservative from Pennsylvania, in the history he wrote in 1780 after his move to England, gave his impression of the approach of the various schools of thought present that fall of 1774 in Philadelphia:

> Upon the meeting of Congress, two parties were immediately formed, with different views, and determined to act upon different principles. One intended candidly and clearly to define American rights, and explicitly and dutifully to petition for the remedy

2. The First Continental Congress

which would redress the grievances justly complained of—to form a more solid and constitutional union between the two countries, and to avoid every measure which tended to sedition, or acts of violent opposition. The other consisted of persons, whose design, from the beginning of their opposition to the Stamp Act, was to throw off all subordination and connection with the Great Britain; who meant by every fiction, falsehood and fraud to delude the people from their due allegiance, to throw the subsisting government into anarchy [Henry's state of Nature], to incite the ignorant and vulgar to arms, and with those arms to establish American Independence.[43]

Galloway and John (or Samuel) Adams can be seen as the two opposing leaders of the camps at the First Congress. It has already been mentioned that despite their protestations to the contrary, independence, confrontation, and conflict with Britain was what the radicals wanted. In fact, as we have seen, Patrick Henry claimed that all connection between America and Britain was already severed. While Henry's language may have been in the minority at this point, his thoughts and feelings were not.

Still, on October 7, John Adams wrote to prominent Bostonian William Tudor that in his estimation, Congress would avoid confrontation. "They will not, at this session, vote to raise men or money, or arms or ammunition. Their opinions are fixed against hostilities and rupture, except they should become absolutely necessary; and this necessity they do not yet see."[44] Still, they rejected outright Galloway's Plan of Union, met in an extra-legal congress, and had been destroying British property (and other private property) for some years already; it is not clear what Adams was trying to say—except that he was trying have it both ways. Furthermore, Congress was preparing to engage in economic warfare through embargoes. Adams and his radical colleagues were hard to follow in the First Congress. They would not hit their stride until the Second Continental Congress convened in May 1775, after hostilities had already begun. Adams ended his letter to Tudor:

> They dread the thoughts of an action, because it would make a wound which would never be healed; it would fix and establish a rancor which would descend to the latest generations; ... it would light up the flames of war, perhaps through the whole continent.[45]

Having passed the Declaration of Rights, the Congress quickly passed the Articles of Association which called for the boycott of exports and imports, along with other measures designed to impact Britain financially. The Articles were for internal colonial consumption as a means to ensure the focus of the colonies was being brought to bear in the resolve generated to be carried on beyond the meeting of the First Congress. Finally, the last document produced by Congress was an address to the people of Great Britain. This letter sought to bypass Parliament and the King and appeal directly to the people and ask them for their support and understanding. A letter to the King was also sent. Lastly, to further this idea that all would suffer or prosper together, Congress called for a second congress to meet on May 1, 1775, should the situation not improve, or even worsen.

Before adjourning, Congress agreed to have their written proceedings printed and published for all to see—an early variant of transparency. However, this transparency only reached so far. Congress did not want anyone to see writings that showed a less than robust response to the growing rebellion, such as Joseph Galloway's Plan of Union, which was removed from the official record as mentioned. The final act was left to Secretary Charles Thomson, who was entrusted to send the various addresses to Benjamin Franklin in London for him to deliver to the appropriate recipient. Thomson wrote to Franklin, "This day [October 26, 1774] the Congress broke up, the papers are not all got ready but will be sent to you by the next opportunity. As a vessel sails tomorrow morning early I am ordered to forward to you the petition to the King."[46]

Many of the individual delegations felt compelled to report back to their respective legislatures. Most took a tone of bravado expected from such gatherings. Individual delegates too reported on the end of proceedings. John Dickinson of Pennsylvania wrote to Arthur Lee:

> Yesterday the Congress broke up. You will immediately know their proceedings from publications.
> The colonists have now taken such grounds that Great Britain must relax, or inevitably involve herself in a civil war....
> A determined and unanimous resolution animates this continent, firmly and faithfully to support the common cause to the utmost extremity....
> I wish for peace ardently; but must say, delightful as it is, it will come more grateful by being unexpected. The first act of violence on the part of Administration in America ... will put the whole continent in arms, from Nova Scotia to Georgia.[47]

The Law

Wrapped into all the discussion about freedom, liberty, no taxation without representation, etc., were the nuts-and-bolts issues of law and government. As John Adams had pointed out, nearly one-third of the delegates to the first Congress were lawyers.

The calling of the First Continental Congress followed nearly a decade of increasingly bitter debate over the nature of imperial power and the legal foundation of that power between Britain and the American Colonies. This concerned the relationship between constitutional limits on power and colonial law. From the colonial perspective, that limitation was grounded in a centuries' old, but ill-defined notion of individual liberty and freedom from excessive governmental control. By contrast, the Crown saw little need for limitation as it already possessed virtually unlimited power as imperial administrators. Increasingly, the American dispute was pitting the contours of medieval law against the stark modernity and heady ideas of the burgeoning Enlightenment.

The contested issues, especially on the colonial side, had been deftly distilled by a handful of leaders by 1774 to simple phrases designed to create a devoted mass following. On the surface, it seemed a somewhat simplistic argument; the colonial leaders struggled over whether the Crown or the Parliament had control over the law and legislation, and ultimately over the colonies. In theory though, it was a rather complicated debate regarding where the foundations of law resided.

During the seventeenth century Puritan Revolution in England, the seat of power, and hence law, toggled back and forth between the Crown and Parliament. These very same arguments reappeared nearly a century later (spurned on in part by the arrival of Enlightenment thinking upon American shores) and found new cause in the buildup to the American Revolution. According to historian Charles Mullett, "Anyone who has examined the pamphlets emanating from the preliminaries of the American Revolution must have been impressed by the references to revolutionary England."[48] As he further wrote, "Bacon, Coke, Selden, Harrington, Locke, and Sidney, are great names in the history of law and politics," and it is their "dicta, scattered through controversial writings or embedded in weighty decisions [that] clutter up the pages of American pamphlets."[49] Historian Bernard Bailyn wrote that "The colonists identified themselves with these seventeenth-century heroes of liberty."[50] When the Crown eventually "refused to adopt the view that the Imperial Parliament could not bind the colonies ... war became inevitable."[51] To the colonists, the British were disavowing a constitutional political heritage which they themselves invoked nearly a century before in the English Civil War.[52] The lessons of history would be employed in short order in the colonial struggle.

"The Literature of Revolution"[53]*: Thomas Jefferson, James Wilson, and the Distillation of History*

Thomas Jefferson's *Summary View of the Rights of British America* and James Wilson's *Considerations on the Nature and Extent of the Legislative*

Authority of the British Parliament are representative of the type of historical-based writing that flourished during the early years of the Revolution in an attempt to find an intellectual foundation for the rebellion taking shape against Britain.

Twenty years prior to his work on the Supreme Court, James Wilson (not yet a congressman) wrote *Considerations on the Nature and Extent of the Legislative Authority of the British Parliament.* This work, which was published in 1774, closely paralleled the great English jurist William Blackstone's *Commentaries on the Laws of England* in design and similarly provided an opposing argument to Blackstone's relating to British colonial power. It would be Wilson's study of the essence or location of authority which would define him as a champion of a secular, constitutional, non–Natural Law approach to not only independence, but also to later constitutional development.[54] Wilson was not alone:

> Out of the ferment, Americans in the late colonial period and the first years of national existence developed an ethics of secular benevolence, a deistic theology, a faith in the perfectibility of man and in the progress of science, and democratic political theory, and a *laissez-faire* theory of economics, all culminating in a cosmopolitan ideal of world citizenship.[55]

Wilson himself wrote, "the consent of those whose obedience the law requires" forms the basis for the law.[56] Consent therefore, not submission under a king, should form the foundation of American life and law and would require human adjudication.[57] Wilson, steeped in the ideas of the Scottish Enlightenment (to be covered later), was at the vanguard of constitutional thinking a decade before the formal debates on a constitution began and well ahead of many of his colleagues.

The inherent elements of Wilson's argument about the British Parliament not having a legal claim to legislate the colonies found expression in Jefferson's *Summary View,* which was immediately greeted with critical acclaim from the colonists. As historian Trevor Colbourn has written, "the *Summary View* was an instant popular success with colonial patriots and sympathetic English Whigs because Jefferson was telling men what they wanted to believe and arguing the American cause in language immediately familiar."[58] Jefferson's attempt to compare Americans to the ancient Saxons who immigrated to England a millennium prior formed a focal point for his argument.[59]

The Saxons who emigrated from the forests of Germany were not bound by the German laws they left behind. Invoking history, Jefferson argued the American colonists should likewise not be bound by the laws they left behind. However, what Jefferson did not say was that the colonists had lived nearly one hundred and fifty years under British laws with few upheavals (implicit is the question, "why revolt now?"). This fact was elaborated more fully by James Wilson, whose "conception of sovereignty, tempered by a century of American experience ... [and] not Blackstone's English orthodoxy," ultimately prevailed.[60] It was Wilson's view of sovereignty, which envisioned the colonies as independent entities in part due to their development so far removed geographically from Britain that became the dominant intellectual argument. In many ways, this makes the forgotten Wilson the architect of American independence.

There were a handful of reasoned discourses reflecting on the parameters of the constitutional governance debate prior to Thomas Jefferson's drafting of a *Summary View of the Rights of British America* in 1774. But in the effort to provide written justification for opposing Crown policies (and ultimately for war), Jefferson's work quickly came to be seen as the manual which argued the unconstitutionality of Parliament's actions.[61] The need to establish constitutional parameters for themselves would be an issue which would occupy the Americans until 1787.[62]

Jefferson was one of the first to make the constitutional differences between American and English approaches to colonial governance an argument for war. As historian Joseph Ellis explains, "Jefferson staked out the constitutional ground just as it was becoming the only tenable position for the opponents of British imperial policy to stand on."[63] However, Jefferson was questioned, both at the time and subsequently, about the accuracy of his depictions of British policy affecting the colonies. As Mullett writes, however, "colonial readers [in general] were not [necessarily] after historical facts, they were after historical notions, and notions made respectable by great names."[64] Interestingly, historian Dumas Malone, the authority on Jefferson, has found little value in the work and has written that "as a contemporary indictment of British policy it [the *Summary View*] bordered on recklessness."[65]

Many prominent writers prior to and during the Revolution went on to further careers as leaders of the new American government whose arguments would shape the debates over the Constitution and in particular the judiciary. Included in this group would be John Dickinson (to be discussed in chapter 3), Richard Bland, Arthur Lee, James Otis, William Henry Drayton, Charles Carroll, the three co-authors of *The Federalist* papers (Madison, Hamilton, and Jay) and James Wilson. In fact, Wilson made some of the more succinct claims respecting British legal control in the colonies, stating flatly during the Revolution, "the colonies were not bound by English statues."[66] Wilson also argued, using the Irish system as an example, that English law did in fact "show expressly, or by a necessary implication, that the colonies are not bound by the Acts of the British Parliament; because they have no share in the British Legislature."[67] Wilson cited as evidence of his argument a 1484 case where the judges found that Ireland was not bound by English statues.[68]

According to legal historian Martin Horowitz, the First Continental Congress argued "that Americans were 'entitled to the common law' as well as to English statues at the time of colonization."[69] On one level, this was further indication of how far ahead of his colleagues Wilson was in the area of constitutional thought; many of them still saw the common law as a viable system of jurisprudence. Horowitz quotes the Continental Congress stating that Americans were entitled to the common law. This would seem to imply that the adoption of English common law by the colonists was optional. An entitlement generally is something which can, or cannot, be taken. This approach viewing the common law as an entitlement was something the British would not accept as the colonists were Englishmen (as far as the British were concerned) and were consequently bound by the common law; they had no choice. In fact, during the Revolutionary period, "eleven of the thirteen original states adopted, directly or indirectly, some provisions for the reception of the common law as well as of limited classes of British statutes."[70] This suggests how unprepared the colonies were, and thus by default dependent on, English common law, and clearly not ready for the constitutionalism which Wilson was promoting; this topic will be explored much more in depth in chapters 6 and 8, looking at the Constitutional Convention and *The Federalist* papers.

Throughout much of the eighteenth century, American law relied on "English authority [to settle] virtually all questions for which there was no legislative rule."[71] The absence of legislative rule meant the continual reliance on common law, and to an extent, on some elements of natural law, which was bound with the common law. The common law reflected the way people behaved as it was (and is) based on precedent from earlier cases and thus to a certain extent can reflect the moral principles (in the secular sense) under which they functioned. The common law is understood to be the law derived from judicial decisions over centuries of case law, as opposed to law from a written, codified document.[72] These issues all pointed to the need for an American approach to law, which the Continental Congress was woefully incapable of preparing, and which ultimately led to the Constitutional Convention and *The Federalist* papers.[73]

John Rutledge, delegate from South Carolina, educated at Middle Temple London, and future Supreme Court Chief Justice, gave this view

2. The First Continental Congress 63

of the American legal scene and how the English common law should, and should not, impact Americans:

> The Colonists in the several Colonies are bound by and entitled to the benefit of those parts of the Common Law of England, of the civil and maritime law used there; and of the statutes of that kingdom of force there at the settlement of the Colonies which are applicable to them and from their local circumstances are not impracticable here, and the like parts of the statutes of Great Britain made from time to time for securing the rights and liberties of the subject.... They are also entitled to the [immunities] and privileges which have been from time to time granted to them respectively by royal charters; and to a free and inclusive power of legislation in all cases of taxation and internal policy. Such parts of the common civil and maritime law and of the statutes of Great Britain the acts of our several assemblies and the charters granted to the colonies and these only constitute the law of the land and the rights and privileges of the peoples in the Colonies. These cannot be altered or abridged by any authority but our respective legislatures.[74]

Over the winter of 1774–1775, Britain failed to respond to the requests of the First Continental Congress. This was not a surprise to most observers. Britain had no intention of coming to terms with its colonies even though there were many British leaders who called for greater recognition of Colonial America within the British Empire. One of the most famous Englishmen (he was actually Irish) to side with the American cause was the influential member of Parliament Edmund Burke. Burke spoke in the House of Commons in the spring of 1774, several months before the First Continental Congress met. The Trinity College and Middle Temple educated Burke was known as a profound thinker even early in his career. Burke sought a way as early as the Stamp Act crisis to combine civil liberty for the colonies with the power of the British Empire and Parliament. In some measure, this is the idea the conservative delegates would have at the First Continental Congress, and it is somewhat evident in Galloway's Plan of Union.

The attitude towards the colonies in Burke's speeches was not without parallel. Many of Britain's leaders, and the public, questioned the course the government of Prime Minister Lord North was pursuing in the colonies. "In 1775, Britain became increasingly divided over the subject of America.... The debate raged in the newspapers."[75] After news of the First Continental Congress reached Britain, the debate raged even more. In 1775, petitions on the growing crisis with America circulated which garnered some 45,000 signatures, an incredible number; with more than half in favor of the colonies.[76] Burke's speech in the spring of 1774 in the House of Commons on the subject of American taxation, when distilled down from theory, practically called for an understanding that British imperial sovereignty meant just that: Britain, by its adherence to its constitution and the rules of international law, had rights over its dominions. That right included not only the right to take action—in this case in reference to taxation—but the right to *not* take action as well. Naturally, this struck many observers as nonsense. However, Burke put into a theoretical framework a means by which Britain could still *claim* the right to tax, but not actually *engage* in the practice. This is vaguely similar to the Declaratory Act of 1766, which Burke was certainly aware of. His efforts to find a middle ground, however philosophically tangled, would continue for the duration of the American War for Independence.[77]

Burke's idea of sovereignty rested along with the colonist's theory that their rights to tax themselves came from their Crown Charters and therefore as subordinates to the Crown, Parliament could not tax the colonies. In November of 1776, Burke even proposed legislation that came down from his philosophical highs. He "presented a bill to end the dispute [this was already after the Declaration of Independence in the Second Continental Congress] with America. It proposed renunciation by Britain of the right to tax the colonists for revenue, repeal of the Coercive Acts and the Townshend tax on tea, and pardon to all Americans who had participated in rebellion."[78] The measure failed.

What Burke, and Joseph Galloway, and others on both sides of the Atlantic missed was the power of radical elements who, through plain talk and simple ideas, led their respective countries to war. Once war commenced, there was no turning back. Debates flowed back and forth endlessly in America and Britain. As we know, it did not end until Yorktown, and then another year-and-a-half of peace negotiations before all was said and done.

These were exceedingly complicated times. We today like the simple, binary approach: black/white, true/false, up/down, left/right, etc. History is not simple because life is not simple. The history of the First Continental Congress proves this: "Few would disagree that the history of the Continental Congress from its first hesitant steps toward revolution (1774) to the rise of the Washington administration (1789) was terribly complicated and remains inadequately understood."[79]

Understanding of the post–Revolutionary period over the decades by historians has generally held to the two approaches delineated by the Founders themselves (such as Galloway and Henry at the First Congress and Jefferson and Dickinson at the Second Congress). Much like the Federalists and Anti-Federalists, nineteenth-century historians began to coalesce around the two interpretations of the Constitution.[80] The historical process is not simple, and history does not yield up its story without a fight. Facts can be known, but motivations and human desires cannot. Historians, like virtually every other type of professional, rarely agree on every aspect of a particular topic, and thus it is with the post–Revolutionary period when the newly independent United States operated under the Articles of Confederation.

Chapter 3

The Articles of Confederation

The Articles of Confederation began life in the summer of 1776 during the Second Continental Congress. The First Continental Congress was in session barely two months (September-October 1774) and saw the coming together of the colonies' delegates in Philadelphia to discuss (and most importantly meet one another) the grave issues with Great Britain. Most of the big names in Colonial America were in attendance. Some who were not in attendance, like Thomas Jefferson, were nonetheless making themselves known by their writings, in Jefferson's case for his pamphlet *A Summary View of the Rights of British North America*. A second Continental Congress was called for by the Articles of Association drafted by the First Congress should the situation with Britain not improve. The Second Congress took their seats in May 1775 as the situation had indeed worsened, and would not be disbanded until 1789, when the new Constitution went into effect.

The Second Continental Congress Begins

The Articles of Association from the First Continental Congress held good to its promise to hold a second congress beginning in May 1775 should the situation with Britain not improve. When no progress was reported, and indeed the situation even worsened with the beginning of hostilities at Lexington and Concord, the Second Congress began to assemble in Philadelphia. Richard Henry Lee was one of the first delegates to arrive and wrote to his brother William on May 10:

> I am exceedingly pressed with business and therefore must be short.... The Virginia delegation arrived here yesterday where they find all those from the Southward.... In

3. The Articles of Confederation

an hour all the delegates from the Colonies North of this will be here and then the Congress will be opened. There never appeared more perfect unanimity among any set of men....[1]

As in the First Congress, Silas Deane of Connecticut kept his wife Elizabeth informed of events in Philadelphia. On May 11, he wrote:

> ... but you may depend all will be well; that is if I may judge from appearance; but believe nothing you hear reported of us, for our doings will not be published but by authority of the whole. The scenes before us are so vast that I can give no kind of judgment as to the term we shall be detained here, and I tremble when I think of their vast importance.[2]

The Second Congress may indeed, unlike the first, have had scenes of members with graven faces, blank expressions, and greatly perspiring. The Second Congress was essentially left with the task of dealing with what the First Congress had wrought. Members of the Second Congress could justly have uttered "be careful what you wish for, you might get it." And get it, they did. Most delegates, especially moderates, got far more than bargained for. As John Adams (a radical and a rebel in all but name at this point) wrote to James Warren, "such a vast multitude of objects, civil, political, commercial, and military, press and crowd upon us so fast, that we know not what to do first."[3]

The two stars at the beginning of the Second Congress, Thomas Jefferson (fresh off the success of the *Summary View*) and John Dickinson (still widely known as "The Farmer," for his *Letters from a Farmer in Pennsylvania* from ten years earlier), occupied two distinct poles within the American aristocracy. Much is already known about Jefferson; he was from a prominent family, was exceptionally wealthy after his 1772 marriage to Martha Wayles, was the primary author of the Declaration of Independence, and would not stay long in the Second Congress before heading back to Virginia.

John Dickinson was born in Maryland in 1732, grew up in Delaware, and represented Pennsylvania (although he did represent Delaware later). He was nearly ten years older than Jefferson. Dickinson had spent five years studying in England whereas Jefferson was Virginia born, bred, and educated. Jefferson's wealth was mainly derived from his slaves; Dickinson (also a slave owner but much more diversified) manumitted most of his slaves in 1777, and all, unconditionally, in 1786. Dickinson, unlike Jefferson, was a highly successful businessman. Dickinson spent long periods at his beautiful estate outside Dover, Delaware, overlooking his agricultural interests. He was alone, as his wife Mary detested the Dover estate where Dickinson grew up. A pious Quaker from an extremely tight-knit family, Mary

John Dickinson house, Dover, Delaware (Historic American Buildings Survey).

Dickinson never acclimated to life in rural Delaware. Dickinson himself was a Quaker, although he never formally joined a Meeting House.

These two men, Jefferson and Dickinson, provided the framework that would guide Congress and the states through six years of war and six years of peace before the Constitution finally brought the ideals of their two documents (the Declaration of Independence and the Articles of Confederation) together and created a true, functioning, national government. The two documents they created, vastly different yet similar, explained the why of revolution, and the mechanism for revolution. Mechanism, in this sense, is used to mean the operating of the gears, pulleys, and machinery necessary to plan and carry through not just a war, but a peace. In many ways, Dickinson was a much better choice than Jefferson to prepare the mechanism. While both were fluid with a pen, Dickinson was less political and pedantic than Jefferson.

The first week or so of the Second Congress was taken up with members offering various statements as to their view of the predicament they and their fellow delegates found themselves facing. James Duane wrote one of the longest overviews on the conflict with Britain on May 25, and titled it *On the State of the Colonies*. His first point was to say what was at stake, "The importance of the subject ... concerns our liberties, our lives, and property."[4] These three objectives would be a recurring theme and famously would appear in the Declaration of Independence. Duane continued and expressed the viewpoint that "the eyes of Europe and America are fixed on this assembly.... On our side we tremble for the dearest and most inestimable of all earthly blessings, our liberty and for those rights ... and free government."[5] Among other common phrases from the period, Duane set the debate in place a year before the Declaration of Independence. Duane's efforts to produce the *State of the Colonies* helped focus the delegates with the realities they now faced of having to fight a war, create a government, and finally to take responsibility for their actions. And as everyone knew, those responsibilities would be taking a turn for the worse with more bloodshed the inevitable consequence. As John Adams wrote Abigail on May 29, "Colonel Washington appears at Congress in his uniform, and, by his great experience and abilities in military matters, is of much service to us."[6]

John Dickinson, through his writing of the Articles of Confederation, provided something the First Congress lacked: legal authority. The Second Congress too was actually extra-legal (from the British perspective), but by then it was pointless to attempt and follow colonial laws regarding gatherings like the Second Congress. And of course, with the Articles of Confederation not being approved until 1781, America could be said to lack a legal, functioning government. No less a personage than Benedict Arnold, seeking to explain his treason, wrote to his former countrymen in October 1780 to remind them of this lack of a government. In referring also to the treaty with the French that the Americans had signed, he wrote:

> In the plainness of Common Sense, for I pretend to no casuistry, did the pretended treaty with the Court of Versailles amount to more than an overture to America? Certainly not, because as authority had been given by the people to conclude it, nor to this very hour have they authorized its ratification—the Articles of Confederation remain still unsigned.[7]

In many ways this was hair-splitting, as there was no chance whatsoever of America going back to Britain. And while technically a government did not exist in America, in practice the Second Congress, with or without the Articles, was the government.

The Articles of Confederation were not approved by all of the states until March 1, 1781, just seven months before the Battle of Yorktown. Still, prior to 1781, the Articles, even without all of the states approving them, were the best the former colonies could offer as a new form of government. Until that time, Congress operated in an almost hap-hazard manner, with each state as its own sovereign entity, superior to Congress. Great Britain in some respects had thirteen separate revolts to deal with. If the British had succeeded in crushing Washington, who would have surrendered on behalf of the Continentals? The legal framework linking the states together was not yet formally established. A theoretical framework existed through the Declaration of Independence, but an actual legal framework did not exist binding the states into a nation. In many ways it is no wonder that it took until 1781 for the Articles to finally become ratified. There was a war on, and expediency was what was needed in government affairs, not a ponderous legal infrastructure. The effort to define a new government and successfully break from a colonial master would have been too much to undertake, especially when roughly two-thirds of the population was either against the idea or apathetic to the idea of independence, much less a new form of government.

1774–1789

For fifteen years, the Continental Congress was the ultimate governmental entity in the colonies soon to be states. It produced the Articles of Confederation, ran a revolution, and provided many of the greatest political, economic, and military leaders a platform to hone their skills and test their ideas. This was a group born of necessity which has been described as "a single governmental authority with ill-defined powers, it exercised, as occasion arose, the functions of an executive, of a legislative, and of a judicial body, but not always in like degrees of efficiency."[8] Even after the adoption of the Articles of Confederation in 1781, the last eight years of Congress' life (sometimes referred to as the Confederation Congress) was fraught with nearly the same issues that faced the pre–Articles Congress. The lumping of all functions (executive, legislative, and judicial) in one ill-defined body was bound to cause problems.

As noted earlier, many scholars like to distinguish between the Second Congress pre–Articles and post–Articles, calling the latter the Confederation Congress. While this is a good argument, it belabors the point and significance of the Second Continental Congress. The debate has dragged on for decades. In 1932, Frank Harmon Garver wrote, "The rather common practice of giving the name 'Continental Congress' to the chief governing body of the country from 1775 to 1789 owes much to the fact that one secretary, namely, Charles Thomson, served continuously throughout the period."[9] This debate can be seen as part of a larger discussion of the foundation of American law. The delegates to both the First and Second

Congresses saw law as the bedrock of their argument against Britain and as the starting point for any American government. While the debate over whether it should be the Second Continental Congress or the Confederation Congress after 1781 is to a certain extent an academic exercise, it does not lessen the larger attempt to understand when and where American law began. While some claim the drafting of the Constitution and the rejection of English common law, many states at the time still held on to the vestiges of common law (and still do).

Whatever its faults, this was the governing authority for the thirteen colonies (states after 1777), assembled. It had many faults, many delegates, many presidents, and many different meeting locations over fifteen years. For by the time the Constitutional Convention met in 1787, the delegates had endless examples of the types of problems of governing they wanted to change and those they wanted to avoid altogether in creating a new government through the Constitution. In that respect, the Continental Congress was a success—it had shown America's leaders what not to do and how not to structure a government.

The Continental Congress during its life was a unicameral body of about thirty members at any given time. They were sworn to secrecy.[10] Some were elected by their state legislators, some by the people, and some by the Committee of Correspondence for their colony; a considerable number chose not the serve even though they were elected, as was discussed earlier. William Paterson of New Jersey, future senator and Supreme Court Justice, was just one example. The Congress was not necessarily considered prominent. Most members would have considered serving in their state legislatures much more important and honorable, and many did just that, such as Thomas Jefferson.

Attendance

One issue facing Congress, similar to Washington's problem of keeping enlisted soldiers in the ranks through a full enlistment and beyond, (such as led to the mutiny at the Morristown camp) was elected members actually showing up at the Congress and participating in the work at hand. In all, over the course of the fifteen years the Continental Congress was in session, nearly ninety members failed to serve, although they were elected. That equals six members per year who did not attend proceedings—and no reason was required. This non-attendance could cripple Congress, and in turn, the American war effort, and every other effort requiring Congress' attention. On August 25, 1781, the president of Congress, Thomas McKean of Delaware, wrote a letter to several states:

> The Act of Congress of the 23rd instant, of which you have a copy enclosed, was occasioned by five states being unrepresented on this important period. We are at the Eve of great events, and the collected wisdom of the United States was perhaps seldom more wanted. I flatter myself therefore the public good will so far prevail over every other consideration that the Delegates from your states, or two of them at least, will give their attendance without delay.[11]

Fortunately, the President of Congress lacked the authority and temper of Washington and could not execute "a few" recalcitrant congressmen as an example to the rest to serve when elected.[12] Actually, over the course of the Congress, especially during the time of the surrender at Yorktown, "we will learn [from the record] that a body of about twenty-five men controlled the destinies of the nation; that their number often fell below twenty-five, but never rose to more than thirty-five."[13]

As late as September 26, 1781, less than a month before Cornwallis' surrender, the United States Congress, even with a formal Articles of Confederation, had trouble filling all of its seats. The New York delegation, writing to Governor Clinton, commented that "Congress have remained so thin that a single dissentient would have frustrated any proposition which we might have offered."[14] Once again, it was fortuitous that the President of Congress, Thomas McKean, did not have the power to execute "a few" members of Congress to bring the other members in line and force them to serve.[15] To add insult to injury, members still wanted their salary, just like the soldiers wanted theirs. Congressman George Walton, of Georgia, upon leaving on October 10, wrote to the President of Congress:

> Intending to return to Georgia as soon as I can make some little establishment for my family, I request Congress will order me a sum of money for that purpose, in like manner as was done for my late colleagues Colonel Few and Mr. Howly.
>
> When provision was lately made for discharging the necessary debts of the Delegates of the three Southern States, I owed the sum of fifty-six pounds: this I did not draw for, proposing to have paid it by economizing the monthly allowance: but going soon after out of office, that debt, (which ought to be considered upon a footing with those of the other delegates), is left upon me undischarged.[16]

Ironically, the President of Congress, Thomas McKean of Delaware, resigned from Congress in a letter to Washington the day before Cornwallis surrendered. With quicker communication, McKean probably would have stayed for the victory. He wrote to Washington, "I shall be under a necessity of attending the Supreme Court next week: besides my health requires a ride into the country, and my mind some relaxation: I shall therefore resign the chair of Congress."[17]

By the end of the American War in 1781 and certainly by the Peace Treaty of 1783, the relative ineffectualness of the Continental Congress was well known. During the eight years (1775–1783) of the American Revolution, Washington wrote thousands of letters to Congress begging for them to act, to move from inaction to action—as he saw it—in helping the army wage the revolt against Britain. Washington's letters are by far the most famous, although there was no shortage of observers critical of the apparent ineptitude of the Congress. For most, the problem lay in the lack of power of Congress over the states. One who saw this, and addressed the issue, was Alexander Hamilton.

Hamilton's Theory of Power

The recognition of the need for a powerful central government can be traced back in part to Alexander Hamilton in the late 1770s. Even before the Paris Peace Treaty of 1783 formally ended the American Revolution, and in fact even before the battle at Yorktown, young Alexander Hamilton, who will figure greatly in later chapters, wrote several essays under the pseudonym "Continentalist" wherein he argued for a more powerful central government. (See appendix 2)

Hamilton's call was not widely embraced by the formal end of the war in 1783, when sentiments for a stronger, more coordinated central government were not overly prevalent. Many felt that the new states had just overthrown a powerful central government; and why would they then impose a new one so soon, if ever at all? Most patriot leaders felt that they had done their job in so far as securing independence and thus a recapturing of the ancient liberties they felt had been taken from them by the British monarch and Parliament. Ancient liberties meant not just the ancient English practice of liberty; it was an understanding of the historical process from ancient times to their time. It is fairly well known that most of the Founders were not only familiar with the ancient Greeks and Romans, they in many cases tried to model their lives, or at least aspects, on writings of the ancients.

For those with access beyond the Bible (which would have included nearly all of the Founders), the classical writers offered more than simple instructions for daily living. More astute Founders looked to the distant past to learn about history, and thereby tried to fathom the place their contributions and the Revolution had in the grand sweep of human events. The writings of secular ancients were just as useful as the religious ancients in helping to justify the Revolution to the American victors. (Throughout the eighteenth and nineteenth century, orators would sprinkle references to ancient writers and biblical references in what became ever more mythologized remembrances of the past.) Even obscure, ancient writers, like the historian Polybius (second century BCE) were occasionally quoted. Legal historian John Maxcy Zane has written, "This conception of the social aggregate as a reversion to the ideas of the ancient Greek and Roman world shows how it is that great and fundamental ideas are rarely entirely lost in the story of the law."[18]

In a Fourth of July oration in 1783—three months before the formal end of the Revolution with the Treaty of Paris—Dr. John Warren stated that, inspired by the theory of history embodied in Polybius, "to revert to first principles is so essentially requisite to public happiness and safety, that Polybius has laid down as an incontrovertible axiom, that every State must decline more or less rapidly, in proportion as she recedes from the principles on which she was founded."[19] In this view, adapted to the American experience, the colonies had, according to Warren, already receded from the principles on which she was founded by Britain and Britain was solely to blame for the resulting war. Therefore, the only alternative left to the colonists was revolt, but justified revolt to restore ancient, preexisting liberties in fulfillment of an inescapable law of history. Of course, what was discovered quickly was that you cannot go back. Once independence was achieved, the ancient liberties upon which the Revolution was fought were difficult to reinstate. Shadows of these concepts became, eventually, enshrined in the American Constitution, but to get there was not as simple as decreeing their return.

In this viewpoint, the resulting Constitution, if seen in a cyclical context, is simply a re-establishment of an order that had already existed. As will be shown in later chapters, the Constitution, and *The Federalist* papers, with all of the arguments back and forth, both sides, form a symmetry (not asymmetry) much like the architectural style so in favor at the time— Georgian. The ideals that the ancient's espoused, and colonist's absorbed, were full of not just liberty and rights, but order, balance, and, for lack of a better term, a sort of harmony with everyone working for the common good—a commonwealth type of approach. If any one section got out of order—too powerful, too weak—the whole establishment was liable to come crashing down. As historian Michael Lienesch has written concerning an imbalance, "In constitutional theory, the fear of excess was pervasive, Constitutional republicans, like all good republicans, assumed that an excess of power would create tyranny."[20] This excess could be found anywhere;

government, private groups like the Society of the Cincinnati, and mobs of disaffected men and women with little to lose and a lot to contend with. It was in part a fear of concentrated power that led the colonies to write the Articles of Confederation which gave the Continental Congress so little power. Yet, it was the Articles of Confederation which set the course for all constitutional national government in the United States. And with that, we will look at the Articles in some depth as the rightful ancestor of the Constitution.

The Thinking Behind the Articles

The first debate on the Articles of Confederation occurred in August 1776 (they were written by committee the previous two months). It was clear from the beginning that the issue of state power and sovereignty would dominate discussion and would slow down confederation and take valuable time away from running the war. This same issue of big state versus small would arise again in 1787 during the Constitutional Convention. It took five years of debate, but John Dickinson's Articles, after much alteration, finally became the law on March 1, 1781.

Historian Merrill Jensen has written of the Articles of Confederation, "Historians old and new have pictured them as the product of inexperience, the parent of chaos, and the basic cause of the need for the creation of the Constitution of 1787."[21] Why is this? The Articles of Confederation are rarely mentioned in textbooks, and even some college American history majors barely know what they were. Where or why were they written? Who wrote them? Answers to these questions will give us some facts, but hardly an insight into why they are viewed with such negativity.

Edmund Randolph offered a typical contemporary complaint of the Articles: it was too weak in the face of democracy.[22] Two co-authors of *The Federalists* Papers, Alexander Hamilton and John Jay, had very similar views. There was a pervading sense in the new states that the Revolution, while beneficial in freeing the colonies from Great Britain, had created too much democracy. In other words, the masses were too much in charge.

Alexander Hamilton is well known for his comments such as "the rich and well born" are the natural leaders and should receive such deference.[23] John Jay is equally well known for his similar maxim: "the people who own the country ought to govern it."[24] These views were not isolated. Many Founders saw this approach as the natural way government (and society) was structured. More so, they saw the Articles of Confederation as endangering that process and enabling too much democracy. Thus, these Founders who agitated for a new constitution were, by today's standards, quite autocratic and not democratic, as we tend to view them in our collective historical consciousness. These men saw an opportunity after the Revolution to fashion a new government to their liking. They sought a government not so much inclusive concerning voters, but rather stable concerning the existing power structure. While they originally championed a state's rights approach during wartime in crafting the Articles of Confederation, they softened that thinking when writing the Constitution and sought more power for the federal government. As Merrill Jensen has written, "Men who believed thus undertook to blacken the reputation of the Articles of Confederation."[25]

Part of the understanding necessary when confronting the Articles of Confederation is to remember that they were written during wartime (indeed at the same time as the Declaration of Independence) without a long term view to the future. They were an expediency to accomplish a task—winning the Revolutionary War. Fiscal historian Robert Wright has written on the inadequacies of the Articles of Confederation to wartime governance:

> A wartime expedient, the Articles of Confederation did not inspire confidence among merchants, manufacturers, or urban artisans. Under this document, the national government could not directly tax, and therefore could not do much of anything. Two attempts to give it the power to collect revenues by taxing imports, the so-called impost, failed due to the intransigence of a single state, Rhode Island in 1781, and New York in 1783.[26]

In a sense, they were destined for failure after independence was achieved because it was an agreement written for war, not peace. Furthermore, the large issues of liberty, democracy, and freedom, became subsumed in the much larger issue of power and economics.

The Articles of Confederation provided an expedient solution to a rapidly escalating problem: opposition to British control. In other words, the armed uprising, or revolution, which occurred between 1775 and 1781, was made more complicated by the theory on which it was premised— upon the sovereignty of the individual states, not upon the sovereignty of the national government via the people. Ideas and theories have consequences. It is impossible to know what would have happened if the Articles had been stronger in their conception. The main issue is that enough leaders realized, as has been stated many times already, a government organized for war is not necessarily inclined to govern in peace.

Yet, a government organized for peace had to take into consideration

3. The Articles of Confederation

those basic principles of government that constituted every idea, argument, or debate that occurred in America since the beginning of the dispute with Britain in 1765 (an admittedly somewhat arbitrary date, but nonetheless acceptable). Twenty years of debate and anguish was not to be distilled in four months. Beyond those twenty years, the delegates grappled with law and government dating back over a millennium—that was the heritage the Founders dealt with and fashioned the American Enlightenment upon. The distillation of the heritage the Founders crafted is our heritage today.

The radical language of the independence faction in Congress repulsed John Dickinson and many of his fellow conservatives. Those who became reluctant patriots had a difficult time assimilating into the radical fold. They recognized that the language of independence was necessary to bring along as many non–Founders as possible (the "common man"). Someone had to actually take up arms and fight. Most of those potential soldiers could not be recruited or motivated by less than over-the-top language mixing elements of liberty, freedom, and independence.

Merril Jensen wrote of this view of the conservative patriots (those who became Loyalist radicals):

> In a general way the conservatives knew what kind of a government they wanted. They wanted a centralized government which would take the place of the British government: a government which would regulate trade, control the disposition of western lands, and provide force to quell internal dissention.[27]

The conservatives were more than just nostalgic of the British system. They feared civil war among the colonies at worst and weak union without foreign recognition at best. A general paralysis would render the new nation incapable of conducting business and advancing its cause. In many ways, the Constitution was the victory of the conservatives who lost the independence debate in 1776; while the same Constitution was a defeat for the radicals who won the independence debate of 1776.

John Adams conflated the two issues of war and peace in his autobiography; he wrote that the Quakers of Pennsylvania "had hitherto acquiesced in the measures of the colonies, or at least had made no professed opposition to them; many of both descriptions had declared themselves with us and had been as explicit and as ardent as we were…. But now these People began to see that Independence was approaching they started back."[28] In many ways, the move on the part of the conservatives in the early Second Continental Congress came back a few years later when the same Congress began to write the Articles of Confederation. The same man, who led the conservative effort prior to independence, was the same man who led the effort to draft the Articles: John Dickinson.

More Than Just Independence

The year 1776 would prove to be a very busy one for the Second Continental Congress. Having reconvened in May of 1775, it had spent its time trying to organize a united military response to the beginning of armed hostilities with Britain. Even though the military aspects were extremely bleak in 1775, Benjamin Franklin proposed a plan of union for the colonies. His plan, recorded May 10, 1775, in the Journals of the Continental Congress (Franklin had just returned to America from England in March 1775) was not considered by the full Congress due to the seemingly incomprehensible thought of American independence at that early date and to the pressing military issues. In January 1776, Franklin's plan was again tabled, but by the summer, when independence was declared, Franklin's earlier suggestions became the outline of a directive for a committee that was formed to write a new plan of government. On June 12, 1776, the Second Continental Congress set about to create a framework of government: "Resolved, that the committee to prepare and digest the forms of a confederation to be entered into between these colonies, consist of a member from each colony."[29] The main members of this committee would be John Dickinson of Pennsylvania (who would be seen as the primary member although ironically he opposed independence and Franklin's plan of union), Samuel Adams of Massachusetts, Roger Sherman of Connecticut, and Robert R. Livingston of New York (the latter two would also serve on the committee to draft the Declaration of Independence). In short, the Dickinson plan:

> called for a one-house American legislature composed of delegates chosen annually by the states ... authority to settle boundary disputes between the states, to set limits to states claiming lands westward to the Mississippi, and to form new states.... The states were to contribute toward the maintenance of the common government in proportion to population.[30]

However, the extremely contentious issue of taxation—an issue which got America into the present war with Britain to begin with—was left to each state to determine and administer how they would provide revenue to the national government. The Continental Congress could impose no tax and raise no money except with the concurrence of all thirteen states. This provision was a direct result of the objections the delegates had to imposition of taxes by a central government. Of course, this objection would cripple the efforts of the Second Congress to wage war on a national level. This oversight would not be resolved until the drafting of the Constitution in 1787 and the explanation of taxation in *The Federalist* papers.

3. The Articles of Confederation 79

There are seemingly endless post-mortems on what was wrong with the Articles of Confederation. In short, they lacked enforcement, and they lacked money. Nothing could be done without money. As the ancient Roman statesman Cicero stated: "Revenues: The sinews of the state."[31] Strangely, the congressional leaders would send some of America's best and brightest to Europe to negotiate for loans rather than push states harder for revenue. It was an odd arrangement:

> In the absence of other means of obtaining funds Congress had resorted early to the unfortunate expedient of issuing paper money based solely on the good faith of the states to redeem it. This fiat money held its value for some little time; then it began to shrink and, once started on the downward path, its fall was rapid.[32]

Thankfully for the Americans, some European powers were happy to poke a finger in Britain's eye over the colonial revolt. Depending on highly fluid monetary rates and the calculations based on those rates, the United States might have borrowed more money than generated internally. In its own way, that was unfortunate, but ultimately necessary. Americans let others invest more in their future than they did themselves.

One example of the states' unwillingness to comply with requests from Congress for revenue: "In 1782 Congress asked for $8,000,000 and the following year for $2,000,000 more, but by the end of 1783 less than $1,500,000 had been paid in" to Congress.[33] As will be seen in chapter 8, Hamilton, the arch-conservative rebel, was exceptionally critical of Congress's inability to raise revenue. Without revenue, there was no point in having a country. Without jumping too much ahead of our story, Hamilton, in *Federalist* thirty-one, highlights several points arguing for the ability of Congress, or the national government, to tax:

> A government ought to contain in itself every power requisite to the full accomplishment of the objects committed to its care, and to the complete execution of the trusts for which it is responsible, free from every other control but a regard to the public good and to the sense of the people.
> As the duties of superintending the national defense and of securing the public peace against foreign or domestic violence involve a provision for casualties and dangers to which no possible limits can be assigned, the power of making that provision ought to know no other bounds than the exigencies of the nation and the resources of the community.
> As revenue is the essential engine by which the means of answering the national exigencies must be procured, the power of procuring that article in its full extent must necessarily be comprehended in that of providing for those exigencies.
> As theory and practice conspire to prove that the power of procuring revenue is unavailing when exercised over the States in their collective capacities, the federal government must of necessity be invested with an unqualified power of taxation in the ordinary modes.[34]

As we have already seen, "Congress had been given the authority to contract debts without the means of discharging them. It was entrusted with securing treaties without the authority to execute them. Most disturbing of all, it was charged with the "common defense" but lacked the power to…" raise and equip a proper army or navy.[35]

One of the better overviews of the problems with the Articles of Confederation is by Max Farrand, a giant in the scholarship of the Constitutional era. He wrote:

> The plan of government was there but it lacked any driving force. Congress might declare war but the states might decline to participate in it; Congress might enter into treaties but it could not make the states line up to them; Congress might borrow money but it could not be sure of repaying it; and Congress might decide disputes without being able to make the parties accept the decision.[36]

On July 12, 1776, nearly two weeks after Richard Henry Lee introduced a resolution calling for independence, and little over a week after the Declaration of Independence was first read aloud, Congress noted that "the committee appointed to prepare articles of confederation brought in a draught, which was read."[37] It seemed a natural flow to the order of events—independence first being declared, then the plan of government being presented. These two committees, the Articles and Declaration, were unquestionably busy during June and July of 1776. Neither of these proposals was taken lightly either. After the Articles were presented—the draft in the hand of John Dickinson—Congress directed that

> eighty copies, and no more, of the confederation, as brought in by the committee, be immediately printed, and deposited with the secretary, who shall deliver one copy to each member.
> That the printer be under oath to deliver all the copies, which he shall print, together with the copy sheet, to the secretary, and not disclose either directly or indirectly, the contents of the said confederation.[38]

With the issue of taxation safely left out of the Articles, the topic that caused the most unrest was that of western lands. Many of the new states claimed land that in theory stretched to the Pacific Ocean. Ironically, these claims came from the colonial-era charters, which established the colonies. This contention pitted the haves (states with extensive claims) against the have-nots (states without extensive claims). In fact, this sore point would delay ratification of the Articles for five years. Other factors, such as absenteeism in Congress, threats of British invasion into Philadelphia, and military business conspired to keep the Articles from ratification during those years as well.

Not everyone saw the final ratification of the Articles as a necessary good. Some saw the ratification as signaling an end to the struggle of Congress over the states and thus precluding opportunity to draft something better. "For from the nationalist point of view, the essential power lacked was the power of coercion over the states and their citizens."[39]

There was also over a century of prior mistrust of colonial powers, past treatment which the newly declared states did not easily forget. The surrendering of partial sovereignty (which is what the radicals saw the Articles as doing) to a national government was a move that could not be rushed. Yet, there was a sense of urgency. The Second Congress sent the Articles to the states for official consideration on November 17, 1777, over a year after it was drafted. In a letter of transmittal, Congress wrote to the states asking them to be ready to consider ratification in Congress on March 10, 1778. Congress wrote:

> The Congress will permit us, then, earnestly to recommend these articles to the immediate and dispassionate attention of the legislatures of the respective states. Let them be candidly reviewed under a sense of the difficulty of combining in one general system the various sentiments and interests of a continent divided into so many sovereign and independent communities, under a conviction of the absolute necessity of uniting all our councils and all our strength, to maintain and defend our common liberties: let them be examined with a liberality becoming brethren and fellow-citizens surrounded by the same imminent dangers, contending for the same illustrious prize, and deeply interested in being forever bound and connected together by ties the most intimate and indissoluble; and finally, let them be adjusted with the temper and magnanimity of wise and patriotic legislators, who, while they are concerned for the prosperity of their own more immediate circle, are capable of rising superior to local attachments, when they may be incompatible with the safety, happiness, and glory of the general confederacy.[40]

Writing from York, Pennsylvania, where the Congress had sought refuge from the British, Richard Henry Lee wrote to Samuel Adams:

> We have at length finished the Confederation and shall send it to the different states in a few days with strong exhortation to give it quick consideration and speedy return. Taxation, finance, and recruiting the Army will also be strongly recommended. Your utmost aid will no doubt be cordially applied to the expediting these important points.[41]

Lee captures nearly every point that would vex the states until the Constitutional Convention ten years later. Taxation, finance, and Congress having more authority over the states than just recommending this or that would render the Articles fragmentary at best. All three topics would imperil the peace after Yorktown and not subside until *The Federalist* papers would explain it ten years later.

By March 10, 1778, only Virginia was prepared to sign the Articles of Confederation. Congress postponed until June the deadline as so few members were in attendance. Finally, on June 26, 1778, Congress printed a separate form for delegates to sign indicating their state's approval and ratification. The Articles themselves were printed on parchment:

> The ratification of the Articles of Confederation, engrossed on a roll of parchment being laid before Congress, ... the same was signed on the part and in behalf of their respective states by the delegates of New Hampshire, Massachusetts Bay, Rhode Island and Providence Plantations, Connecticut, Pennsylvania, Virginia, and South Carolina, ... The delegates of the states of New Jersey, Delaware, and Maryland informed Congress that they have not yet received powers to ratify and sign."[42]

Eight states signed on July 9 and by the end of July a total of ten states had signed. New Jersey, Delaware, and Maryland were the holdouts, and the Articles required unanimous consent for ratification. Congress appointed Richard Henry Lee, Francis Dana, and Gouverneur Morris to prepare a letter to be sent to the three states that still had not signed. New Jersey signed on November 26, 1778, and Delaware on February 22, 1779. Maryland would hold out until March 1, 1781, as mentioned previously over the issue of western lands. Maryland also had an issue over the destitute of another state: it did not want them. As early as December 22, 1777, the Maryland legislature instructed its delegates to the Second Congress to amend the fourth Article, "by striking out the word 'paupers' and inserting a provision, 'that one state shall not be burthened with the maintenance of poor persons who may remove from another state."[43]

On November 20, 1777, North Carolina Congressman Cornelius Harnett wrote to fellow Congressman Thomas Burke:

> Your favorite Confederation is at last finished. It only waits several states for their approbation, with a pressing letter from Congress on that subject, which you will soon see. Our finances are in such a situation, that unless the States agree immediately, to tax as high as the people can possibly bear [they did not], the credit of our money must be ruined [it was].[44]

Harnett too, like Lee, recognized the weakness of the American cause without revenue. It was looking more and more that without foreign aid, the Americans could not be seen as fielding a proper army, among other things, and thus would eventually fail in their goal. As was seen in chapter 1, geo-political concerns in Europe ensured American victory with French assistance. Harnett's and Lee's letters also point out that the American attempt at independence was in no way a foregone conclusion. Two-hundred years later, that notion or inevitability makes us feel comfortable and secure in our past and present, but at the time, there was nothing comfortable and secure about the American attempt at independence.

Finally, Congressman Harnett illuminated another issue with the Second Congress. After the giddiness, the almost naughty feeling of the First

Continental Congress had worn off, the Second Congress was faced with the actual work of governing. Most can agree that while fighting is easy, listening, compromising, and governing, is not so easy. As has been pointed out, it is all too easy (it is almost a sport) to dismiss politicians (again, easily forgetting that somebody had to vote for these people) and part of that sentiment was at play as early as the Second Congress. Congressman Harnett wrote home "For God's sake endeavor to get some Gentlemen appointed in my stead. I can not stay any longer with any pleasure."[45] Harnett would write separately to an associate named William Wilkinson, "If I once more can return to my family all the Devils in Hell shall not separate us. The honor of being once a member of Congress is sufficient for me, I acknowledge it is the highest honor a free state can bestow on one of its members."[46] (Sadly, Harnett was captured by the British and suffered imprisonment before being released and dying in 1781, before the surrender at Yorktown.)

A further bone of contention that would rip apart the Union a century later was noted in the reaction to the Articles as well. Congressman Nathaniel Folsom of New Hampshire wrote to the president of that state, Meshech Weare. The topic of slavery caused Folsom concern:

> Inclosed I send you a copy of the Confederation, the eighth article of which respects taxation, and has given me great uneasiness, as I cannot see any justice in the rule therein laid down for proportioning the several states with the charges of the present war. In the first place, it appears to me that one third part of the wealth of the Southern States which consists in Negroes, is entirely left out, and no notice taken of them in determining their ability to pay taxes.[47]

Not only was Fulsom concerned about the burden the War would impose on individual (sovereign) states, the specter of slavery had already entered the national governing vocabulary and would not depart from the nomenclature for nearly one-hundred years.

Conclusion

There are many fine studies that review the Articles simply as the Articles in a lineal, narrative, approach. The Articles are without question the most important aspect to appear from the churning mass of chaos unleashed by America's dispute with Britain. This statement can be made with the understanding that a national government was the end goal of the colonists' cause. Likewise, with that understanding in mind, it can be said with some confidence, not total, that the Continental Congress was a failure. It would be difficult to point to any substantive accomplishments that truly impacted, in a time-sensitive manner, contemporary issues and correspondingly had impacts for the future of the country as they (the members) knew or understood it to be. In a manner of speaking, was the Continental Congress destined or designed to lead a war and subsequently (with luck) the peace? The Continental Congress comes across more as an expedient which could prevent anarchy by claiming to be the repository of the new nation's ancient liberties. (Juxtaposing "new" with "ancient" is intentional, what ancient liberties could the colonists claim beyond the British constitution, which they were rejecting?) In the macro sense, one could argue the overall Revolutionary effort, with its successful conclusion, shows Congress in a positive light. The problem with this is that Congress could be seen just as easily as negating its responsibility. Then again, what were those responsibilities? The Articles of Confederation mention nothing about fighting the War for Independence; where did its legal authority come from, where was it grounded? In this case, how can Congress be seen in a positive light for the Revolution?

In spite of historians' best efforts, the answers cannot be known. There is no such thing as definitive history. Names and dates are easy; the why of history is what is hard. And that "why," as long as people differ, can never be settled. This work overall thus far has looked at the Articles and the Congress through to the Treaty of Paris of 1783, establishing independence, in a more-or-less linear fashion. It is now time to begin the transition to the Constitution and *The Federalist* papers which will culminate in chapters 6 and 8. For now, we will move to chapter 4 and look at how the failures and weaknesses of the Articles and Congress began to generate concern among the more reflective leaders in the states, and their correspondence and smaller gatherings arguing that the current government in 1783 (post–Revolution) was totally inept at facing the challenges of governing their new nation. The results of this agitation were the meetings at Alexandria and Mount Vernon followed by a small convention at Annapolis, Maryland, onetime capital of the United States.

PART II

The Failure of the National Government

As the Second Continental Congress struggled through the peace process brought on by the Yorktown surrender, it was abundantly clear, as if it needed more clarity, that the national government was woefully inadequate to secure the peace. For one, there was no money, and without money, you cannot have a country. You can have inspirational phrases about liberty, and freedom, and the Rights of Man; but without money, they are dead phrases. The Second Congress had to find a way to remedy the situation. They could not; and it was left to a small band of leaders to begin the process of creating a mature, functioning, government with a reliable revenue source.

Chapter 4

Annapolis and Alexandria

A Period for Reflection

The years after the final peace with Great Britain in 1783 were filled with a sense of trial and error gone awry. The Articles of Confederation were proving to be woefully inadequate to not just governing, but more importantly to establishing a sound economic foundation for America to rebuild itself and compete internationally. It was clear by this point too that an actual united government of the states was desired, as opposed to independent sovereign states loosely confederated. (Although a minority held out hope for thirteen separate governments independent from a national government.) Few had an idea or energy to create something from nothing. They all knew the problem existed, but ideas to remedy the problem were scarce.

With independence achieved, the United States faced the prospect of standing on the world stage as a new cast member in the competing jumble of nations. Each one sought to define themselves and gain the upper hand over their rivals. As a former colony of Britain, the United States had a fortunate pedigree. One of the most powerful and admired nations (Britain) had an offspring. That offspring, the United States, had a lot to live up to. Pressure however was mounting both internally and externally for the United States to move beyond its rustic beginnings and assume a role as a world figure. To do this, most of America's leaders knew a functioning, respected, and strong national government had to be in place. The Articles of Confederation proved completely inadequate to national governance—and the majority knew this. Still, there were many powerful voices, even though in the minority, who kept tempting America with the past rather than trying to shape the future. The years between 1783 and 1787 were indeed years of reflection and introspection. During those years, the lines between the past and the future became clearer. This chapter will look at those roughly four years and highlight some of the main arguments being made for a stronger national government with real structure, meaning, purpose, and promise. These years would also see the coming of two young men who will factor so prominently in the remainder of this study—Alexander Hamilton and James Madison. Their efforts on behalf of the national government would mature and be more broadly disseminated, reaching ripeness during the Constitutional Convention in 1787 and *The Federalist* papers project immediately following the Convention.

Revenue

Historian Ben Baack wrote in the *Economic History Review*:

> The Articles of Confederation clearly defined the institutional relationship between the states and Congress. The states were to be free and independent while Congress had only limited and well specified powers. Any alteration by amendment of this structure which enhanced the powers of Congress could come only at the expense of the sovereignty of the states. To avoid this happening without the consent of the states, the framers had incorporated a decision-making rule for Congress requiring unanimity among the states to amend the articles. Granting the power of taxation to Congress would therefore require the unanimous consent of the states.[1]

On January 29, 1783, before the formal signing of the Paris Peace Treaty, Arthur Lee of Virginia wrote to Samuel Adams of Massachusetts and covered two of the topics which dominated the debate from 1784 to 1787. These topics would lead in quick succession to Alexandria, Annapolis, an unhappy, mutinous army, and finally, back to Philadelphia for the Constitutional Convention—and national taxation.[2] Lee wrote:

> Every engine is at work here to obtain permanent taxes and the appointment of Collectors by Congress, in the states. The terror of a mutinying army is played off with considerable efficacy. [There would be several former soldiers leading revolts, the most well-known being Shays' Rebellion.] It is certainly a great misfortune to any country, that their army should be discontented....[3]

Congressman James Madison, a leading figure in post–Revolutionary America, was also highly concerned about the lack of revenue, among other things, to pay for the war recently ended. In February 1783, Madison voiced his concern in a letter to Governor Edmund Randolph of Virginia that he estimated the cost of war and the revenue needed to be three-million dollars; Madison called this an "enormous" sum, and it was—although he was actually off by quite a bit.[4] Madison elaborated on the revenue question in Congress to Randolph: "The generality of the members are convinced of the necessity of a continental revenue for an honorable discharge of the continental engagements, and for making future provision for the war."[5]

Madison ended his missive by identifying the weaknesses and impediments to revenue generation, which he saw were the individual states. As historian Robert Wright has written, states "refused to give the national government the power to tax though they had given it the power to borrow."[6] And, borrow it did. "Congress estimated that its foreign debt had reached nearly $8 million while its domestic debt was just over $42 million."[7] This was slightly more than Madison estimated—however, to be fair, no one could hardly have accurately calculated the debt given the fluid nature of the fluctuating value of the paper currency and bonds. Without a central bank or financial authority, no true estimate could stand scrutiny.

Throughout February 1783, Madison struck the theme of taxation and army revolt (as did others), writing again to Edmund Randolph on February 25, 1783: "It is now whispered, that they have not only resolved not to lay their arms till justice shall be done them, but that, to prevent surprise, a public declaration will be made to that effect."[8]

Madison and his fellow Congressional colleagues (and those outside Congress too) were growing ever more concerned about the risk of mutiny and civil uprising. Soldiers could be easily discharged, but of course they could just as easily incite a civil riot back home then. This is exactly what happened in several instances from 1784 to 1787, the year of the Constitutional Convention. The most well known was Shays' Rebellion, which will be the subject of chapter 5.

Joseph Jones, member of Congress from Virginia, wrote to George Washington in February 1783, with perhaps a different outlook than Madison concerning taxation. Jones wrote:

> A short time will bring to a conclusion our efforts on this business [taxation], which I am in hopes will terminate in the adoption of such measures as may be acceptable to the states, and produce the granting of such funds as will restore public credit, give value to the great mass of depreciated certificates, and enable Congress to render, to every class of the public creditors, ample justice.[9]

Keeping on the tax theme, the North Carolina delegates to Congress wrote to their governor Alexander Martin in March 1783:

> In the mean while attempts have been made to lay a general tax on lands, houses, etc. as you will see.... We presume that no such tax will be recommended to the states because we think that the states should be left to tax lands and other permanent property in such manner and at such rates as they think best.[10]

On April 23, 1783, Congress prepared a resolution "for granting an impost, and Excise, and to change an Article of the Confederation...."[11]

Literally hundreds, if not thousands, of letters crisscrossed the states, in the effort to figure out how best to deal with raising revenue and decide whether or not raising revenue somehow violated state sovereignty. On the positive side, the one aspect in which Congress did not lack during this period was its level of correspondence. The members kept couriers and postal workers busy for over a decade, writing on both public and private topics, writing as a group, or simply writing to report on the tedium of Congress.

On April 18, 1783, Congress was considering a report on finance. The big question was the national government financial situation. As recorded in the Journals of the Continental Congress:

> That as a further mean, as well of hastening the extinguishment of the debts, as of establishing the harmony of the United States.... That it be recommended to the several states, as indispensably necessary to the restoration of public credit, and to the punctual and honorable discharge of public debts, to invest the United States in Congress assembled with a power to levy for the use of the United States the following duties upon goods imported into the said states....[12]

Among those imports which were proposed to be taxed by the new United States was tea—the one commodity we associate so completely today with the rebellion against Britain.

The issue of revenue was so great that Robert Morris, the secretary of finance for the Second Congress, resigned on November 1, 1784, out of disgust (Morris was replaced by a treasury board, which was completely overwhelmed).[13] Morris, one of the most gifted men in finance next to Alexander Hamilton at the time, fought for greater revenue and was frustrated at every turn. Morris was in fact so seminal to the avoidance of financial collapse that his contribution deserves a closer appreciation. Morris had extensive national and international contacts. As mentioned, next to Hamilton, "he was one of the few American statesmen who could fully grasp the implications of England's financial structures."[14] This was crucial as Americans where reliant on the English system as that was all they knew.

With few native financial resources on hand, Morris set about in 1781 "to stabilize the Bank of North America ... [which was] the very first stock bank in America."[15] Morris did more than just talk about theory. He personally placed not just his reputation on the line, but his own money:

> At great personal risk, Morris put his full energy into this program. In his new position as Superintendent of Finance, he personally guaranteed the newly issued notes, using his private credit as a merchant to stop the decline of industry when it became clear that this was the only means of winning acceptance. These "Morris Notes" were known

colloquially as "Roberts," and were generally referred to as "short Bobs" or "long Bobs," according to the length of their term.[16]

Morris expressed his frustration, and those of his colleagues, with the oratorical "wind-bags" who seemed to slow progress on financial matters through their loquacious reliance on theoretical opposition to practical undertakings. Morris, like many of his more mature colleagues, quickly tired of the theoretical ramblings that afflicted some of the delegates. In a letter to the state governors on July 25, 1781, two months before Yorktown, Morris wrote:

> To suppose this expensive war can be carried on without joint and strenuous efforts [for raising revenues] is beneath the wisdom of those who are called to the high offices of legislation. Those who inculcate maxims which tend to relax these efforts, most certainly injure the common cause whatever may be the motives which inspire their conduct.[17]

His plan for a national tax was stymied by the agrarian delegates, who, with "their poor grasp of economic matters" had worked to defeat Morris' proposal.[18] By 1786 nearly all had collapsed:

> Congress could not sell *any* of the $500,000 worth of domestic bonds it needed to bolster the federal army in the aftermath of Shays' Rebellion, and the state governments could have borrowed in Europe only on terms so ruinous no republican government would countenance them in peacetime. Congress found it difficult to muster a quorum much less a decent revenue.[19]

Morris' anger was expressed countless times in letters and correspondence with members of Congress back home hinting at talk of national taxation but vowing that it could never pass the Congress. Here again is a perfect example of a Janus-like approach the Congress had to revenue. Members can be seen as saying, "we know we need revenue, just don't ask for it from the states, or at least not my state." Morris sought all along for a national tax, one that could respond to the financial crisis facing the still warring Untied States. Morris saw (much like Hamilton as Secretary of the Treasury) "Public debts [as] an important impetus to raise taxes at the national level. The higher the national public debt, the more urgent it was that congress institute its own tax system if it was to avoid bankruptcy."[20]

On May 5, 1786, Rufus King of Massachusetts wrote to John Adams (in England as American Ambassador) about yet another slight to America over its inability to raise revenue: "It has undoubtedly been said in England that the act of Congress of the 15th of February relative to the federal revenues, is full proof that the United States are in the utmost confusion, and that the Union is nearly dissolved."[21] The Journal of the Continental Congress for February 15 records the Act to which King referred:

> In the course of this enquiry, it most clearly appeared, that the requisitions of Congress, for eight years past, have been so irregular in their operation, so uncertain in their collection, and so evidently unproductive, that a reliance on them in future as a source from whence moneys are to be drawn to discharge the engagements of the Confederacy, definite as they are in time and amount, would be not less dishonorable to the understandings of those who entertain such confidence, than it would be dangerous to the welfare and peace of the Union: The Committee are therefore seriously impressed with the indispensable obligation that Congress are under, of representing to the immediate and impartial consideration of the several States, the utter impossibility of maintaining and preserving the faith of the federal Government, by temporary requisitions on the States, and the consequent necessity of an early and complete accession of all the States to the revenue system of the 18th of April, 1783.[22]

King continued that he felt the British were not aware of American resolve though to figure something out. Yet it could not be denied that the situation was bleak. King went on:

> That there exists a criminal neglect of several of the states in their most important duties to the confederacy cannot be denied. I hope a reform will take place. The people generally through the confederacy, remark that we are in a crisis…. But there is good reason to expect that our finances, will be strengthened and made certain, and a proposition has originated in Virginia, for a convention of delegates, in September, from the several states to agree on such commercial regulations as shall extend the American navigation and promote the trade of the union.[23]

King, at the early point in 1786, saw the Annapolis gathering purely in light of the trade consequences related to revenue. In his analysis he did not approach the idea of reform of the Articles to end the revenue stalemate.

The final embarrassment for Congress occurred in the spring of 1786. An investigation into the financial strength of the country revealed that it was quite weak. Since 1781, the states had paid only $2.4 million of a total requisition from Congress of $15.6 million. This was an appalling figure and genuinely stunned most members of Congress.

Additionally, John Adams, in England as the American Ambassador, wrote to Foreign Secretary John Jay that the British would not evacuate their northwestern garrisons until the Americans fulfilled their treaty obligations to repay British creditors and compensate Loyalists for lost property. This could not happen without national legal pressure applied to the states requiring them to honor national treaties. Individual states were operating at this time as though they could simply ignore national treaties. No doubt there was an element of foot-dragging on the part of the states; unfortunately, it went well beyond juvenile delays. These issues were compounded because each state operated as its own virtual nation and could impose what laws it wanted in connection with former Loyalists and in repaying

British creditors. Or, more likely, they did not impose any at all and simply ignored the national laws. Many of these topics would not be settled until the Constitution compelled adherence to national treaties. Many of the Loyalist and British creditor cases would wind up before the new Supreme Court in a few years' time and would also be part of the 1794 Jay Treaty with Britain.

Alexandria and Mount Vernon

Amidst all the swirl of debate, fear, and apprehension, two states decided to come together to try to improve the commercial relations of their region. One of the few studies that can be found that looks exclusively at the Mount Vernon Compact (the meeting actually occurred in Alexandria, but George Washington invited the negotiators to Mount Vernon to sign the final agreement and the name Mount Vernon has been attached to it ever since) states: "From a trade compact between two states to a political union between thirteen there are wide spaces of no needful logical connection, though the first be practically the latter's sponsor and progenitor."[24] Perhaps there is the typical nineteenth century penchant for flowery, embellished language (this study dates to 1888), but it nonetheless points to a larger truth: the Mount Vernon Compact, while extra-legal, was the first step toward a fuller contemplation of American national government.[25] George Washington had long been interested in capitalizing on the navigation of American waterways, especially those waterways literally right outside his back door, to provide access to his land in the west.[26] With the failure of the Second Congress to act on such issues, Washington sought to build support for a regional gathering of representatives. In a March 29, 1784, letter, Washington, enjoying retirement at Mount Vernon, wrote to Thomas Jefferson (a few months before Jefferson embarked for France):

> More than ten years ago I was struck with the importance of it [a navigation plan], and despairing of any aid from the public, I became a principle mover of a bill to empower a number of subscribers to undertake, at their own expense ... the extension of the navigation from the tidewater to Will's Creek ... and I devoutly wish that this may not be the only expedient by which it can be effected now.... The plan however, was in a tolerable train when I set out for Cambridge in 1775, and would have been in an excellent way had it not been for the difficulties which were met with in the Maryland Assembly.[27]

Washington wrote numerous letters to state leaders throughout 1784 encouraging them to support efforts to create a more binding network of canals and navigational aids allowing greater access to the products from the western lands. Some of these improvements would be financed through a toll on using the waterways. Great effort was expended to get not only Virginia leaders interested, but Maryland as well. Furthermore, issues of boundary claims between neighboring states were impacting negotiations into the navigation of the Potomac. The Virginia Assembly in June 1784 agreed with Washington: "Whereas great inconveniences are found to result from the want of some concerted regulations between this state and the state of Maryland touching the jurisdiction and navigation of the river Potomac."[28]

The resolution further named George Mason, Edmund Randolph, James Madison, and Alexander Henderson, as commissioners to meet with the commissioners of Maryland in Alexandria.[29] The Maryland commissioners were Thomas Johnson, Thomas Stone, Samuel Chase, and Daniel of St. Thomas Jenifer.[30] With Washington's assistance, the commissioners actually completed their work at the end of 1784—thus resulting in the Potomac and James River Companies. James Madison took the initiative to move this agreement onto the larger stage. Madison wrote to Washington in December 1784, "It seems naturally to grow out of the proposed appointment of commissioners for Virginia and Maryland, concerted at Mount Vernon, for keeping up harmony in the commercial regulations of the two states. Maryland has ratified the report, but has invited into the plan Delaware and Pennsylvania, who will naturally pay the same compliment to their neighbors"[31]

What became known as the Mount Vernon Compact of March 1785 was a success, so successful in fact that the original Maryland and Virginia agreement now included Pennsylvania, joining in their effort to connect the Potomac and Ohio rivers by canals, and thus creating a most formidable commercial artery to the American West. "The compact was confirmed in due time, settling points as to tolls and fisheries, light-houses, buoys, and kindred matters."[32] Thus secured, Virginia, Maryland, and Pennsylvania were business partners. Simultaneously, Virginia and Maryland discussed navigation of the Chesapeake Bay as well, given its huge economic potential. Washington certainly added his prestige, but Madison created the plan "to consider how far a uniform system in their [the states] commercial regulations may be necessary to their common interest and permanent harmony" and rightly deserves the credit for moving the arrangement to the next level.[33]

From this persistence of Madison, the Annapolis Convention of 1786 was conceived. Born of the need for trade and commerce (and revenue), it ended up masquerading as a trade deal but in reality took aim at the structure of the Articles of Confederation and ultimately the government of the United States. One of the most succinct statements on the Annapolis Convention of 1786 comes from historian Edmund Burnett: "The Annapolis Convention derives its origin directly from an effort on the part of Virginia and Maryland to adjust their own problems relating to the commerce of the Potomac, while indirectly it was an outgrowth of the movement for a general regulation of trade by Congress."[34]

General Discontent Before Annapolis

While the Alexandria meeting was the lone bright spot during this time, much angst existed among America's leaders. Although the Alexandria meeting involved only two states, James Madison took the momentum of Alexandria and began to agitate for a nationwide gathering in Annapolis.

On May 11, 1786, James Monroe (Virginia delegate to the Continental Congress) wrote a lengthy letter to Thomas Jefferson in France. Again, as with his colleagues, Monroe talked about revenue and complained about delegate attendance: "Since my last I have received yours of 11th December and 27th January last until lately we have had so thin a Congress that few acts of consequence have passed, a very pointed recommendation to those states who have hitherto declined to accede to the recommendation of respecting a revenue system only excepted."[35] Monroe continued with other political news and updated Jefferson before he ended with a mention of the upcoming Annapolis convention and the central role played by Virginia: "The plan of a convention at Annapolis which I believe will be carried into effect has taken the subject [revenue] from before Congress, as it originated with our state we think it our duty to promote its object by all the means in our power."[36]

Striking a similar tone to Monroe was Charles Pettit of New Jersey. Writing to Jeremiah Wadsworth of Connecticut on May 15, 1786, Pettit wrote: "I am now at a loss to answer your other question as to what we are doing in Congress. It has been but a short time that we have had a Congress adequate to the important parts of business and the greater part of the time has been spent in forming opinions on various subjects without maturing scarcely anything."[37]

In May 1786, William Grayson of Virginia wrote to his colleague James Madison expressing nearly identical sentiments about the upcoming Annapolis Convention. Certainly Grayson must have known that Madison was the main promoter of the gathering. Grayson informed Madison he saw a larger purpose to the gathering beyond just trade issues "so as to comprehend all the grievances of the Union, and to combine the commercial arrangements with them, and make them dependant on each other...."[38] In Grayson, Madison found a kindred spirit.

A month after his letter to John Adams sounding the themes of commerce and reform, Rufus King wrote to Jonathan Jackson repeating, even more forcefully, similar concerns:

> The views of individuals are so various, and the imaginary interests of the states are so opposite, that without the danger of some evil that will affect each member of the Confederacy, a reasonable hope cannot be indulged of a reform.
> The situation of the federal government is now critical; the authority of the confederation is found to be inadequate to bringing money into the common treasury, and the credit of the states is not sufficient to procure loans at home or abroad....
> I fear that the commercial convention, proposed to be held in Maryland in September, will go but a little way in effecting those measures essentially necessary for the prosperity and safety of the states.[39]

King commented further on the plan originating in Virginia and that the Virginia delegates might have more in mind than just commerce.[40] This gives a clear indication of just how well communications were moving among the states that King could be so well informed of the motivations for the Annapolis Convention in such a short period of time.

Theodore Sedgwick also represented the tenor of the times when he wrote to Caleb Strong on August 6, 1786:

> Even the appearance of a union cannot in the way we now are long to be preserved. It becomes us seriously to contemplate a substitute; for if we do not control events we shall be miserably controlled by them. No other substitute can be devised than that of contracting the limits of the confederacy to such as are natural and reasonable, and within those limits instead of a nominal to institute a real, and an efficient government.[41]

As late as August 1786, less than a month before the Annapolis Convention, James Monroe sent letters to state leaders encouraging them to send delegates. He wrote to John Sullivan of New Hampshire, "It is with concern I have been informed it is probable commissioners will not attend the convention at Annapolis from your state. I hope this is not the case. I have looked forward to that convention as the source of infinite blessings to this country."[42]

By the beginning of September 1786, Rufus King was again declaring the potential gloom of the United States and the ardent hope that something will come of the Annapolis gathering. He again pointed to Madison as the chief thinker behind the event: "He (Madison) does not discover or propose any plan than that of investing congress with full powers for the regulation of commerce foreign and domestic. But this power will run deep into the authorities of the individual states.... The reform must necessarily be extensive."[43]

Annapolis Considered

Maryland and Virginia had already met in March 1785 at Alexandria and at Mount Vernon to work out their trade differences. Largely successful, the two states wanted to broaden their work into a more regional undertaking. With the Second Congress unable to act, these states, guided primarily by Virginia and James Madison, sought out the means to strengthen the economic ties of the states.

The lead-up to the Annapolis Convention as seen was fraught with worries over money, trade, and commerce. These topics would dominate concerns over not just national financial well-being, but national prestige too. American leaders, especially those who served abroad, were keenly aware of the need for the new country to be able to get its financial affairs in order.

It is clear that James Madison gave extensive consideration to the Annapolis Convention. Not only was Madison a prime leader in the effort to promote the gathering, develop its agenda, and provide a framework for something larger than a commercial gathering, he even helped pick the location. Writing to Thomas Jefferson (serving in France as American Ambassador) Madison stated:

> ... it has been agreed to propose Annapolis for the place, and the first Monday in September for the time of holding the convention. It was thought prudent to avoid the neighborhood of Congress, and the large commercial towns, in order to disarm the adversaries to the object, of insinuations of influence from either of these quarters.... If it should come to nothing, it will I fear confirm G.[reat] B.[ritain] and all the world in the belief that we are not to be respected, nor apprehended as a nation in matters of commerce....
>
> I consider the event therefore as extremely uncertain, or rather, considering that the States must first agree to the proposition for sending deputies—that these must agree in a plan to be sent back to the States, and that these again must agree unanimously in a ratification of it. I almost despair of success. It is necessary however that something should be tried and if this be not the best possible expedient, it is the best that could possibly be carried through the legislature here.[44]

Congress itself was generally favorable to the idea of a nationwide gathering to study trade and commerce, and most of the states did appoint delegates to Annapolis. Unfortunately, when the convention met in Annapolis on the first Monday of September 1786, only five states had representatives in attendance. Four other states had appointed members, but their travels were not expeditious enough to get them to Annapolis on schedule. At the time, the French minister to the United States, Louis-Guillaume Otto, took a keen interest in the proceedings in Annapolis and reported back to France on the progress and evolution of the meeting—proceeding as it did from an ostensible discussion on trade and commerce to much more, perhaps even reforming the Articles of Confederation.

As with the Continental Congress, the stars of Annapolis were clearly the young men. One was from Virginia, James Madison, and one from New York, Alexander Hamilton (both future *The Federalist* co-authors). It is hard to imagine two men who had the same goal being so different. Madison, the calm and cool scholar, seemingly unable to break a sweat even in one-hundred-degree weather; Hamilton, while brilliant, no scholar. He was impetuous, rash, and often spoke before thinking. One of the fascinating sidebars of the entire Revolutionary generation was the types of figures it produced as leaders.

Reporting to Congress

The Annapolis Convention produced a report that went far beyond trade and commerce.[45] Reflecting the urgency of Hamilton and the intense research of Madison, the report called for a new gathering of commissioners from every state to gather in Philadelphia on the second Monday in May of 1787. This was the first appearance in print of the call to the Constitutional Convention. (See appendix 1) The stated goal was to "devise such further provisions as shall appear to them necessary to render the Constitution [Articles] of the Federal Government adequate to the exigencies of the Union...."[46] The Congress approved the Annapolis recommendation for a Philadelphia convention on February 21, 1787. Rhode Island was the only state not to appoint a delegation for Philadelphia, as was their usual approach to such gatherings. Interestingly, the Newport and Providence deputies to the General Assembly openly protested the actions of the majority of the Assembly with a letter attempting to counter the reasoning of the majority. The Newport and Providence deputies wrote:

> ... it has never been thought heretofore by the legislature of this state, or while it was a colony, inconsistent with or any innovation upon the rights and liberties of the citizens of this state to concur with the sister states or colonies in appointing members or delegates to any convention proposed for the general benefit, but with the highest approbation

of the good people of this state and while a colony, the legislature have at various times agreed to conventions with the sister states or colonies and found their interests greatly served thereby.[47]

The Annapolis Convention was something akin to letting the genie out of the bottle. Once out, it cannot easily be put back. The report of the Annapolis commissioners was delivered to Congress on September 20, 1786. Under the hand of the convention president, John Dickinson, the report listed it could not conduct its business due to a lack of participation—very much the similar problem with Congress. Those present, however, felt a duty to draw up a listing of their discussions even though they were non-binding. The report stated:

> ... Your commissioners cannot forebear to indulge an expression of their earnest and unanimous wish that speedy measures may be taken to effect a general meeting of the states in a future convention...
> ... Your commissioners submit an opinion, that the idea of extending the powers of their deputies to other objects than those of commerce ... will deserve to be incorporated into that of a future convention....
> That there are important defects in the system of the Federal Government, is acknowledged by the Acts of all those states which have concurred in the present meeting....
> ... your commissioners ... beg leave to suggest their unanimous conviction ... in the appointment of commissioners to meet at Philadelphia on the second Monday in May next, to take into consideration the situation of the United States.[48]

When the full Congress took up the proposal on February 21, 1787, it was determined that:

> in the opinion of Congress it is expedient that on the second Monday in May next a Convention of delegates who shall have been appointed by the several states be held at Philadelphia for the sole and express purpose of revising the Articles of Confederation and reporting to Congress and the several legislatures such alterations and provisions therein....[49]

Reactions

Rufus King, much more than a passive observer in these events, wrote to Massachusetts governor James Bowdoin on September 17, 1786, immediately after the Annapolis Convention concluded (he was not an attendee). King began by lamenting the state of revenue and the lack of interest on the part of the states in Congress. King wrote:

> I am here on a committee from Congress, soliciting the legislature on the subject of revenue, the temper of the times, and the systems of many of the states, are very unfavorable to the honest and just views of the United States. The Delegates from New

York to the Annapolis Convention passed through this place this morning on their return home. From them I learn that Delegates from only five states assembled at Annapolis, that the powers of even these five were materially different ... that a convention of Delegates should be held at Philadelphia in May next for the purpose of a *general revision* of the confederation ... [emphasis in original].[50]

King was the most vocal of all members of the Second Congress. He wrote to John Adams in England on October 2, 1786:

> The convention proposed to have been held at Annapolis in the last month on the subject of commerce has terminated without credit or prospect of having done much good. I enclose you the report which they addressed to their constituents. They were founded in the opinion that an adjustment of the commercial powers of the several states is intimately connected with the other authorities of the Confederacy and the respective states.[51]

Similarly, Nathan Dane delivered an address before the Massachusetts House of Representatives on November 9, 1786. He struck many of the same themes as his colleague Rufus King. Dane stated: "That the gentlemen in their report [from Annapolis] had made use of very general and indefinite expressions, that seem, however, to suggest the propriety of submitting the federal system of government in general to a revision, or to be changed."[52]

It is abundantly clear that between 1784 and 1786 a fundamental shift was taking place in the United State, and not just in Congress; indeed, much of the impetus was generated by forces outside of Congress. Likewise, much was generated outside of the United States. While realities drove delegates one way, theory and the past drove them another. Fear, jealousy, and practical circumstances like making a living kept many delegates reticent on the prospect of changing the system. Yet, it was inescapable. If the United States was going to survive as a country, a country on the world stage, it had to have a government with the ability to collect revenue and pursue a national agenda, among other tasks.

Hamilton and Madison

James Madison was probably the most studious and determined American legislator in the mid–1780s. Having been supplied with books by Jefferson, who was in France as the American Ambassador, Madison quickly set out to study the history of confederacies, much like the one the United States operated under in 1785. His goal was to prepare a plan in time for the proposed convention in Philadelphia. His outline of study was most ambitious for even the most learned scholar.

His studies ranged from the ancient period up to his own time. Two

4. Annapolis and Alexandria

studies that Madison relied on heavily were the "thirteen-volume edition of Felices *Code de l'humanité*. Heavy reliance also was placed on William Temple, *Observations upon the United Provinces of the Netherlands* ... and the copies of Charles Joseph Panckoucke et al., eds., *Encyclopédie méthodique*, which Jefferson sent from Paris."[53] The confederacies which Madison studied included: the Lycian (ca. fifteenth century BCE); the Amphyctionic (ca. sixteenth century BCE); the Achaean (ca. third century BCE); the Helvetic (ca. late eighteen century CE); the Belgic (ca. third century BCE); and the Germanic (ca. seventeenth century CE). Madison's studies looked at the physical size of confederacies, populations, and the legal, economic, and social policies and attitudes that pervaded each time period and place. His work marked him as a scholar for his generation and throughout history. His legacy is one of not just legislative work and politicking, but one of actual study and analysis of competing contemporary issues.

Among all the thousands of letters and correspondence that exists from the Revolutionary period, a handful stands out as foretelling, or prophetic. One, by Alexander Hamilton, is often described as the first call in print for a more powerful national government than existed under the Articles of Confederation. In a letter written on September 3, 1780, before the Articles even officially went into effect, Hamilton expounded on his theory to James Duane:

> The fundamental defect is a want of power in Congress. It is hardly worthwhile to show in what this consists, as it seems to be universally acknowledged, or to point out how it has happened, as the only question is how to remedy it....
>
> But the confederation itself is defective and requires to be altered; it is neither fit for war nor peace. The idea of an uncontrollable sovereignty in each state, over its internal police, will defeat the other powers given to Congress, and make our union feeble and precarious.[54]

Much like Madison a few years later, Hamilton looked to the Greeks, the Swiss, the Germans, and the Dutch, as he pointed out the failures that had fallen on confederacies which left their constituent parts more powerful than the aggregate whole. Hamilton's long letter is truly one of the masterpieces of the period. He continued:

> The confederation too gives the power of the purse too entirely to the state legislatures ... for without certain revenues, a government can have no power; that power, which holds the purse strings absolutely, must rule....
>
> Another defect in our system is want of method and energy in the administration.... It is impossible such a body, numerous as it is, constantly fluctuating, can ever act with sufficient decision, or with system.[55]

It is interesting to note Hamilton's view of the military, of which he was an integral part in 1780:

> Without a speedy change the army must dissolve; it is now a mob, rather than an army, without clothing, without pay, without provision, without morals, without discipline. We begin to hate the country for its neglect of us; the country begins to hate us for our oppressions of them. Congress have long been jealous of us; we have now lost all confidence in them, and give the worst construction to all they do. Held together by the slenderest ties we are ripening for a dissolution.[56]

This was a stunningly realistic overview of the military situation as it existed in September of 1780. This was a few months after the horrible winter at Morristown, New Jersey (where Hamilton was in residence with Washington at the Jacob Ford, Jr., mansion), and a few months before the Pennsylvania line mutiny of January 1781 which was discussed in chapter 1. The letter shows Hamilton years ahead of his colleagues in thinking (or just having the courage to put pen to paper) about the future of the United States in relation to the present situation. This letter came about ten months before he was to write the series of essays known as the Continentalist. This series of essays has been overlooked in history. They form an arc with Madison's studies on ancient confederacies which together brought the nation to the Constitutional Convention and ultimately saw both Madison and Hamilton co-authoring (with John Jay) *The Federalist* papers. (See appendix 2)

For Hamilton, the present and the future were one. Hamilton also had the benefit of not feeling overly burdened by the American past. Not being a native-born American, he was not prone to the kneejerk responses to perceived injustices by Britain of America's ancient liberties and freedoms. Moreover, Hamilton was one of the most ambitious men in America as well as one of the smartest.

Before Hamilton embarked on his journey to Annapolis in 1786, he planned to dine with Richard Varick in New York. Hamilton's wife, Elizabeth, had other plans however. Hamilton wrote a short note of apology to Varick: "Mrs. Hamilton insists on my dining with her today as this is the day of departure and you ... will know that in such a case implicit obedience on my part is proper."[57]

After all was said and done, on May 7, 1787, eight months after the Annapolis Convention, Alexander Hamilton submitted an invoice for reimbursement for expenses incurred by himself and his colleague Egbert Benson while at Annapolis on behalf of New York. Addressed to "The People of New York," Hamilton wrote, "For our expenses in attending the Convention at Annapolis in September last including the journey thither and back ... £113.1.4."[58]

Sovereignty

The secondary issue behind taxation at Annapolis, which was not an issue at Alexandria, was sovereignty. Who held the upper hand—the states, individually, or the Congress, collectively? That was a question not easily determined. One of the reasons the Congress seemed to fester after the euphoria of achieving independence was the taciturnity of so many delegates to voice their opinion on the sovereignty topic. Vocalizing in favor of the national Congress, empowered by the Articles, was politically dangerous. Many delegates instinctively knew the answer—Congress was sovereign, if one wanted a country—and states would have to be subordinate. This was a difficult admission, if not impossible, for some. It would take Madison, Hamilton, and others, working endlessly, to make the case for Congress.

The prevailing eighteenth-century attitude toward nation-state sovereignty held that independent states, such as New York, North Carolina, etc., could enter into agreements for commercial or political reasons and still maintain their sovereignty. These agreements, whatever the purpose, did not create a more powerful entity via the transfer of individual sovereignty. This may rightly seem complicated, but for the eighteenth century educated leader, it was as second nature as breathing. Three giants of seventeenth and eighteenth century thought who greatly influenced American leaders were John Locke (1632–1704), Emmerich de Vattel (1714–1767), and William Blackstone (1723–1780).[59] All three of these argued similarly that states (i.e., Pennsylvania, Great Britain, Spain, Connecticut) did not forfeit their sovereign power by entering into a confederation, or league, or agreement: "the mere fact that each of the thirteen states agreed to what the Articles called a 'perpetual union' in no way negated each state's continuing sovereign status."[60]

It is well-known that American leaders at this time who spoke of their country generally meant their home state, not the United States. As we have seen, this created a host of problems for the waging of a war and for securing the peace. These issues led to agonizing debates in Congress following the final peace of 1783; ultimately, the sovereignty issue by necessity took second place to concerns over commerce and national identity both of which were also part of sovereignty.

In large measure, the Virginia leaders were some of the more progressive thinkers, just as the Massachusetts leaders were some of the more active radicals before the Revolution. George Washington, surprisingly, seemed little concerned over the minutiae involved in discussion of sovereignty. His colleague James Madison, however, was the foremost thinker on this topic and was as much an agitator for greater national power as Samuel Adams was an agitator for independence well before the First Continental Congress.

The Mount Vernon (Alexandria) Compact and the Annapolis Convention, while real and valuable in their own right, served much larger purposes. Both gatherings prepared the eighteenth century mind for something quite extraordinary—the transfer of sovereignty from a state to a larger state even though all theory held this could not occur.

Conclusion

The road which led from the euphoria over the Peace Treaty of 1783 to the Mount Vernon trade compact, the Annapolis Convention, and ultimately back to Philadelphia for the Constitutional Convention was mired in debt. Not that the debt did not already exist, it did. It was largely ignored by all but a handful during the Revolution as a side bar to the much larger concern of winning the War. That approach was perhaps the best that could be hoped for. Yet, the debt would not go away; and it could not go away without revenue. And revenue had to come from somewhere. National and state debt drove the thinking and actions of many members. Some states had even resorted to printing their own paper money, much as the Continental Congress did. "State and section showed themselves jealous, preferring to fight each other over boundaries as yet unsettled and to pass tariff laws against each other."[61] Some states even went so far as to maintain their own navies. The states of Maryland and Virginia however led the way to a more determined future when they decided to work out their navigational differences along the Potomac and the larger Chesapeake Bay. This gathering was technically illegal, and under the Articles of Confederation and in theory any agreement would be worthless, as the Articles required all states to agree to commercial ties.[62]

Still, the period of the Alexandria and Annapolis Conventions prior to the Constitutional Convention was filled with great distress over the rapidly mounting revenue problem; the political problem; the international problem; and the perception or prestige problem. To use a modern analogy, by this point Congress was running on fumes. It could not make good on its loans, could not get new loans, it could barely even negotiate—as a nation, the United States had very little to offer. A handful of visionary leaders, including James Madison and Alexander Hamilton, stoked the

4. Annapolis and Alexandria **105**

fires for greater reform. George Washington, by lending his name to the navigation and commerce issue, inadvertently became associated with the reform-minded Virginians. There was yet one more challenge to confront the Americans, even as all seemed to be collapsing around them: A farmer from Western Massachusetts was determined to make the elected officials listen to him.

CHAPTER 5

Shays' Rebellion

When John Jay reported on public affairs to Thomas Jefferson in France, he made mention of a rising problem in Massachusetts without naming it directly. In a letter written on October 27, 1786, just after the Annapolis Convention, Jay told Jefferson:

> The inefficacy of our government becomes daily more and more apparent. Our treasury and our credit are in a sad situation; and it is probable that either the wisdom or the passions of the people will produce changes. A spirit of licentiousness has infected Massachusetts, which appears more formidable than some at first apprehended. Whether similar symptoms will not soon mask a like disease in several other states is very problematical.[1]

The path from the Annapolis Convention to the Constitutional Convention seemed a seamless, logical progression. In a manner of speaking, it was. Yet, on that straight, flat, thoroughfare, a dramatic lay-by enticed American leaders. Shays' Rebellion had very little chance to disrupt the evolving sense of American development. That sense was far too strong an urge to be easily curtailed. The need for reform or complete overhaul of the system of government was too widely ingrained to fall at the first sign of trouble. In fact, the participants in Shays' Rebellion showed no interest whatsoever in America's larger development, in that it did not, in their eyes, impact their grievances. They were interested in local issues. They wanted a new legislature to amend laws they saw as being predatory upon the agrarian interests they represented. America's leaders however, reacted to Shays through the lens of the larger American scene. Shays' timing just happened to coincide with tense American themes playing out on the national level.

As if the financial turmoil was not enough of an impetus to get the United States to acknowledge that it had a governing crisis on its hands, civil unrest erupted to provide graphic visuals of the need for change. Regrettably, more than Shays' Rebellion occurred throughout the country and certainly more were threatened but did not come to pass. Yet, all it took was an armed revolt to actually signal to America's leaders that all was not well with the "masses" in America's cities, towns, and villages. As with the Pennsylvania Line mutiny of 1781, one of the complaints voiced in Shays centered on money—whether about not being paid, or about having to pay too much through taxation. Either way, money was a potent ingredient in the turbulent governing landscape in America in 1786–1787. Congress simply could not raise money enough to operate a national government in a responsible manner relative to other nations. The Articles of Confederation explicitly prohibited the Congress from enacting any revenue-generating legislation without the concurrence of all thirteen states.[2] This virtually ensured nothing of a monetary nature would pass due to infighting and jealousy among the states over the proper role of a national government. Before his resignation, the Superintendent of Finance, Robert Morris, came very close to achieving unanimity in 1783 for a national tax plan, but Rhode Island, and then Virginia, refused to consent. Such situations created endless worries for leaders at home and embarrassment, frustration, and anger for American diplomats overseas trying to build creditable ties with allies.

The American Revolutionaries of 1776 were not in any mood to view an uprising favorably; in fact, they were quite underwhelmed. A revolutionary is only so until their goal is met (or lost), upon which they establish themselves by quite non-revolutionary principles and outlaw the very actions that brought them to power. The revolutionary impulses they espoused to gain power become treasonable acts. "Not amused" was too benign a phrase to describe the reaction to Shays and his followers when news of their actions spread.

The beginnings of Shays' Rebellion lay in the financial arrangement mandated by the Articles of Confederation. By requiring all thirteen states to agree to nearly anything the Congress attempted virtually ensured failure, especially when proposals concerned revenue. Not just the Congress ultimately faced insolvency, but the individual states as well. Each state had begun printing paper money without reserves to secure it. The problems simply multiplied from there. Nearly every state, as mentioned, had some type of civil unrest during the period, but not all were violent. In Massachusetts, there was an exception. In a way, this was predictable. Massachusetts was, after all, the colony that most stridently sought a separation from Britain over a decade before. Max Farrand has written about the causes of Shays' Rebellion:

> It is doubtful if a satisfactory explanation ever will be found [he wrote this in 1921], at least one which will be universally accepted, as to the causes and origin of Shays' Rebellion. Some historians maintain that the uprising resulted primarily from a scarcity of money ... that, while the eastern counties were keeping up their foreign trade sufficiently at least to bring in enough metallic currency to relieve ... credit, the western counties had no such remedies.[3]

Farrand also cited theories concerning the smaller harvests after several boom years during the Revolution; and finally there is the ever-popular conspiracy theory which holds that those wanting a stronger national government incited the farmers to violent action in the hopes of strengthening resolve to scrap the Articles of Confederation for a stronger system of national government.[4] This lack of a clear motive is partly why Shays still has a somewhat mythic hold on the American psyche. How can we as a nation put the colonies collectively on a pedestal for rising in revolt against a tyrannical British government but yet condemn Shays and his followers for nearly the same thing? Shays and the agrarian faction were unrepresented in the Massachusetts legislature, much as the colonies were not represented in Parliament. True, Shays and his followers at least had an option to elect legislators more favorable to their cause. The parallels are not perfect, but neither are they perpendicular.

The generally accepted outline of events holds that a twin convergence of factors drove some to open revolt. The two issues were back debts due to creditors, which were suspended during the war, and new taxes that accompanied independence:

> State extraction took the form of direct taxes on property and polls, which placed a disproportionate burden on farmers with small holdings. Duties were imposed on land regardless of its value, and almost forty percent of tax revenue came from a head tax, with equal amounts due from rich and poor. The farmers' fiscal problems were compounded by the requirement that taxes be paid in specie.[5]

The farmers (most participants in the rebellion were agrarian) sought relief originally in 1786 to prevent the courts from operating, thereby preventing seizure of land for non-payment of debt or back taxes, or both. Henry Lee wrote to George Washington in October 1786, as the rebellion was gaining momentum, speculating on the causes: "This event produces much suggestion as to its causes. Some attribute it to the weight of taxes and the decay of commerce, which has produced universal idleness. Others, to ... the fondness for novelty which always has and ever will possess more or less influence on man."[6]

In a December 23, 1786, David Cobb wrote to Massachusetts Governor Bowdoin about the closure of the courts:

> I have the honor to inform your Excellency that the courts of Common Pleas and General Sessions of the peace, which by law were to have been held here on Tuesday last, were adjourned by proclamation to the fourth Tuesday of January next.... The insurgents did not make their appearance upon this occasion, whether they are intimidated by the late spirited measures of government or whether they mean to reserve themselves until a new election, is very uncertain, but from their ridiculing and unnoticing the late Act of Indemnity it is evident that their principle of opposition still continues.[7]

At first, to prevent bloodshed, local authorities complied and tried to negotiate with the farmers. The strategy of preventing the courts from operating was quite effective from the start. Without orders from the courts, local authorities could not act to foreclose on property. When Massachusetts asked the national Congress for assistance to resist the revolt, Congress declined as several states rejected the request.[8] This action provided yet another example of the weakness of the national government in that it had to rely on all the states to agree, rather than Congress being able to act as its own entity on behalf of the country as a whole. In the end Governor Bowdoin had to rely on wealthy Bostonians to pay for a force to resist Shays and his followers. He raised a force of four-thousand troops on the fear-induced generosity of wealthy Bostonians. However, this failed to quell their anger or determination.

John Woodward, writing from Newton on August 21, 1786, wrote to John Nutting, chairman of a committee from the several towns of Groton, Shirley, Townsend, and Ashby, in an attempt to entice him to participate in the revolt. Woodward, not swayed by Nutting's appeal, replied:

> We should have been happy had you [been] more explicit on the subject, and pointed out the grievances to which you alluded—the town would then have been able, after knowing your object to have judged of the propriety of the measures. At present, it appears to be involved in uncertainty and although we would not wish to entertain uncharitable sentiments of any of our fellow citizens, yet we are constrained, and do observe that this transaction has created suspicions in our mind, rather unfavorable to the author.[9]

As the farmers gained strength and organization, they acquired a leader in Daniel Shays, a captain during the Revolution. The unrest quickly spread from its origin in the western counties towards the east with its wealthy merchants and sea traders. As the rebels moved east in December 1786, they were stymied by poor weather conditions and abandoned plans for an attack on Cambridge, site of Washington's first taking command of the Continental Army in 1775—which in 1786 must have seemed an eternity ago.

Governor Bowdoin named General Benjamin Lincoln, another veteran

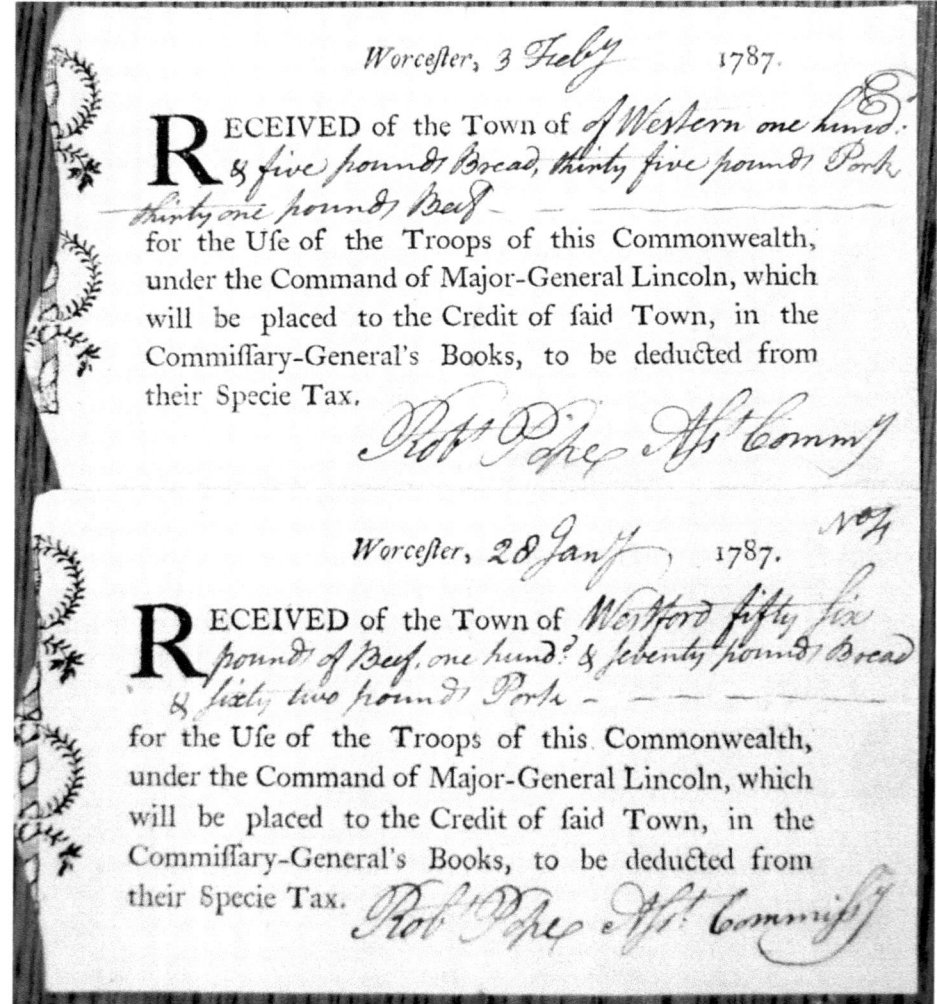

Receipts to the town of Westford for delivery of foodstuffs to the private army under General Lincoln (Morristown National Historical Park).

of the Revolution (and onetime commander of Daniel Shays) as commander of the privately funded army. Governor Bowdoin's letter (labeled His Excellency's Instructions) of January 19, 1787, appointing Lincoln as commander, was quite clear as to his intents for Lincoln's troops:

> You will take command of the militia detached in obedience to my orders of the fourth instant. The great objects to be effected are to protect the judicial courts, particularly those next to be held in the County of Worcester, if the justices of said courts should

request your aid, to assist the civil magistrates in executing the laws; and in repelling or apprehending all and every such person and persons as shall in a hostile manner attempt or enterprise the destruction ... of this Commonwealth."[10]

After failing to enter Cambridge, the rebels headed west in an attempt to attack the United States arsenal at Springfield (made famous in the Longfellow poem years later).[11]

One entry in the Journals of the Continental Congress that is hard to imagine involves the moving of munitions from Connecticut to Springfield, Massachusetts, where they were considered to be more secure. This was before the attack on the arsenal occurred but well into the uprising, and it seems that the news of more, and bigger, munitions arriving at the arsenal would have been identified by the War Office as a potential target by the rebels and prove a reason for placing the munitions elsewhere. It seems as though this would have made the already tempting arsenal even more tempting in the eyes of Shays and his followers. Whatever the thinking, it makes for strange reading in hindsight, "that in consequence of some representations of the insecure situation of a large quantity of shot and shells at Salisbury in Connecticut, amounting to about two hundred tons, they have been removed to the arsenal at Springfield."[12] The knowledge of this material at Springfield made it a target simply too great to ignore.

In addition to the munitions mentioned, a War Office report of September 20, 1786, lists "new arms and bayonets about seven thousand in number ... in perfect condition for use. The powder amounting to upwards of thirteen hundred barrels of excellent quality has been shifted, dried, and repacked."[13]

Slightly more than a week later, on September 28, 1786, the report from Springfield was a bit ominous: "Enough of a lawless and desperate spirit had been manifested to alarm the well affected to government for the safety of the stores. The malcontents openly avowed the idea, that should the government attempt to punish them, that they easily could obtain the means of defense from the arsenal."[14] The report continued that due to the lack of a national standing army, and a lack of funding to pay for such an army, the precariousness of the situation was needlessly compounded.[15]

As to be expected, the British government took a keen interest in Shays' Rebellion, much as they did the Pennsylvania Line mutiny of 1781. Edward Carrington of Virginia wrote to Governor Edmund Randolph on December 8, 1786, "It is an undoubted truth that communications are held by Lord Dorchester with ... the insurgents of Massachusetts, and that a direct offer has been made to the latter, of the protection and government

Part II. The Failure of the National Government

of Great Britain, which they are at present to decline, but hold ... as a last resort in case future events may place them in desperate circumstances."[16] Timothy Newall reported on the latest updates on the rebellion from Great Barrington, Massachusetts. Newall wrote to Dwight Foster in Brookfield, Massachusetts on April 4, 1787:

> Nothing very extraordinary for news, the rebels, on and near the lines of New York and Vermont are very insulting and threaten much. Six persons have been tried here for high treason, five found guilty and one acquitted, one tried for setting fire to a barn in Egremont, found guilty. Judge Whiling indicted for inflammatory words and for publishing a seditious libel and was tried this day, the judges gave ... decidedly against him....[17]

George Washington, on March 10, 1787, from Mount Vernon, wrote to Thomas Cushing, a noted jurist in Massachusetts. Washington ended the letter by commenting on the rebellion: "I am happy to find by the last accounts from the Northward that the disturbances in your state were almost totally suppressed and I hope before this that peace and good order are again restored."[18]

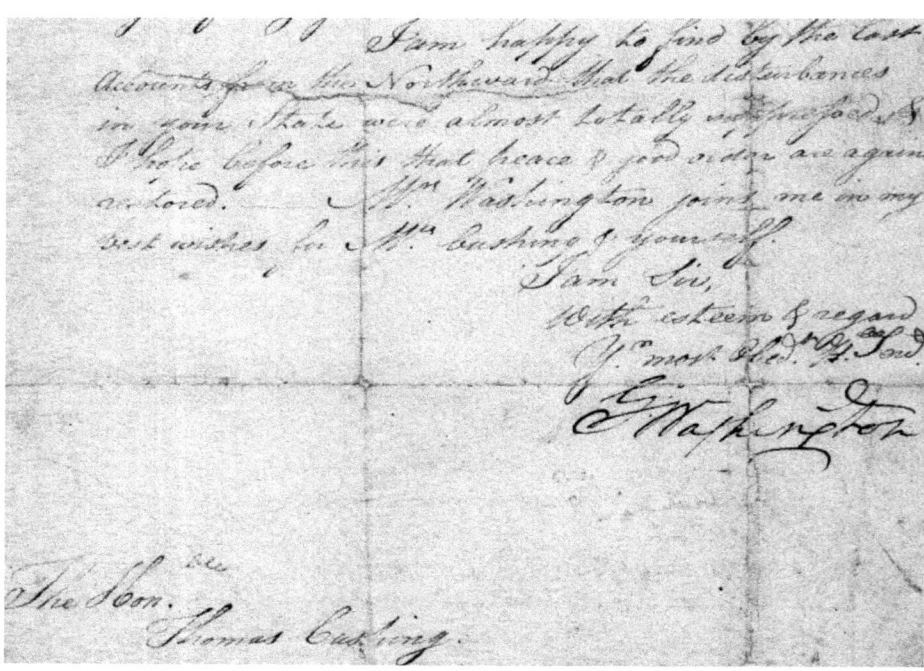

George Washington writing to Thomas Cushing, commenting upon his relief that the rebellion is nearly suppressed (Morristown National Historical Park).

Reflecting on Shays' Rebellion months after it ended (and after the new Constitution had been drafted) in a letter to James Madison, Thomas Jefferson wrote from France on December 20, 1787: "The late rebellion in Massachusetts has given more alarm than I think it should have done. Calculate that one rebellion in 13 states in the course of 11 years, is but one for each state in a century and a half. No country should be so long without one. Nor will any degree of power in the hands of government prevent insurrections."[19]

Clearly, had Jefferson not been in France the Constitution would have had a much different tone; presuming one would have been written at all. (The same holds true for John Adams, who was in England during the Constitutional Convention.)

The End

By October 1, 1786, Henry Knox of the War Office felt confident enough to write to Congress "that the malcontents to the government of Massachusetts who had assembled at Springfield, had dispensed to their respective homes."[20] Knox would make the first account of rebellion to Congress in a letter of October 3, 1786, immediately after his arrival and following his surveying of the scene:

> The malcontents were much more numerous, but not well armed. They were headed by a captain Shays of the militia, and formerly in the continental army, but who resigned a considerable time before the conclusion of the war. They were embodied in a military manner, and exceedingly eager to be led to action, but the prudence of their leader prevented an attack on the government troops…. The horror of a civil war was a powerful consideration to restrain the government party from commencing an attack…. The disaffection to the government … is risen to an alarming height, and will probably terminate most seriously.[21]

A week later, Knox was in Boston meeting with Governor Bowdoin. The two men agreed that securing the Springfield armory against attack was to be accomplished by "the highest exertions."[22] Yet, Knox feared that trying to add a considerable force to the arsenal would only inflame the rebels who were still in the vicinity.[23] On October 18, 1786, Knox again wrote Congress with an update on the standoff. Although both sides had dispersed from Springfield, he feared "that unless the present commotions are checked with a strong hand, that an armed tyranny may be established on the ruins of the present constitutions."[24]

Here the rebels were repulsed fairly quickly by the garrison and General Lincoln's private army. A brief, early account, of the skirmish appeared

114 Part II. The Failure of the National Government

in a letter by Jedidiah Baldwin, writing to General Lincoln on January 25, 1787:

> We are this instant informed that Mr. Shays marched up about 4 O'clock this afternoon in full force against General Shepard,, on the plain near the magazine and General Shepard brought their body to a halt with a few shot from his field pieces. Captain Shaw of this place, my informant, says that he saw 3 or four men that were killed and several wounded. That Shays retreated to Chapin and they were halted, where he left them, it is probable you may have a better account soon.[25]

Citizens, too, were writing to General Lincoln, to inform him of what they felt about Shays. One such citizen was Caleb Strong from Northampton, who wrote on January 24, 1787. Aaron Graves, writing on the same date sought to inform General Lincoln of Shays movements. Jonathan Brooks too informed Lincoln of the whereabouts of members of the rebellion.[26] Major General Shepard, who was defending the Springfield arsenal and the general area, sent several hurried letters to General Lincoln during the early days of late January 1787 when it looked like Shays was much more of a threat than he was. Given Shepard's weak position and fewer men, he naturally sounded an alarm: "If you should think advisable, perhaps it would be well to send a party detached from your troops, at least as far as Pelham, to make their movements according as circumstances shall vary and require, that if Shays should pursue his plan as I have drawn it, this body might then follow him in rear, or come and reinforce me at this post."[27]

Although an armed uprising was technically underway, General Lincoln did not forego the pleasures of life. While General Shepard was writing to Lincoln urging him to send reinforcements, Richard Devens, the Commissary General, sent Lincoln a treat for his dining table: "I have ventured to send on a cask of wine for your honorable table. Should it meet a disapprobation, I have directed the Deputy Commissary General to take care of it."[28]

That was essentially the end of the uprising after the failure of the rebels at Springfield. There was never real concern, as mentioned already, that the rebels would do actual harm. Some of the rebels were armed with nothing more than farm implements. Nothing ever ends easily though, especially when armed force is resorted to. Shays, writing from Pelham (at least that is where he labeled his letter as being written) on January 30, 1787, to General Lincoln, offers some terms for a final solution to the standoff:

> The people assembled in arms from the counties of Middlesex, Worcester, Hampshire, and Berkshire, taking in to serious consideration the purport of the flag [presumably asking the rebels to surrender] just received.

5. Shays' Rebellion

Proclamation of Massachusetts Governor James Bowdoin concerning the aftermath of Shays' Rebellion (Morristown National Historical Park).

> Return for answer, however unjustifiable the measure may be which the people have adapted, in having recourse to arms, various circumstances hath induced them ... we are sensible of the embarrassments the people are under, but that virtue which truly characterizes the citizens of a Republican government hath hitherto marked our paths with a degree of innocence, and we wish and trust it will still be the case; at the same time the people are willing to lay down their arms on the condition of a general pardon, and return to their respective homes, as they are unwilling to stain the land which we in the late war purchased at so dear a rate with the blood of our brethren and neighbor men, therefore we pray that hostilities may cease on your part until our united prayers may be presented to the general court, and we receive an answer....[29]

Lincoln and his men however hounded the fleeing rebels for weeks and Massachusetts asked neighboring states to help with locating the rebels and returning them for trial. Most states did not fully comply, sending further shockwaves through America's leaders over the fate of the nation.[30] One of General Lincoln's men was Israel Chapin. He notified Lincoln on February 5, 1787, from Springfield:

> I have sent out horsemen, who have been as far as Amherst to the north and as far as Palmer to the east, and can get no intelligence of the place in which Shays at present is fixed, nor can we know very nearly where your army is. In this situation I wait your orders, whether any men from this post are to join you, or march elsewhere, or whether any of our men may be furloughed or discharged, as there seems to be no great demand here at present for so many men.[31]

While the revolt fizzled, the sentiments did not. The greatest fears of Congress, much as with an army mutiny, had come to pass. Civil unrest was the worst kind and the impotent Congress could only stand by and watch with its mouth hanging open in amazement. Much like the causes of Shays' Rebellion never fully being known, it may also never be fully known how much Shays acted as a catalyst to the 1787 Constitutional Convention. On the surface, Shays can be seen as having a causal impact on the Constitution. Still, debate endures. Richard Morris has written that "perhaps more than any single condition or event, it [Shays' Rebellion] produced a sense of crisis that had a profound effect on the forthcoming deliberations in Philadelphia."[32]

Daniel Shays and his followers had their supporters (or at least sympathizers). The revolt led to several of Thomas Jefferson's most quotable quotes from a letter to James Madison on January 30, 1787: "A little rebellion now and then is a good thing."[33] In another letter to William Smith from Paris on November 13, 1787, Jefferson wrote concerning the claim that the new Constitution would help prevent civil unrest. Jefferson saw differently:

> Yet where does this anarchy exist? Where did it ever exist, except in the single instance of Massachusetts? And can history produce an instance of rebellion so honorably conducted? I say nothing of its motives. They were founded in ignorance, not wickedness. God forbid we should ever be 20 years without such a rebellion. The people cannot be all, and always, well informed…. If they remain quiet under such misconceptions it is a lethargy, the forerunner of death to the public liberty…. What country before ever existed a century and half without a rebellion? And what country can preserve its liberties if their rulers are not warned from time to time that their people preserve the spirit of resistance? Let them take arms. The remedy is to set them right as to facts, pardon and pacify them.[34]

Jefferson was very much in the minority in this opinion. Even his best friend and confidant James Madison had a completely different view. Jefferson could have been more lenient due to his being in France. Leaders from Washington, to Madison, to William Cushing and Samuel Adams in Massachusetts saw the revolt as evil and Shays himself as evil. Naturally, the "money-men" in Boston and the port cities who owned the mortgages were aghast at the events of Shays and his followers. These men did not fear the chaos in Congress over revenue, but they did fear the armed farmer who owed them money. And that fear was translated in to calls for a stronger national government. In the end, Governor John Hancock pardoned those convicted in 1787, much as Jefferson had earlier mused should occur.

Debates

Shays' Rebellion was not a significant military threat to the state of Massachusetts or the United States. Shays greatest threat was what he and his followers' represented. It is easy to compare Daniel Shays to Samuel Adams and his taking on the British Empire. (Samuel Adams said there was no comparison for taking up arms against a king, as he did, and a democratic government, as Shays did.) Naturally, one could say that Adams was exhibiting characteristics of a Tory who came to power as a Whig. Americans have long had a fear of internal rebellion by the masses (and slaves in the South). The debates over Shays and his followers cover some familiar terrain. Certain historians or writers can predictably be seen as either sympathizing with Shays or abhorring him and what he stood for. Is it possible Shays was both correct and incorrect in what he did? Daniel Shays can easily be cast as a parallel figure to a Karl Marx, Robin Hood, or Benedict Arnold. It really boils down to one's sensibilities and understanding of the forces at play within human nature and the American psyche. One thing that is certain is that Shays was very much like Charles Dickens' ghost of Christmas Future. The Rebellion was a foreshadowing of what to expect in America if something was not done at the national level to stop the slide into financial ruin and anarchy.

In 1948, the highly regarded *William and Mary Quarterly* published a talk given in 1905 by Jonathan Smith to the Clinton, Massachusetts, Historical Society. Smith fashioned himself as an objective voice, believing that "an impartial examination of the facts, and of the motives of the men who took arms, will compel the revision of any judgment based upon the opinions of those who suppressed the movement."[35] Smith saw three reasons for the rebellion:

> 1st—The absence of a strong national government, commanding the confidence and obedience of the people; 2nd—The issue by the Confederation and by the state governments of large quantities of worthless and hopelessly irredeemable paper currency; 3rd—The extreme poverty of the people, resulting from the long war of the Revolution, the total absence of manufacturing industries, the ruin of American commerce, and the crushing burdens of public and private indebtedness.[36]

Over one hundred years old, Smith's thesis has garnered attention from some who viewed his conclusions as outdated and not in keeping with the evidence. Smith's study is important because it was one of the first to look at Shays' Rebellion since the "official" history of the event was prepared shortly after it was neutralized. Many times the historiography of a topic is just as interesting as the event itself, especially when that event pertains to a national event that impacts our collective feeling of self-worth. In many ways history is a viewfinder based on our perspective—which is why there really is no such thing as definitive history. Seeming to neutralize Smith's argument was a 2002 book by historian Leonard Richards. In a review of the book, Thomas Humphrey wrote:

> Richards contends that long-accepted conclusions about the rebellion can no longer stand. Richards argues that most rebels were not debt-ridden, not all were poor, and not all came from towns at odds over religion.... The rebels sought to regulate the political tyranny of the Massachusetts legislature personified by the tax man, making Shays' Rebellion more of a political regulation than an economic uprising.[37]

Yet, one hundred years ago, Jonathan Smith thought he was being definitive. After laying out his methodology and reasons for the uprising, he set out to analyze not just actual events of what took place, but the issues surrounding the events and why they occurred. The economy was in complete shambles and the "farmer's barn and cellar were full, but they afforded him no relief, for he could not realize on them enough to pay his taxes.... The condition of the laborer was even worse; for the little work he could find to do was paid for in produce which was worthless on his hands."[38]

One of the odd facts with Shays' Rebellion was that Daniel Shays had very little to do with it in the beginning. Those who actively fomented the rebellion were not leaders of men. Shays, a veteran of the Revolution with five years' service to his name as an officer, came the closest to fulfilling that requirement. Still, Shays himself was poor, uneducated, and probably even less motivated to war against his home state than were his neighbors. Yet he saw a duty to perform, and he did. His seems to have been a case of seeking justice when the constituted justice (the court system and elected officials) had failed to protect his followers from destitution under what can only be described as unbearable taxation created for a commercial economy, not an agrarian one. Shays was a signatory to several petitions asking the local courts not to conduct business until after the upcoming elections, in order to prevent more debtors' property from being seized before the new legislature could amend the laws.[39] Naturally, the courts did not comply. Shays and his followers also took issue with the 1780 Massachusetts State Constitution, which they saw as undemocratic and was why many wanted to forego the court cases until a new legislature was seated which might amend the most egregiously undemocratic sections which the rebels saw as unduly enriching the non-agrarian class.

The Specter of Shays

Even after the Constitution was written and sent to the states for ratification, the topic of Shays' Rebellion came up many times in the debates surrounding its merits. In an essay from November 2, 1787, John Stevens, Jr., writing under the pseudonym "Americanus," argued that, contrary to popular understanding holding that a republic could only function over small territories, they could in fact function in large ones as proposed by the new Constitution. In his essay, which appeared in the New York *Daily Advertiser*, he wrote: "Had the commotion, which Shays excited in Massachusetts, happened in a state of *small territory*, what would have been the probable consequences? Before the people had recovered from their madness, perhaps all would have been lost [emphasis in original]."[40]

Another instance occurred in an essay by Oliver Ellsworth, future Supreme Court Chief Justice. In his essay of November 26, 1787, Ellsworth wrote a reply to an essay by Elbridge Gerry, who opposed the new Constitution. Ellsworth, a proponent of the Constitution who was a vital member of the Convention in Philadelphia (he had to leave at the end of August, thus missing being able to sign the document), writing as "A Land Owner" in the Hartford *Connecticut Courant* stated:

> Had Shays, the malcontent of Massachusetts, been a man of genius, fortune and address, he might have conquered that state, and by the aid of a little sedition in the other states, and an army proud by victory, became the monarch and tyrant of America. Fortunately he was checked; but should jealousy prevent vesting these powers, in the hands of men chosen by yourselves, who are under every constitutional restraint, accident or design will in all probability raise up some future Shays to be the tyrant of your children.
>
> A people cannot long retain their freedom, whose government is incapable of protecting them.[41]

Without getting too far ahead in our story, Shays' Rebellion is recounted in several of *The Federalist* papers as well. In number six, by Alexander Hamilton and published on November 14, 1787, in the New York *Independent Journal*, Hamilton, as Publius, wrote, "If Shays had not been a *desperate debtor* it is much to be doubted whether Massachusetts would have been plunged into a civil war [emphasis in original]."[42] Hamilton was reflecting on the evils of human nature and what prompts action in some and that without a strong national government such as proposed by the new Constitution the country would forever be dealing with Shays-like incidents.

Hamilton again looked to Shays a month later in another *Federalist* essay, number twenty-one, from December 12, 1787. Again in the *Independent Journal*, Hamilton wrote:

> The tempestuous situation, from which Massachusetts has scarcely emerged, evinces that dangers of this kind are not merely speculative. Who can determine what might have been the issue of her late convulsions, if the malcontents had been headed by a Caesar or by a Cromwell? Who can predict what effect a despotism established in Massachusetts, would have upon the liberties of New Hampshire or Rhode Island; of Connecticut or New York?[43]

Hamilton, in general, in *Federalist* twenty-one, was arguing about the weakness of the Articles and thus the national government to check the evils of human nature. Hamilton again referenced Shays in *Federalist* twenty-five, which appeared in the *New York Packet* on December 21, 1787. Again, Hamilton was using the rebellion to highlight the weakness of the national government and thus favoring the need for a professional, national, standing army: "The conduct of Massachusetts affords a lesson on the same subject.... That state (without waiting for the sanction of Congress, as the Articles of the Confederation require) was compelled to raise troops to quell a domestic insurrection, and still keeps a corps in pay to prevent a revival of the spirit of revolt."[44]

Shays' Rebellion was also a point made in several state constitutional ratifying conventions, all using Shays in support of the proposed Constitution. There was one essay however against the Constitution which used Shays in its argument. An essay by "Cato" (the writer has never been positively identified, although New York Governor George Clinton is a prime candidate) appeared in the *New York Journal* on October 25, 1787. Cato argued that the United States was simply too large a land mass to contemplate the establishment of a republic, which the proposed Constitution called for. Cato argued that a republic would not have been able to prevent or respond to Shays because:

> ... the wheels of a free republic are necessarily slow in their operation; hence in large free republics, the evil sometimes is not only begun, but almost completed, before they are in a situation to turn the current into a contrary progression: the extremes are also too remote from the usual seat of government, and the laws therefore too feeble to afford protection to all its parts, and insure *domestic tranquility* without the aid of another principle [emphasis in original].[45]

Members of Congress were not immune either to commenting on Shays' Rebellion. The Virginia delegates seemed quite taken with the whole affair.

This may not be too strange as Virginia was in the forefront of the push for a stronger national government and consequently monitored situations around the country.

Naturally, the Massachusetts delegates to Congress were very concerned over the events in their home state. On February 21, 1787, they wrote to Governor James Bowdoin:

> The secretary at war having ordered the troops raised in Connecticut under the resolution of the 20th of October last to repair to Springfield, for the protection of the federal magazine, and having authority likewise to direct those raised in Massachusetts to take post at the same place ... we have thought it prudent under present circumstances to rest satisfied with these arrangements.[46]

James Madison, it seems, mentioned Shays in nearly every letter he wrote in early 1787. The frequency with which Madison referred to Shays is indicative of how troubling he found the whole affair. (Yet, in *The Federalist* papers, it is Hamilton, not Madison, who mentioned Shays.) Madison seemed taken aback by how the local population treated Shays and his followers. In a letter to Edmund Randolph on March 19, 1787, Madison wrote with dismay:

> Notwithstanding the apparent victory in Massachusetts over the spirit of rebellion, it is said that at least half the offenders choose rather to defy the consequences of treason, than accept of the amnesty on the conditions annexed to it; that they not only appear openly on public occasions, but have the insolence to wear badges of their character, and that this boldness is countenanced in many places by popular elections of them to local offices.[47]

Cotton Tufts, writing to John Adams (both prominent Massachusetts men) in London on June 30, 1787, expressed similar frustrations:

> What shall I say to you my friend with respect to the state of my country, with respect to the complexion of our new court and the measures pursuing and pursued by it. The spirit of the day has brought into public life characters that in sober times would have been hissed off the stage and been expelled as members unfit to grace the seats of legislators. Fomenters of the late rebellion are found in council, senate and in the House of Representatives. In the House are some who from the beginning were enemies to the late Revolution, secret in opposition when it could best serve their purposes and open when prospects of success presented, avowed friends to monarchy and to despotism, that have taken every advantage of discontents and encouraged every kind of faction, disappointed Whigs, convention men and debtors not a few. The object of the first is to throw all into confusion and introduce a new form of government, the disappointed Whigs & convention men are most of them mushrooms that have sprung up on a sudden are tools of the former but in principle levelers. The debtors join their force hoping for an annihilation of public and private debts, among these are some whose characters once shone with luster. But are now meanly courting the populace and practicing the arts of corruption. These characters came to court with a determination, and from many towns with instructions, if possible to undo the measures of the late administration

to remove the troops stationed for the suppression of the rebellion and the protection of the western counties, to remove all disqualifications, to obtain a general goal delivery of all state prisoners and a general indemnity and pardon as well to those condemned to death as those that have not come in and accepted former terms of mercy and pardon, although the latter have been and are daily making depredations. The removal of the court from the town of Boston—as more *liberal* Tender Act—or a continuation of the former—with some an emission of paper money, with others a discharge of public securities at the going price are favorite objects. It is doubtful whether, the court will be removed from Boston. The Tender Act so called will be continued till January next. Paper money is reprobated and the further reduction of public securities will not be attempted this session.[48]

Abigail Adams, writing to her sister Mary Smith Cranch from London on March 8, 1787, expressed her displeasure as well with the outcome of events relating to Shays:

I lament that so atrocious an offender as Shays should escape least he should in future create more disturbances; the measures which government appear now to pursue will give a permanency to it, and I hope suppress every tendency to future rebellion, at the same time that every rational and reasonable redress of grievances will be granted, that the community in general are suffering from a want of confidence in the public faith is a sorrowful truth, and this distrust creates an artificial scarcity of a circulating medium, could confidence be restored, you would soon find this evil diminished....[49]

Conclusion

Of the Founders, it can be easily argued that George Washington had the most to lose should the United States falter in their attempt at independence. The Father of the Country would have been a bad parent indeed should the American experiment have failed. This could be why he was so alarmed at the state of affairs in post–Revolutionary America. His letters to peers such as Thomas Jefferson, James Madison, Henry Knox, Richard Henry Lee, and many others echo his deep apprehension over the paralysis of the government under the Articles. This sense of doom and urgency reached a near crescendo during Shays' Rebellion. Writing to James Madison on November 5, 1786, Washington wrote that the states "are fast verging to anarchy and confusion."[50] Should the United States falter completely, our failure would fulfill the prophecy of Great Britain. Washington continued, "How melancholy is the reflection that in so short a space, we should have made such large strides towards fulfilling the prediction of our transatlantic foes."[51] Still, there were those unpersuaded by Washington's fear of anarchy. At the Pennsylvania Constitutional Ratifying Convention in December 1787, several Antifederalists—such as William Findley, Robert

Whitehill, and John Simile, among others—argued the anarchy charge was a canard to dupe people into accepting the new Constitution.[52]

This approach also hurt the young country at the very moment it needed foreign investment, and recognition, the most. American ministers abroad at this time had a difficult task explaining both positive and negative attitudes coming from American writers and observers. George Washington himself was not above projecting a "glass-half-full" image to the Chevalier de la Luzerne at the same time he was speaking of "glass-half-empty" anarchy to Madison.[53] On August 1, 1786, Washington wrote to Luzerne that, "in short the foundation of a great Empire is laid, and I please myself with a persuasion that Providence will not leave its work imperfect."[54]

Washington, a Federalist in terms of his overall support for the new Constitution in 1787, was far from being the only Founder who saw both sides of the coin with equal clarity. The Founders left behind a trail of writings that can be interpreted, for the most part, in maddening variety. This apprehension, apart from being basic human nature, was naturally appropriated by later historians, who have spent the last two hundred and thirty years trying to interpret the Revolution, Confederation period, and the Constitution. Their efforts reflect the searing personal debates that occurred between the Founders, and indeed, within themselves in many cases.

CHAPTER 6

The Constitutional Convention of 1787

It might seem odd that this chapter is included in the section titled Failure. While we know today that the convention was successful, nothing at the time would in any way lead the delegates to declare the Constitution a "done deal" following the Philadelphia Convention. In fact, so precarious was the ultimate passing of the Constitution through state conventions that *The Federalist* papers were produced to help persuade the New York State Ratifying Convention, which met in Poughkeepsie in June and July 1788, to support the new plan. Still, we find books and speakers today attributing all manner of glorious and honorific attributes to the Philadelphia Convention of the summer of 1787, giving the impression that it was a *fait accompli*. This is no doubt partly natural; we all want to feel good about our past. Moreover, it cannot be denied that the Constitution that was created in Philadelphia was (and is) extraordinary. However, the fact remains that the delegates themselves had no way of knowing what the future would hold for their work after they left Philadelphia in September 1787. The actual Convention, when it ended, had an unknown prospect. Its work hung in the balance. Some delegates refused to sign. Others wrote essays vehemently opposing the proposed Constitution. Naturally, we today know how the story ends, but in the summer of 1787, that was not the case. Even from within the Continental Congress, serious reservations were heard. In a letter from April 8, 1787 (before the Convention), Rufus King, writing to Theophilus Parsons, stated:

> ... I wish it was in my power to say that the affairs of the union bore a more favorable appearance than when I saw you last; but the contrary is the fact. What the convention may do at Philadelphia is very doubtful. There are many well disposed men from the Southern states who will attend the convention; but the projects are so various, and all so short of the best, that my fears are by no means inferior to my hopes on this subject.[1]

6. The Constitutional Convention of 1787   125

Throughout all the postwar years especially, American officials and non-officials struggled to come to grips with the meaning of independence and the meaning of government. It took America six years of open warfare, and two years of negotiating, to achieve peace and independence. It took them less than four years to get a new government. However, those four years were filled with great energy and activity. The Constitutional Convention of 1787, the result of those four years of angst, burst in to action in May, and spent the next four months in a whirlwind of activity. In many ways, no new ground as such was covered in Philadelphia; most delegates arrived with finely honed beliefs, experiences, and even more finely honed debate skills. Some were so ensconced in their beliefs and viewpoints that their intransigence led them to leave the Convention early in frustration when their points were not adopted. Others stayed the course and recognized that compromise was the key to a brighter future for everyone. In fact, the entire Constitution was, and is, an example of compromise. In some measure, calling it the Compromise Convention would not be all too inaccurate. There was no way every delegate would be happy with the outcome. The fact that no one member was totally satisfied was a good thing—it meant the process of listening, give and take, and respectful disagreement was present to ensure the delegates worked together to produce a plan that all could at least support, if not fully embrace.

Representative of much of the thinking outside the committed nationalists by 1785 was that of the Massachusetts delegates to the Continental Congress. Writing on September 3, 1785, to Governor James Bowdoin, they told him their opinions of revising the Articles of Confederation as opposed to creating something new:

> It may be necessary previously to observe, that many are of opinion, the states have not yet had experience sufficient to determine the extent of powers vested in Congress by the Confederation; and therefore, that every measure at this time, proposing an alteration, is premature. But admitting the necessity, of immediately investing Congress with more commercial powers, it may be expedient to enquire.[2]

It is often said that discretion is the better part of valor; and Massachusetts cannot be criticized for advising caution. The United States, it was true, did not have the luxury of being able to engage in much trial and error, or an extensive testing period prior to adopting the Articles of Confederation—for eight years straight (1775–1783) the country was at war. Conflict is not an ideal incubator to gestate a government structure. The Americans were partly making it up as they went while clinging to the outlines of the Articles. The Massachusetts delegates touched on another topic fraught with apprehension, the clever ability of people to get around laws and regulations written in a constitution. They told Governor Bowdoin, "but experience teaches us, that in the formation of Constitutions and laws, the wisest men have not been able to foresee the evasions and abuses, which in the operation have resulted from vague terms and expressions; latent inconsistencies, artful constructions, and from too full and unguarded a delegation of powers."[3]

Massachusetts delegate Rufus King, a perennial political player who has been referenced many times already, had his concerns about any attempt to amend or revise the Articles of Confederation. Writing to Nathan Dane on September 17, 1785, King asked a favor: "I pray you to re-examine the motives of the legislature in recommending to Congress, to propose to the several states a convention of delegates for the express purpose of *a general revision of the confederation*, and to communicate to me the result of such investigation [emphasis in original]."[4]

The jockeying and politicking that occurred was nothing new, even in 1785. Each state, still jealous and covetous of its sovereignty, saw itself as an independent entity apart from the national government. Few states wanted to go on record, without good cause, as supporting a revision of the system existing at that time. Furthermore, there were many individuals who were making good livings off the way the system operated under the Articles of Confederation and they were not in a hurry to change things.

There were many heroes of the Convention. One of the greatest was James Madison, often referred to as the "Father of the Constitution," and rightly so, in part because of his role in bringing the convention together, and his overall agitation for a stronger, more formal national government. His notes of the Convention form the single best resource extant on those four months shrouded in secrecy in Philadelphia.[5] Finally, Madison played seminal roles in two state ratifying conventions—New York, where he was not a resident but was residing when a co-author of *The Federalist* papers, and in his home state of Virginia, where he fought off the attacks of opponents such as Patrick Henry and his windy oratorical theatrics.

One delegate in particular, George Washington, seemed baffled by the whole event. He barely uttered one word throughout the entire Convention, yet all portrayals depict him as physically dominating the scene, like a mute Zeus. Washington was not given to rapid-fire exchanges of thought and lacked the debate skills his highly educated colleagues possessed (Washington always had a reticence in public due to his lack of a formal education). Washington also had to scrupulously guard his reputation, a reputation that rested upon a manufactured image, a likeness he wished to portray to others based purely upon his physical presence; his was a remarkable piece of showmanship.

Philadelphia, May 1787

As has been discussed, the Constitutional Convention was called for during the Annapolis Convention as one of the recommendations of that body. The date of May 1787 was decided upon by the fall of 1786, after having been outlined in the report from Annapolis. Throughout the several years after independence was formally recognized, leaders from Madison, to Hamilton, to Jay, to Charles Pickney, to William Grayson, and others, sought to take the temperature of their colleagues and the nation for a general convention to revise the Articles of Confederation. The word revise was a euphemism actually used by many nationalists who sought a whole new governmental system. A revision of the Articles was a much easier sell than the wholesale creation of a new government, but for most nationalists that was indeed their goal, and more and more of their colleagues came to agree with them.

James Madison was the first delegate to arrive in Philadelphia, on May 5, 1787. He had made the trip from Montpelier in three days. With him, he brought his voluminous notes and a few reference volumes. Madison was ideally suited for such a life. His family were wealthy planters with an extensive plantation. He had no need for a career in the conventional sense; he was not married, and had no worries or needs that could not be handled by his family's wealth or large slave population. Although he was smiled upon by fate and had no material care or want, he devoted himself to the new nation completely. He had advantages not all the Founders could rely on, and he took those advantages and put them to extensive use. What's more, he seems to never have enriched himself through public service, and died deep in debt in 1836 (albeit this was partly the fault of his irresponsible stepson).

The summer of 1787 was unusually hot and humid, and the delegates met in strict secrecy with doors and windows shut and guarded at the Pennsylvania State House, now known as Independence Hall, making for unimaginably uncomfortable sessions. Nathan Dane, writing to Rufus King on June 19, 1787, admitted secrecy was the best policy and that the public should not know of the debates, just the final product: "I fully agree to the propriety of the Convention order restraining its members from communicating its doings…. I think the public never ought to see anything but the final report of the Convention…."[6]

Dane felt the public knowing which delegates or national section "won" concessions would be detrimental to the trust of the public in the final document. Richard Henry Lee, Jr., commented that, although working in secrecy, "it is certain that this august body is plying assiduously to their great work...."[7]

It is well-known that James Madison prepared the Virginia Plan, and that this prompted the creation of the Connecticut Plan, and the New Jersey Plan. It is widely accepted that the resulting Constitution was the product of many compromises and additions and deletions to the Virginia Plan, making Madison the indispensable man. Slavery was an issue which was compromised endlessly to accommodate slave owners (the word is not actually used in the Constitution), especially in the South—some of whom threatened the entire Convention with failure if they did not get their concessions.

The oldest delegate was Benjamin Franklin of Pennsylvania, the youngest Jonathan Dayton of New Jersey. Over half were trained in the law; many were, or had been, members of the Continental Congress, and many had served in the Revolutionary War. Most were comfortably well off, with several on the lower end of the well-off scale and some on the opposite end. The general outlines which are a part of every study of the Convention really do not need repeating. However, before moving on to the two seminal themes surrounding every discussion relating to the Congress or the Convention—sovereignty and taxation—a basic outline follows.

From the beginning, the Continental Congress had been in favor of the proposed Convention called for at the Annapolis gathering of September 1786. On February 22, 1787, it was recorded in the Journal of the Continental Congress:

> Congress having had under consideration the letter of John Dickinson esqr. Chairman of the Commissioners who assembled at Annapolis during the last year also the proceedings of the said commissioners and entirely coinciding with them as to the inefficiency of the federal government and the necessity of devising such farther provisions as shall render the same adequate to the exigencies of the Union do strongly recommend to the different legislatures to send forward delegates to meet the proposed convention on the second Monday in May next at the city of Philadelphia.[8]

Throughout the spring of 1787, the states notified the Congress of their interest to participate (or not) in the proposed Convention (it was not known as the Constitutional Convention yet) in Philadelphia. They also sent the names of those delegates who would represent their state at the convention. In this sense, Congress, as the existing constituted authority

6. The Constitutional Convention of 1787

in America, played an organizing role in the lead up to the May meeting.

With preparations in full swing, Edmund Randolph, governor of Virginia and one of Madison's staunchest supporters, wrote to him on March 27, 1787:

> I have turned my mind somewhat to the business of May next: but am hourly interrupted. At present I conceive 1. That the alterations should be grafted on the old confederation; 2. That what is best in itself, not merely what can be obtained from the assemblies, be adopted; 3. That the points of power to be granted be so detached from each other, as to permit a state to reject one part, without mutilating the whole ... ought not some general propositions to be prepared for feeling the pulse of the convention on the subject at large?[9]

George Washington, though quiet throughout the entire convention, was nonetheless anxious for its success. He wrote to James Madison on March 31, 1787:

> It gives me great pleasure to hear that there is probability of a full representation of the states in Convention.... I am anxious to know how this matter really is, as my wish is, that the Convention may adopt no temporizing expedient, but probe the defects of the constitution [Articles] to the bottom, and provide radical cures; whether they are agreed to or not....[10]

In total, the twelve states (Rhode Island did not send delegates) appointed seventy-four delegates, of which fifty-five served at any given time. Most delegates came and went while a handful of the committed and able stayed the entire time. May 14, 1787, is traditionally given as the start of the Convention, although not enough members were present for a quorum. The first quorum was reached on May 25, and four days later the Convention adopted rules to guide it; these rules included each state having one vote, votes were to be decided by a majority of the state's present, and, issues already voted on could be brought back up for debate.

On May 29, Edmund Randolph began the Convention in earnest by presenting what came to be known as the Virginia Plan, which was essentially Madison's plans and ideas brought together as a cohesive whole. This plan called for, among other things, a bicameral legislature of nearly equal status and composition. This plan further called for an executive and a judiciary, the three branches of government we recognize today. The next day, May 30, the Convention debated the Virginia Plan, and immediately discussion centered on the Convention's authority to so dramatically alter the Articles of Confederation. While the question arose, no one refused to participate and no one left after the discussion was over. Into June, much of the debate on the Virginia Plan centered on the makeup and powers of

Assembly Room, Pennsylvania State House, meeting room of the Constitutional Convention (Historic American Buildings Survey).

the proposed legislature and executive. The method of election to the new Congress would prove a contentious point—should there be popular voting for members of Congress or should members be voted on by state legislators? What today is well established, in 1787 was just a thought, and like all topics of government in 1787 it generated a great deal of heated debate.

By mid–June, debate on the Virginia Plan ended; it included language that slaves would be counted for purposes of determining representation in the legislature, although the infamous three-fifths rule was not yet agreed upon. William Paterson of New Jersey, already working on an alternate plan to preserve small-state prerogatives against the Virginia Plan and not to fully discard the Articles of Confederation, introduced his design (popularly known as the New Jersey Plan) in mid–June. Some delegates were encouraged by Paterson's plan because they thought it preserved more state sovereignty, much as they saw the Articles of Confederation doing.

By this point, nearly a month into the Convention, the delegates were becoming aware of who was on what side of the critical question—would the Articles be amended or completely replaced? It was clear that support for the Articles was still strong, and that feeling would be hard to overcome. Those factions would continue throughout the summer to coalesce and hone their respective arguments which would spill out after the Convention in the hundreds of essays written for and against the Constitution.

Madison was the clear leader of the Constitution faction, arguing repeatedly that amending the Articles would be worthless and a waste of time. By the end of June it was clear that the New Jersey Plan did not have enough support and the Virginia Plan was the framework of record which would be debated going forward. Throughout the last weeks of June, the concern turned to the place of the states in the Virginia Plan framework and the important concept of sovereignty. The fine points of the bicameral legislature too were beginning to take shape out of the existing loose framework. Representatives would serve for two years (with all standing for election every two years) and senators serving for six years (with one-third standing for election every two years).

Some by this point however, including the aged Franklin, were becoming worried that the course of events were not going well. Seeming to confirm Franklin's doubts, William Blount referred to the Philadelphia proceedings in a June 15, 1787, letter to John Gray Blount which hinted at a lack of progress:

> Major Pierce returned here last night from the convention of which he is a member and says it is probable and that it is the general opinion of the members of that body that it will not rise before the middle of October.
> I have not learned from him what in particular is done but he says in general terms very little is done and nothing definite ... the members are under an injunction not [to] disclose by writing or otherwise any part of their proceedings to any persons but sitting members.[11]

Most however, dismissed Franklin's concerns and moved on with the work of the Convention, heading into the dangerously hot month of July.

July was the month of no turning back. It was clear by now, as if it was not all along, that the Convention was moving well beyond simply revising the Articles. (Whatever the Convention came up with would only be a recommendation. Anything they proposed had to be adopted by the states.) Madison would hit upon this point a year later in *The Federalist* papers. In *Federalist* forty, he responded directly to those opponents of the Constitution who said the Convention only had the authority to amend the Articles. In the *New York Packet* on January 18, 1788, Madison wrote:

> ... that the object of the convention was to establish, ... a *firm national government*; 2nd, that this government was to be such as would be *adequate to the exigencies of government* and *the preservation of the union*; 3d, that these purposes were to be effected by *alterations and provisions in the articles of confederation*, as it is expressed in the act of Congress, or by *such further provisions as should appear necessary*, as it stands in the recommendatory act from Annapolis; 4th, that the alteration and provisions were to be reported to Congress, and to the states, in order to be agreed to by the former and confirmed by the latter [emphasis in original].[12]

Madison was reminding his readers that the Convention did not overstep its authority in drafting the proposed Constitution and that the document produced by the Convention was, at the end of the day, just a recommendation. It still had to be approved by the states. Madison continued:

> Let them [opponents of the Constitution] declare, whether it was of most importance to the happiness of the people of America, that the articles of confederation should be disregarded, and an adequate government be provided and the Union preserved; or that an adequate government should be omitted, and the articles of confederation preserved. Let them declare, whether the preservation of these articles was the end, for securing which a reform of the government was to be introduced as the means; or whether the establishment of government, adequate to the national happiness, was the end at which these articles themselves originally aimed, and to which they ought, as insufficient means, to have been sacrificed.[13]

Drafting a new Constitution, creating a new government, was without a doubt what was taking shape. Delegates knew the time for making a decision was upon them. The framework of government existing under the Articles was no longer viable long-term. The time for ideas was now, they had one chance left and enough stepped forward to get the work done.

An interesting exchange of letters occurred at the height of the Convention in the summer of 1787. As mentioned, Thomas Jefferson was in France as the American Ambassador. Although removed by thousands of miles, he was still very well informed of events to the extent that mail travel allowed at that time. On June 9, 1787, around the time the delegates were coming to understand that the Convention was creating a wholly new document rather than revising the Articles of Confederation, Edward Carrington wrote a letter to Jefferson giving his perspective on rapidly unfolding events. Carrington wrote, contrary to some of the more negative comments seen earlier, that things were actually quite upbeat. "The importance of this event [the assembling of the Philadelphia Convention] is every day growing in the public mind, and it will, in all probability, produce a happy era of our existence...."[14] Carrington blamed the bad conduct of America's elected representatives not on a deficiency in mankind, but on a deficiency in the system of government since the end of the war. He told Jefferson that "delinquencies of the states in their federal obligations; acts of their legislatures violating public treaties and private contracts, and universal imbecility in the public administration ... have resulted rather from constitutional defects, and accidental causes than the natural dispositions of the people."[15] This pure belief in the ability and soundness of the people no doubt found favor with Jefferson, the people's ultimate champion among the Founders. Carrington pointed out the inherent risk of democracy when good people prefer not to enter public life: "Men whose ability and integrities had gained the entire popular confidence ... retired from the public scene.... Demagogues of desperate fortunes, mere adventurers in fraud, were left to act unopposed."[16]

Jefferson wrote his reply to Carrington on August 4, 1787. Ever the optimist, Jefferson told Carrington, "But with all the imperfections of our present government, it is without comparison the best existing or that ever did exist."[17] No doubt there was some truth to this, the problem was, the system did not work. Jefferson was not in the United States and was only reading and hearing accounts of what was going on and acquiesced that "...if the convention should adopt such propositions I shall suppose them necessary."[18] Jefferson was however very concerned about giving Congress power expressly to raise money. He argued that this requirement existed in law as part of the legal fabric of contracts, not necessarily within a government. In a contract it does not say how something is to be done, just that it is to be done. Jefferson took the same approach to the states and national government. There was no need, in his mind, to spell out how the money was to be generated and paid to the Congress.

The work to flesh out the three branches of government was well under way by July 4, a date which did not pass unnoticed by the delegates. The order in which they appear in the Constitution—legislative, executive, and judicial—are pretty much the way they were dealt with in the Convention. The greatest power, raising revenue, was left with the House of Representatives. Although the toughest question was representation among the states and would not be completely resolved until the Connecticut Compromise was offered, giving proportional representation in the House, and equal representation in the Senate. The lower chamber of Congress—the House of Representatives—would have membership based on state population; the upper chamber—the Senate—would have equal representation among the states. Until that compromise states were split over how to allot congressional representation among themselves. Big states favored proportional representation, small states equal representation.

The one issue settled rather quickly when determining population was the counting of slaves as three-fifths of a white person for representation purposes. This is widely seen as having been acceded to in order to keep the Southern delegates from leaving en masse and rendering the Convention an absolute failure. July also saw the departure of the New York delegation (Robert Yates and John Lansing—Hamilton had left earlier to attend to his law practice) in frustration, leaving a critical state without representation.

One sidebar in the steamy summer occurred outside of the Convention in the all but seemingly irrelevant Continental Congress, then meeting in New York. In what must have been an important moment for Thomas Jefferson (serving in France as ambassador), Congress passed the Northwest Ordinance on July 13 for administering the lands beyond the Ohio River. Nathan Dane of Massachusetts was the main sponsor and drafter of the legislation which was modeled after Jefferson's original plan of 1784. The future states of Ohio, Indiana, Illinois, Michigan, Wisconsin, and some of Minnesota, would come from this territory. The Ordinance was a remarkably democratic (for the period) piece of governance reflecting Jefferson's and Dane's expansive views for the future of America. Uniquely, as per Jefferson's original plan, slavery was prohibited from the area. Also, again reflecting Jefferson, freedom of worship with no religious requirements for public service were features of the Ordinance—these guarantees would be a part of the Constitution as well. While this vote in Congress may have been a sidebar in 1787 to the Philadelphia Convention, it was a sidebar with enormous consequences for tens-of-thousands of people at the time and tens-of-millions today. It was one of the more positive and far-reaching pieces of work to emerge from the Continental Congress over its fifteen-year history. It was slightly ahead of the developing Constitution by having a Bill of Rights and containing the centuries-old Magna Carta guarantee of trial by a jury of one's peers according to the law of the land. (Of course in Magna Carta's guarantee it originally only applied to knights and other high level individuals, but, the idea was there.) Certain other elements that reflected the thinking found in the Constitution (again, the Jefferson imprint was on these) included no primogeniture; it reduced sex discrimination in land ownership and it encouraged the establishment of schools and the protection of Native American land.

Returning to the Convention, the discussion in late July turned to what would become the topic of Article III of the Constitution, the judiciary. The debate revolved around who would appoint judges; the executive, the House of Representatives, the senate? Also, not far behind the appointment issue was the power to determine the legality of laws; in other words, could the proposed Supreme Court declare legislation unconstitutional?

6. The Constitutional Convention of 1787   135

While that specific language did not make it into the Constitution, the idea was certainly there. The concept of nullification of legislation by a supreme judiciary was nothing new, and every lawyer and educated delegate was aware of its existence. Nullification had a long history in English common law and could be traced back to the great English jurist Edward Coke in the sixteenth century. The Convention also began to debate how the new Constitution would, once finalized, be approved or disapproved. Would state legislatures have the final say, or the people through a general vote; should the Continental Congress be involved?

The Convention took a week-and-a-half break at the end of July and the beginning of August to allow a Committee of Detail to put all of the agreements reached thus far into a draft document so they could be seen together as one whole. This first draft version would already be very familiar to us as the outlines, if not always the language, were very much discernible in the final product we are familiar with. The famous "We the People" opening was in place at this point already. The Convention had indeed accomplished a tremendous amount of work in slightly over two months.

Philadelphia in August 1787 was oppressive, especially with the unusually hot weather. South Carolina statesman Pierce Butler, writing from outside of Philadelphia to Englishman Weedon Butler (no relation) on August 1, 1787, during the break, commented on the dangers of such warm conditions in a crowded city. Butler said "we adjourned for one week—having placed my family here [outside the city], Philadelphia not being so healthy, I embraced the opportunity of visiting them."[19]

Among the existing manuscript references the delegates drew from to craft the first draft of the Constitution were the Articles of Confederation, the various state constitutions, Madison's Virginia Plan, and certain pieces of legislation from the Continental Congress. As much as we like to see the Constitution as unique and having sprung wholly from that Philadelphia summer of 1787, from men sequestered behind guarded, closed doors and windows, the fact is, it did not suddenly spring from nothingness. To an extent, it did spring from a uniquely American set of circumstances forged through war and political, economic, and social upheaval, and we as a people can take pride in the Convention's work. However, the Constitution was not created out of nothing. Indeed, we have seen that Madison studied extensively prior to the Convention the history of republican government over the course of two millennia.

This notion that the Constitution was not something from nothing was the topic of an essay by an early and important Constitutional scholar named Max Farrand, who has already been referred to several times. Writing in 1908 for *The American Political Science Review*, Farrand undertook to show that it could "be found that every single provision of the federal Constitution can be accounted for in American experience between 1776 and 1787."[20] Farrand quoted John Dickinson as being finished with the windy theorist whose eloquent maxims helped fight the war for independence but were hopelessly useless in the practical business of government, as stating "experience must be our only guide. Reason may mislead us."[21] Even James Madison, the most important man at the Convention, later wrote in *The Federalist* papers, in *Federalist* forty, on January 18, 1788, in the *New York Packet*:

> The truth is, that the great principles of the Constitution proposed by the convention may be considered less as absolutely new, than as the expansion of principles which are found in the Articles of Confederation. The misfortune under the latter system has been, that these principles are so feeble and confined as to justify all the charges of inefficiency which have been urged against it, and to require a degree of enlargement which gives to the new system the aspect of an entire transformation of the old.
> In one particular it is admitted that the convention have departed from the tenor of their commission. Instead of reporting a plan requiring the confirmation *of the legislatures of all the states*, they have reported a plan which is to be confirmed by the *people*, and may be carried into effect by *nine states only*. It is worthy of remark that this objection, though the most plausible, has been the least urged in the publications which have swarmed against the convention [emphasis in original].[22]

Madison again returned to the subject in *Federalist* forty-five, on January 26, 1788, in the *Independent Journal*: "If the new Constitution be examined with accuracy and candor, it will be found that the change which it proposes consists much less in the addition of *new powers* to the Union, than in the invigoration of its *original powers* [emphasis in original]."[23]

Madison, in *Federalist* forty especially, goes to great lengths to show that the Constitution is part and parcel of what has existed and been experienced since the beginning of the war. As Farrand expressed it in his 1908 essay: "Our Constitution was a practical piece of work for very practical purposes. It arose from the necessity of existing conditions. It was designed to meet certain specific needs and when those were provided for, the work was completed."[24]

Other delegates, alumni of the English legal system of learning at the Inns of Court, had invaluable expertise in framing practical and theoretical law. The Inns of Court, mentioned numerous times already, are described by legal historian Edward White as:

> After becoming affiliated with an Inn, a prospective barrister then needed to become associated with an office of barristers, called a chambers, to which solicitors would

bring cases to be argued in court. Solicitors typically did not attend universities: they received on-the-job training in a solicitor's office. They needed to become conversant with the law of various subjects in order to render advice and determine whether their clients would profit through litigation. There were no Inns of Court in the British Colonies, and the barrister/solicitor distinction quickly disappeared.[25]

Compromise

The middle of August saw the beginning in earnest of the debate on taxation and revenue generation. This included commerce among states to the extent that it reflected the strong desire of states to have a regulatory body which would help strengthen the commercial ties among the states and between the United States and foreign powers. And, as usual, the issue of slavery was never far from anyone's mind with loyalties falling upon familiar fault lines between north and south. The compromise over what to do about slavery and the slave trade called for a termination of slave importation after 1808, an admittedly arbitrary date suggested by South Carolinian Charles Cotesworth Pinckney.

One of the most important and often forgotten prohibitions in the Constitution passed unanimously at the end of August—a statement prohibiting religious tests (as already existed in the Northwest Ordinance) for holding office ensured that a theocratic approach to the American system of government would never occur. The absence of religious controls was as revolutionary as was America's independence from Britain: "The sovereign secular state created a new problem in political theory. The state and its sovereign attributes could not be explained or justified by any notion of a divinely ordained political order as had medieval governments, for the new nations had renounced theocratic controls."[26]

Rather than divinely ordained rulers and countries functioning within some cosmic structure wherein mortals were only playing parts, American and other leaders looked to replace the loss of seeming orderliness with the concept of Natural Law. This is most clearly seen in Jefferson's Declaration of Independence and its reliance on the Laws of Nature. By the time of the Revolution, Jefferson was not the only American thinker captivated with these ideas:

> Colonial theories of natural law and natural rights, ... written constitutions, and the right of revolution bore fruit in the Revolutionary era, when they formed the legal basis of the colonial argument against England. Patrick Henry.... John Dickinson, ... and Jefferson ... were applications of well-matured colonial ideas upon natural law and natural rights.[27]

At the beginning of September one of the strangest compromises emerged and was adopted—the presidential elector. This position was created to prevent direct election of the president by the public for fear the people could be too easily swayed by those with great wealth or those with great oratorical ability.

As the Convention was drawing to a close myriad agreed upon topics were polished and finalized. It was agreed that the Continental Congress would not have a say on the proposed Constitution (and their future as an organization) once signed by the Convention. Rather, the Constitution would be sent to the states via the Continental Congress for approval or disapproval by state ratifying conventions whose delegates would be chosen by the voters of each state. Most of the language and writing of the Constitution as known came from the Pennsylvania delegate Gouverneur Morris. After the Committee of Style submitted its final draft, the effort moved towards acquiring signatures on the document. Ideally, Convention leaders would have liked to have had an unanimous showing of support for the recently drafted Constitution. Realistically, this was not to be. Even Washington, who sat mute and Zeus like through the stifling summer, was finally moved to say that he supported a last minute amendment concerning population and representation in the House of Representatives. This change increased the number of representatives each state would have and Washington hoped this move might persuade some of those delegates who were unsure about supporting the Constitution to support it. Franklin too encouraged support for the document, and even suggested that if a member disapproved of the plan of government, to at least sign as a witness to the work done. Franklin had limited if any success persuading the most obstinate opponents.

On September 17, 1787, forty-one delegates present began to sign the Constitution. Of those forty-one, Elbridge Gerry of Massachusetts, Edmund Randolph and George Mason of Virginia refused to sign. (Ironically, Randolph was one of the strongest supporters of the Convention and even led the effort on behalf of Madison and the Virginia Plan when the Convention had begun earlier that year in May.) The Constitution was then sent to the Continental Congress to be communicated to the states for an up or down vote in state ratifying conventions with delegates chosen by the voters. The Philadelphia Convention dissolved itself within a week after September 17. The public debate, which would rage in the newspapers for nearly a year, now began.

As president of the Constitutional Convention, George Washington had the task of transmitting the proposed Constitution to Congress and ultimately the states, in his letter of transmittal, Washington wrote:

> The friends of our Country have long seen and desired, that the power of making war, peace and treaties, that of levying money and regulating commerce, and the correspondent executive and judicial authorities should be fully and effectually vested in the general government of the Union: but the impropriety of delegating such extensive trust to one body of men is evident. Hence results the necessity of a different organization.
>
> It is obviously impracticable in the federal government of these States, to secure all rights of independent sovereignty to each, and yet provide for the interest and safety of all. Individuals entering into society must give up a share of liberty to preserve the rest. The magnitude of the sacrifice must depend as well on situation and circumstance, as on the object to be obtained. It is at all times difficult to draw with precision the line between those rights which must be surrendered, and those which may be reserved; and on the present occasion this difficulty was increased by a difference among the several States as to their situation, extent, habits, and particular interests.[28]

Inkwell used to sign the Constitution at the end of the Convention, September, 1787 (courtesy of Independence National Historic Park).

This was such an important letter. Washington enunciated the major points which led the United States to the point they faced in 1787—taxation and sovereignty. And, he flatly states what no one else in the country could have gotten away with, namely, "Individuals entering into society must give up a share of liberty to preserve the rest."[29] Naturally, not everyone was convinced by Washington's lecture (which were frequently written by Hamilton or Madison), but his sentiment expressed the frustration of the more mature heads at the Convention who probably had enough of the political theory version of "fire and brimstone" which some of the more theatrical delegates were engaging in and would continue to in essays and at state ratifying conventions.

Sample Reactions

Less than a week after the delegates affixed their signatures to the parchment on which the new Constitution was placed, David Redick (an opponent of the Constitution) wrote to William Irvine on September 24, 1787, mocking his fellow Philadelphians for their reaction to the newly published document: "The new plan of government proposed by the convention has made a bustle in the city and its vicinity. All people, almost, are for swallowing it down at once without examining its tendencies."[30]

In an essay which could be seen as trying to neutralize *The Federalist* papers, an anonymous writer, calling himself "A Plebian," sought to cast doubts on many of the claims the supporters of the Constitution were making. This writer, contrary to other commentators, saw the United States under the Articles of Confederation in a more positive light. Conditions were not as bad as many were led to believe. He wrote:

> It is insisted, that the present situation of our country is such, as not to admit of a delay in forming a new government, or of time sufficient to deliberate and agree upon the amendments which are proper, without involving ourselves in a state of anarchy and confusion.... We are told, that agriculture is without encouragement; trade is languishing; private faith and credit are disregarded, and public credit is prostrate ... that private embarrassments and distresses invade the house of every man of middling property, and insecurity threatens every man in affluent circumstances: in short, that we are in a state of the most grievous calamity at home, and that we are contemptible abroad, the scorn of foreign nations, and the ridicule of the world.[31]

The writer argued that the United States just emerged from an expensive war with pre-war debts still to be paid. Naturally, problems were to be expected. This was somewhat similar to Jefferson's "the glass is half full" approach to the American situation. The supporters of the new Constitution identified a much larger issue at stake however—national versus state sovereignty. The "A Plebian" writer had other like-minded essayists to comingle with too. An "Impartial Examiner" from June 1788 struck a similar note of wondering whether the country was rushing too quickly into the new system of government.[32]

Likewise, an anonymous writer called "Federal Farmer," in his essay number seventeen on January 23, 1788, spent considerable space explaining why he felt Congress had no need of the power to tax as called for in the new Constitution. He wrote: "Heretofore we do not seem to have seen danger anywhere, but in giving power to Congress, and now nowhere but in Congress wanting powers; and, without examining the extent of the evils to be remedied, by one step, we are for giving up to Congress almost all powers of any importance without limitation."[33]

One opponent of the Constitution, writing as "John Humble," placed an essay in the Philadelphia *Independent Gazetteer* on October 29, 1787. Although not directly related to the taxation issue, "John Humble" raised some interesting points: "Now we the *low born*, that is, all the people of the United States except 600 or thereabouts, *well born*, and most solemnly engage, that we will allow and admit the 600 *well born*, immediately to establish and confirm this most noble, most excellent and truly divine constitution ... [emphasis in original]."[34]

The writing of letters throughout the country became more intense once the Convention disbanded and the new proposed Constitution was sent out to the states for approval or disapproval. On September 23, 1787, barely a week after the Convention dissolved itself, Edward Carrington wrote to James Madison concerning the activities of the New York delegation in Congress. Carrington, a Congressman from Virginia, wrote:

> The New York faction is rather active in spreading the seeds of opposition. This, however, has been expected, and will not make an impression so injurious as the same circumstance would in some other states. Colonel Hamilton has boldly taken his ground in the public papers and, having truth and propriety on his side, it is to be hoped he will stem the torment of folly and iniquity.[35]

As we have seen, the New York delegation left the Convention early in frustration, leaving Hamilton the sole, but powerless, member of their delegation once he returned from his absence attending to his law practice.

On September 28, 1787, the secretary of the Continental Congress formally sent the proposed Constitution to the individual state governors. The accompanying letter stated:

> In obedience to an unanimous resolution of the United States in Congress assembled, a copy of which is annexed, I have the honor to transmit to Your Excellency, the report of the Convention lately assembled in Philadelphia, together with the resolutions and letter accompanying the same; and have to request that Your Excellency will be pleased to lay the same before the legislature, in order that it may be submitted to a convention of delegates chosen in your state by the people of the state in conformity to the resolves of the convention, made and provided in that case.[36]

James Madison sent Thomas Jefferson a detailed outline of the proposed Constitution on October 24, 1787. Madison wrote to Jefferson (still in France):

> I take the liberty of making some observations on the subject, which will help to make up a letter, if they should answer no other purpose.
> It appeared to be the sincere and unanimous wish of the Convention to cherish and preserve the Union of the States. No proposition was made, no suggestion was thrown out, in favor of a partition of the Empire into two or more Confederacies....
> When the plan came before Congress for their sanction, a very serious effort was made by R. H. Lee and Mr. Dane from Massachusetts to embarrass it.[37]

Richard Henry Lee was not a fan of the proposed Constitution. He felt it left the states powerless in the face of the federal government. He had written earlier in October to Samuel Adams saying: "Having long toiled with you my dear friend in the vineyard of liberty, I do with great pleasure submit to your wisdom and patriotism, the objections that prevail in my mind against the new Constitution proposed for federal government."[38]

Lee would lead a faction against ratification in the Virginia Ratifying Convention with Patrick Henry where he squared off against Madison, John Marshall, Bushrod Washington, and other supporters in an attempt to hold back America's new attempt at government.

In an October 24, 1787, letter to William Short, James Madison touched on some of the issues indicating how difficult it was for the delegates in Philadelphia to find common ground given the multitude of competing interests. Madison informed Short: "The nature of the subject, the diversity of human opinion, and the collision of local interests, and of the pretensions of the large and small states, will not only account for the length of the time consumed in the work, but for the irregularities which may be discovered in its structure and form."[39]

Madison truly identified a uniquely American approach to governance: compromise. Diversity of opinion had to be allowed to flourish if participatory, representative democracy was to work. To Madison, compromise was not a shameful occurrence, but rather a significant, necessary occurrence.

James Madison lamented to Thomas Jefferson on December 20, 1787, about the usual problems facing the Continental Congress and how the prospect of a new government under the Constitution has exacerbated the problem. Madison wrote: "...the states seem to be either wholly omitting to provide for the federal treasury; or to be withdrawing the scanty appropriations made to it.... The treasury board seem to be in despair of maintaining the shadow of government much longer."[40]

So the same issues that in part contributed to the Constitutional Convention still plagued the Congress and the country after the Convention concluded its work as the new proposed government caused the old to hold its collective breath.

On February 19, 1788, five months into *The Federalist* papers project, James Madison wrote to Thomas Jefferson in France:

> The Public here continues to be much agitated by the proposed federal Constitution and to be attentive to little else....
> Congress have done no business of consequence yet, nor is it probable that much more of any sort will precede the event of the great question before the public.[41]

Madison here was clearly concerned about the fate of the Constitution. He would soon leave New York, and *The Federalist* papers project, and return to Virginia to prepare for the state ratifying convention later in 1788.

Virginia Congressman Cyrus Griffin wrote to James Madison on March 4, 1788. Madison had already returned to his home in Orange County, Virginia, to prepare for the state convention on the proposed Constitution. Griffin struck familiar themes of Congress not having enough delegates present to conduct business and that the prospect of a change in government had rendered Congress helpless. Griffin wrote: "A prospect of the new Constitution seems to deaden the activity of the human mind as to all other matters; and yet I greatly fear that constitution may never take place; a melancholy judgment most certainly—and would to heaven that nothing under the sun shall be more erroneous."[42]

It is easy to overlook the fact the Congress was still extant and meeting in New York when the Constitutional Convention was working and for the whole period that *The Federalist* papers were being written and published. In fact, James Madison was a member of the Congress at the same time that he was authoring multiple *Federalist* essays. The proposed Constitution was predicated on the dissolution of the Continental Congress. The Constitution did not contain explicit language to this effect, but its meaning was clear, you cannot have two governments. The Continental Congress would enter the annals of history upon the passage of the Constitution.

The years which abut the Constitutional Convention in time on either side of that summer of 1787 did not go by totally unnoticed in the Continental Congress. In fact, as has already been seen, Congress passed the Northwest Ordinance—perhaps the single most important piece of legislation to come out of the Congress in its fifteen-year history. In addition to that legislation, there was plenty of speculation on the proceedings in Philadelphia and what might or might not be accomplished.

Sovereignty

A continually running plot or sub-plot within the entire post–Revolutionary period of American government was what to do about the relationship between the states and national government created in the Articles of Confederation. Concurrently within that question was one that hung over every debate and position taken by a delegate. What was to be the nature of the relationship between the states and the national government as concerned taxation? And, who—states or national government—would set fiscal policy? While endless histories have been written about the four months in Philadelphia trying to make human the activities of the framers, few expand on the debates surrounding the most important questions the framers grappled with: sovereignty and taxation.

Sovereignty in the eighteen century, especially in connection with the states in the Revolutionary period (ca. 1770–1785), was a powerful force. In a way, it is hard for us today to grasp the concept. Most leaders and delegates were terrified of losing control of their destiny. These ideas were intimately intertwined with the Enlightenment concepts which festered all throughout the Revolutionary period and will be examined in depth later. One example to highlight the complexity of this topic is in the very foundation of the definition of the term.

One of the most crucial aspects of sovereignty in the eighteenth century was the right to make treaties and transact diplomatic business on a state to state exchange (state meaning a nation). For instance, if Maryland wanted to conduct diplomacy in 1782 with one of the Germanic principalities, in theory (as the states were viewed as sovereign entities), this could have occurred. However, by the dictates of the Articles of Confederation, this could not occur without the agreement of all the states assembled in Congress. And, even at that, the Congress, as the United States, would be the responsive party in the treaty, not Maryland.[43] So, as per the Articles, the states existed in a state of semi-sovereignty in relation to other political entities—including their fellow states. As we saw in the Mount Vernon Compact, Maryland and Virginia entered in to a commercial agreement that technically violated the Articles of Confederation.

Some leaders, recognizing that the current structure of government was untenable, especially from a financial perspective, proffered the idea of a limited term transfer of sovereignty to the national Congress for the purpose of commercial rehabilitation of America's financial network. Again, Massachusetts statesman Rufus King provides a timely example. In his September 17, 1785, letter to Nathan Dane, he wrote:

> It is true, that additional commercial powers vested in Congress, under proper restrictions, and for a limited time, is an object to be greatly desired; but it is, and I believe will continue to be, the reflected opinion of many, of the most republican, and but informed men, in this country that such delegation of power should be for a limited time.[44]

It seems almost absurd to even contemplate such an arrangement. Yet, the fear of permanently losing sovereignty was something that could not be easily overcome, even though most leaders knew it had to eventually come to that if they wanted a viable country.

One hundred years after these events of 1787, the prolific writer and scholar John Fiske argued in 1888 that the individual states of the Revolutionary period were never sovereign in the sense that Holland or France was. This line of thinking would no doubt have caused a rising of brows among his literary and scholarly ancestors had he made his argument one hundred years earlier. In his book about the post-independence period, *The Critical Period of American History*, Fiske asserted:

> That some kind of union existed between the states was doubted by no one. Ever since the assembling of the first Continental Congress in 1774 the thirteen commonwealths had acted in concert, and sometimes most generously.... It has sometimes been said that the union was in its origin a league of sovereign states, each of which surrendered a specific portion of its sovereignty to the federal government for the sake of the common welfare. Grave political arguments have been based upon this alleged fact, but such an account of the matter is not historically true.... Under the government of England before the Revolution the thirteen commonwealths were independent of one another and were held together, juxtaposed rather than united, only through their allegiance to the British crown.[45]

Another theory stated that sovereignty was held, and flowed from, the people. This was a classic Enlightenment approach to government. But it was only an approach; it was nowhere in the world being attempted in the eighteenth century in its purest form. Thomas Jefferson was its most articulate proponent, and Madison endorsed a version of it.

One of the best reflections on just how sensitive the notion of sovereignty was is the number of times the topic showed up in the debate and ratification of the Constitution that followed its writing. In particular, *The Federalist* papers have multiple references to the idea of power; where does it reside, how is it utilized? In *Federalist* nine, Hamilton, writing in the *Independent Journal* on November 21, 1787, approached sovereignty:

> The proposed Constitution, so far from implying an abolition of the estate governments, makes them constituent parts of the national sovereignty, by allowing them a direct representation in the Senate, and leaves in their possession certain exclusive and very important portions of sovereign power. This fully corresponds, in every rational import of the terms, with the idea of a federal government.[46]

Hamilton sought to assuage the reticence of some who had been wavering about their support of the Constitution because they felt the states would be all but obliterated from the point of practicality into nothing more than impotent partners, doomed to inferiority with no real power. Hamilton struggled to make the case that the states would, under the proposed Constitution, be integral members of the federal system.

Hamilton again took up the topic of sovereignty in *Federalist* sixteen. Again, from the *New York Packet* on December 4, 1787, Hamilton argued that while most lament the weakness of the national government, few wanted to provide it with the appropriate power and authority necessary.

"While they admit that the government of the United States is destitute of energy, they contend against conferring upon it those powers which are requisite to supply that energy."[47] Hamilton likened the government under the Articles to a building whose structural framework is unable to support the façade; the problems with the Articles he continued were "…fundamental errors in the structure of the building, which cannot be amended otherwise than by an alteration in the first principles and main pillars of the fabric."[48]

James Madison (some sources say Hamilton and Madison) entered into the issue of sovereignty in *Federalist* twenty. Published on December 11, 1787, in the *New York Packet*, Madison called for "…a sovereignty over sovereigns…" whereby the people would have power, not a particular state or political entity.[49] Madison, like other proponents of the proposed Constitution, saw sovereignty in the people at large and liked to point to the first three words of the preamble, "We the People" as a sign of the sincerity of their argument that the Constitution was unique in its approach to power and sovereignty.

Hamilton picked up the same theme in *Federalist* twenty-two, from December 14, 1787, in the *New York Packet*. Hamilton speculated on what type of government would emerge in the United States if the Articles were left in place. He imagined something far more rapacious than the proposed Constitution; something that would remove all sovereign authority unto itself without a multi-level approach. Hamilton argued that at some unknown point in the future:

> … we shall finally accumulate, in a single body all the most important prerogatives of sovereignty, and thus entail upon our posterity one of the most execrable forms of government that human infatuation ever contrived. Thus we should create in reality that very tyranny which the adversaries of the new Constitution either are, or affect to be solicitous to avert.[50]

John Jay entered the sovereignty debate as well in *Federalist* sixty-four. On March 7, 1788, in the *New York Packet*, Jay expounded on the notion of a three branch government—legislative, executive, and judicial. Jay was trying to allay concerns about power spread among three equal branches:

> All constitutional acts of power, whether in the executive or the judicial department, have as much legal validity and obligation as if they proceeded from the legislature…. It surely does not follow, that because they have given the power of making laws to the legislature, that therefore they should likewise give them power to do every other act of sovereignty by which the citizens are to be bound and affected.[51]

Hamilton made the final reference to sovereignty in *The Federalist* papers. In *Federalist* seventy-five, from the *Independent Journal* on March

26, 1788, Hamilton took up the topic of America on the world stage and the issue of treaties—a prerogative of a sovereign nation. The Treaty of Paris of 1783 ended the American War for Independence—and it was a treaty with the United States, not with the individual states. It also called for states to reimburse Loyalists and for British creditors to be paid their due from contracts made in good faith prior to the Revolution. Individual states however had chosen to take their own stance in relation to Loyalist and British creditors, in opposition to the treaty, which was negotiated and signed on behalf of all the states within the United States. Hamilton picked up on this point:

> The power of making treaties is, plainly, neither the one or the other [enacting or executing laws]. It relates neither to the execution of the subsisting laws, nor to the enaction of new ones; and still less to an exertion of the common strength. Its objects are *contracts* with foreign nations, which have the force of law, but derive it from obligations of good faith. They are not rules prescribed by the sovereign to the subject, but agreements between sovereign and sovereign [emphasis in original].[52]

There are numerous other references to sovereignty throughout *The Federalist* papers. The ones cited though deal specifically with the role of the proposed federal government. Other references relate to the states and the general nature of political sovereignty. It is fair to say it was a topic which commanded great attention.

John Adams, who was in England (he did not return from England until mid–1788, after the Constitution was in force) as ambassador and missed the Convention, wrote a wonderful letter on sovereignty nearly a year after his return. Writing to Benjamin Lincoln, from New York on May 26, 1789, Adams mused on the nature of sovereignty in relation to the United States:

> In answer to your questions, I ask another—where is the sovereignty of the nation lodged? Is it in the national government, or in the state government? Are there more sovereignties than one? If there is more than one there are eleven. If there are eleven there is no general government—for there cannot be eleven sovereignties against one. Are not the Constitution and laws of the United States, the supreme law of the land? If so, the supreme magistrate of the United States, is the supreme magistrate of the land.[53]

Adams was writing after having taken up the new role of Vice-President of the United States. His response to Lincoln though is entirely in line with his colleagues who wrote similar thoughts on American approaches to sovereignty in the previous two years—the run up to the Constitutional Convention and the year immediately afterward, when states were voting on the Constitution in their respective ratifying conventions. And Adams, as a mature statesman, asked the most basic question—we do, as the United States, want a viable, respected country, do we not?

Outside of *The Federalist* papers, other writers, who supported the Constitution but lacked the literary power of *The Federalist* papers weighed in as well on sovereignty in published essays. Benjamin Rush was a notable Philadelphia physician and longtime proponent of a stronger national government. He was well known and considered a colleague of Jefferson, Madison, and a whole range of Founders in addition to being a Founder himself. As a man of science, he is often overlooked for that other Benjamin associated with Philadelphia—Franklin. In January 1787, Benjamin Rush published "Address to the People of the United States" in a publication entitled *American Museum*. Rush was very prescient to point out that America did not end its development once independence was achieved. Too many people saw independence as the end of the line, nothing further was necessary. As has been brought up many times previously, what did Americans want to do with their independence? It was a question too few asked and even fewer dared to answer. Rush reminded his countrymen:

> There is nothing more common than to confound the terms of *the American revolution* with those of *the late American war*. The American war is over: but this is far from being the case with the American revolution. On the contrary, nothing but the first act of the great drama is closed. It remains yet to establish and perfect our new forms of government ... for these forms of government, after they are established and brought to perfection [emphasis in original].[54]

Rush's address was written much more for the "average" reader than the honed and more scholarly *Federalist* essays. Rush succinctly dealt with sovereignty: "The people of America have mistaken the meaning of the word sovereignty: hence each state pretends to be *sovereign*. In Europe, it is applied only to those states which possess the power of making war and peace—of forming treaties, and the like [emphasis in original]."[55]

This writing shows someone like Rush at their best; communicating complex, even obtuse, concepts into simple to understand explanations. John Dickinson, who published essays in favor of the Constitution in 1788 in Wilmington, Delaware as "Fabius," was another writer who wrote in a more informal approach when explaining the proposed new government. Dickinson continued the theme through three of his Fabius letters, ending with:

> As to the idea, that this superintending sovereign will must of consequence destroy the subordinate sovereignties of the several states, it is begging a concession of the question, by inferring, that a manifest end in abuse; and not only so, but it requires an extinction of the principles of all society ... the federal sovereign will being composed of the subordinate sovereign wills of the several confederated states.[56]

6. The Constitutional Convention of 1787

Many lesser-known names than Dickinson also wrote on the topic. Tench Coxe, writing as "A Freeman," in the *Pennsylvania Gazette* in January and February of 1788, used his essays to highlight the unplaced fears of those Anti-Federalists who seemed to spot a boogeyman behind the proposed Constitution. Coxe, following the lead of so many writers approaching this topic, attempted to assuage the fear of those who thought their state would lose its sovereignty. The Articles, and the new Constitution, were not, according to Coxe, instruments to strengthen national power at the expense of the states.

An interesting addition to the non–Federalist essays promoting the idea of sovereignty in the new Constitution was by William Duer, a man who was part of the original cast of *The Federalist* papers before being replaced (he never published as "Publius"). As "Philo-Publius," Duer, in the New York *Daily Advertiser* on October 30, 1787, wrote: "The powers requisite to constitute sovereignty, must be delegated by every people for their own protection and security. The people of each state have already delegated these powers…. It is not necessary that they should grant greater or new ones."[57]

The goal of Duer, Dickinson, Madison, Hamilton, Jay, and others, was to highlight the fact that the new Constitution would not further erode the state power in relation to the national power. Whether we agree or not with that assessment in hindsight is immaterial from our twenty-first century vantage point. In the eighteenth century, those proponents of the Constitution observed no greater or lesser amount of sovereignty moving between the state and national government. This was a category nearly impossible to gauge anyway. One cannot measure a unit of sovereign identity, what scale had been created to distinguish this? Even at the state ratifying conventions, sovereignty became a contentious issue, as states feared a loss of power and identity.

An example of an Anti-Federalist (one who opposed the Constitution) perspective on sovereignty appeared in the Philadelphia *Independent Gazetteer* on November 10, 1787. The anonymous writer warned:

> The consequence must therefore be, either that the *union* of the states will be destroyed by a violent struggle, or that their sovereignty will be swallowed up by silent encroachments into a universal aristocracy; because it is clear, that if two different *sovereign powers* have a co-equal command over the *purses* of the citizens, they will struggle, for the spoils, and the weakest will be in the end obliged to yield the efforts of the strongest [emphasis in original].[58]

Anti-Federalist writers focused on a more intensive loss of sovereignty in the proposed Constitution. Most of these writers were not even happy with the Articles of Confederation either, and many like Patrick Henry, seemed doomed to being cranks over the issue without being able to compromise. Another Anti-Federalist who had a literary outburst was Arthur Lee of Virginia. Writing as "Cincinnatus," in the *New York Journal*, on November 29, 1787, Lee seemingly yelled from the page:

> Such is the anxiety manifested by the framers of the proposed constitution, for the utter extinction of the state sovereignties, that they were not content with taking from them even the name.... When the whole people of America shall be thus recognized by their own solemn act, as the people of the United States, I beseech you Sir, to tell us over whom the sovereignty, you say you leave to the several states, is to operate?[59]

There were certainly more topics at the Constitutional Convention in Philadelphia than sovereignty, as prickly as that was. But yet nearly every topic was tied in with sovereignty, or taxation.

Taxation

Next to the issue of sovereignty, taxation was the topic which generated the most trepidation. In fact, taxation was simply another word for sovereignty as far as some delegates were concerned. Taxation was not a subset of sovereignty; it was essentially equal to it and was a subject which had to be addressed if the country was to truly be a country and move forward.

Madison wrote in his notes on February 21, 1783, that "Mr. Mercer made some remarks tending to a reconsideration of the act declaring general funds to be necessary, which revived the discussion of that subject."[60] That subject was quite simply a pillar upon which the new government (it was new in the sense of having to cope with a post-war perspective) would either succeed or fail. Merchants, the military, investors, seemingly every facet of American post-war life was clamoring for not just their hand-out due them, but some acknowledgment as to the stability of the larger economic structure which had thus far failed the country. Madison noted on that February day in 1783, that Virginia delegate Richard Henry Lee:

> ... in answer to Mr. Madison said the doctrine maintained by him was pregnant with dangerous consequences to the liberties of the confederated states; that notwithstanding the specious arguments that had been employed it was an established truth that the purse ought not to be put into the same hands with the sword; ... He urged finally as a reason why some states would not and ought not to concur in granting to Congress a permanent revenue....[61]

The doctrine that Lee was referring to dealt with Madison's proposal for greater revenue collecting power for Congress. This was, in 1783, four years

6. The Constitutional Convention of 1787

before the Constitutional Convention, and Madison still had a mountain to climb to get to that point. He had at this date not yet received any of the books Jefferson would send to him for study from France. Madison's mountain would be a high one to conquer. Two years later, Lee expounded on his thinking further in a letter to Samuel Adams. On March 14, 1785, Lee, still distrustful of national power (much like Samuel Adams), wrote:

> ... therefore the confederation should not be presumptuously called an infallible system for all times and all situations—but though this is true, yet as it is a great and fundamental system of union and security, no change should be admitted until proved to be necessary by the fairest, fullest, and most mature experience.... But I can never agree that this body shall dictate the mode of taxation, or that the collection shall in any manner be subject to congressional control.[62]

Finally, in 1787, Lee again wrote about money. Writing to George Mason (who would later refuse to sign the Constitution) on May 15, 1787, just as the Constitutional Convention was beginning, Richard Henry Lee summed up his view of the root cause of the current predicament of the government—money. Lee wrote:

> It has given me much pleasure to be informed that General Washington and yourself have gone to the Convention.... The present causes of complaint seem to be, that Congress cannot command the money necessary for the just purposes of paying debts, or for supporting the federal government; and that they cannot make treaties of commerce, unless power unlimited, of regulating trade be given.[63]

The apprehension these men felt was genuine. And, it came from both north and south. The investment already made in the American journey from colony to country was staggering. The Revolutionary War was fought on the inspiration of profound theoretical quotations, universally understood. Now that the war was successfully concluded, what was the Congress to do? The theory so powerfully relied upon during war had to give way to practical concerns. It was the intersection of theory and practicality that produced the paralysis of 1783–1787. No one trusted anyone else to make the decisions on how to move forward, and when. Yet, it had to be done.

Massachusetts Federalist Samuel Osgood made similar observations in a letter to John Adams on November 14, 1786. Lamenting the petty internecine jealousies that existed among states and within states, Osgood wrote to Adams in England:

> The federal government seems to be as near a crisis as it is possible for it to be. The state governments are weak and selfish enough, and they will of course annihilate the first. Their stubborn dignity will never permit a federal government to exist. There are, however, a few men in every state, who are very seriously impressed with the idea that,

without a proper federal head, the individual states must fall a prey to themselves, or any power that is disposed to injure them.[64]

And, who, in an Osgood letter to John Adams was "seriously impressed" with the gravity of the situation enough to do something about it? Their leader, James Madison. Yet, as John Jay put it in a letter to George Washington on January 7, 1787, "What is to be done is a common question, but it is a question not easy to answer."[65] Jay would partner with Madison and Hamilton later in 1787 to try and make that answer about what to do a bit easier to comprehend.

Revenue, and the ability to raise it, was a cornerstone of a highly functioning nation. Philadelphian David Redick was unconvinced that the national government needed the power given it. Especially, "why will they have power to lay direct taxes?"[66] Two weeks later, James Wilson (a delegate to the Convention and a signer of the Constitution—and the Declaration too) gave a speech at a public meeting in Philadelphia on October 6, 1787. His talk included what could be used as a reply to David Redick:

> The power of direct taxation has likewise been treated as an improper delegation to the federal government; but when we consider it as the duty of that body to provide for the national safety, to support the dignity of the union, and to discharge the debts contracted upon the collective faith of the states for their common benefit, it must be acknowledged, that those upon whom such important obligations are imposed, ought in justice and in policy to possess every means requisite for a faithful performance of their trust.[67]

On October 17, 1787, Noah Webster (of dictionary fame), writing as "A Citizen of America," published an essay in Philadelphia examining the proposed Constitution, of which he was a proponent:

> Permit me to ask those who object to this power of taxation, how shall money be raised to discharge our honest debts; debts which are universally acknowledged to be just? ... Why should a power be more dangerous in Congress than in a legislature? ... I believe life, liberty, and property would be as safe in the hands of a federal legislature, organized in the manner proposed by the convention, as in the hands of any legislature, that has ever been, or ever will be chosen in any particular state.[68]

The writer known as "Brutus," in his fifth essay on December 13, 1787, in the *New York Journal*, spent a considerable amount of time explaining taxation and the theory of it and how it would and could be used to destroy the states. Brutus played into the great fear and insecurities some who opposed the Constitution exhibited. Irrational fears without basis. On one hand, there is a distinct conspiracy theory quality to Brutus and some of his type. They tend to take every utterance and spin it out to unimaginable proportions that only they can see. Their arguments tend to be non sequiturs and at times even Brutus must admit that "it is, perhaps, utterly impossible fully to define this power," as he writes in response to the Constitution's necessary and proper clause.[69] Even Brutus' imagination cannot concoct a scenario that is suitable for his essay, or paranoia.

Much like with the topic of sovereignty, taxation was a central topic of *The Federalist* papers. Alexander Hamilton, writing in *Federalist* thirty on December 28, 1787, in the *New York Packet* declares:

> Money is with propriety considered as the vital principle of the body politic; as that which sustains its life and motion, and enables it to perform its most essential function.... From a deficiency in the particular, one or two evils must ensure; either the people must be subjected to continual plunder as a substitute for a more eligible mode of supplying the public wants, or the government must sink into a fatal atrophy, and in short course of time perish.[70]

Hamilton's argument was that if a regular, existing system of taxation was not implemented, then Americans would be at the mercy of the whim of the national Congress as to when and how taxes would be raised. It would be much better to have a system that is predictable and knowable by all concerned. Hamilton continued:

> What remedy can there be for this situation but, in a change of system, which has produced it? In a change of the fallacious and delusive system of quotas and requisitions? What substitute can there be imagined ... but that of permitting the national government to raise its own revenues by the ordinary methods of taxation, authorized in every well-ordered constitution of civil government?[71]

Conclusion

In so many ways James Madison was the Father of the Constitution. Not just in the pro-creative sense, but also in laying the groundwork for what future generations would understand about how the process worked and indeed providing a written version or script of how to develop and enhance a government. In an age of letter writing, diary keeping, and all manner of written missives, Madison left the most detailed analysis and description of what can only be called the Age of American Understanding. It was during the few post-war years that the United States came to grips with itself and its potential. And Madison provided us with the most articulated reflection of that time. His notes of debates in the Constitutional Convention are only bested by the official Journals of the Continental Congress. And of course his notes on the Constitutional Convention have never been superseded. As we have seen many times already, taxation and sovereignty were the dominating subjects with every other topic radiating off these central themes. As the situation in Congress and the country continued to demand action, a number of influential members of Congress still refused to grant the solution was more power, or more clarity, to the national government.

Whatever the difficulties encountered during the Continental Congress years, it was evident to all but a few that the United States at peace was different than the United States at war. The governing document of war simply could not keep pace in peace. As Max Farrard concluded in 1908:

> However radical the difference between the Articles of Confederation and the federal Constitution, however sweeping the provisions of the later document and however carefully worded, the most potent factor in rendering the new instrument of government effective was the changed attitude of the American people.[72]

Part III

Success

The five men who were involved with the writing of *The Federalist* papers (ultimately only three would actually be published as "Publius") were representative of the most educated men in the young country. All had extensive formal education and were considered leaders in the newly independent United States. Chapter 7 will not provide traditional biographies. Rather, these brief biographical overviews will cover each essayist from their birth until 1787, the year the Constitutional Convention met. From that point, their lives will intermingle in a way that allows for a complete narrative of events leading to the writing of *The Federalist*. In this manner the cumulative life experience from birth to the moment of their greatest triumph (up to that point) can be more fully appreciated without having to try and fathom an entire lifetime of achievement. Chapter 8 will look exclusively at *The Federalist* papers and provide a broad overview of the individual essays and the themes which combine to form a total framework. The final chapter, 9, will approach the world of ideas that helped to form the Constitution and *The Federalist* and will place both within the swirling intellectual hedonism which was the Enlightenment.

CHAPTER 7

The Cast

James Madison

Of all the Founders associated with the Constitution or the writing of *The Federalist* papers, James Madison is the best known. He has not suffered the fate of becoming a "forgotten founder," as have so many of his colleagues. Indeed, his home, Montpelier, in Orange County, Virginia, was restored recently, over several years, the project completed in 2010, at the cost of tens of millions of dollars. Clearly, we have deemed him worthy of remembrance.

Madison was unique among the Founders in not being a lawyer. Of course there were others who didn't practice law, notably George Washington, but Madison was unique in many ways. He had a leading role in preparing countless governmental papers, state and federal, such that he seems a lawyer. His role as Father of the Constitution immediately puts one in mind of the law. Yet, this was not Madison. He disliked the contours of law, while admiring its thoroughness. This served him well in politics when he had to debate the many fine points of law. While not inclined towards courtroom drama—something

James Madison, portrait by James Sharples Senior, 1796–1797 (courtesy of Independence National Historic Park).

his demeanor could not handle—he was as conversant in legal theory and history as any lawyer; and in fact he was probably more learned than many. Madison's studies on republics at his home Montpelier in 1786, in preparation for the Constitutional Convention, ensured his preparedness to discuss not just government and theory, but law in a general sense.

Of the three writers who made up Publius (the pseudonym of the authors of *The Federalist* papers), Madison was the wealthiest and had no real pressing need to earn a living in the conventional sense. As previously noted, he was ideally suited to the type of life he was pursuing. He was a Congressman with few pressing duties, and writing the essays were not much of a burden. He also had his wonderful notes to refer to from the Constitutional Convention. John Jay too was comfortably well off and although not as financially secure as Madison, he had no pressing need for employment. As Secretary of Foreign Affairs, he no doubt had a demanding job, but the added burden of being a member of the Publius trio was not overwhelming. Hamilton, though, needed his career. He was the quintessential self-made man, relying on his inherent abilities to capitalize upon his talents to the fullest. His law office was in the building adjoining his home in New York. He kept a very full business schedule as an attorney in New York City and Albany. Taking on added duties as part of the Publius trio was a great burden. Yet, it was his plan, and though he anticipated more help from Jay, he knew the burden would fall to him as the creator of the plan. Hamilton would work frantically at times to finish an essay and get it to the printer so it could quickly appear in the newspapers. Historian Ron Chernow described Hamilton's intense, hyperactive rate of production:

> Hamilton's mind always worked with perpetual speed. Words were his chief weapons, and his account books are crammed with purchases for thousands of quills, parchments, penknives, slate pencils, reams of foolscap, and wax. His papers show that, Mozart-like, he could transpose complex thought onto paper with few revisions.... He wrote with the speed of a beautifully organized mind that digested ideas thoroughly, slotted them into appropriate pigeonholes, then regurgitated them at will.[1]

James Madison was born at his grandmother's plantation on the Rappahannock River, opposite Port Royal, King George County, Virginia, on March 16, 1751. Named for his father, young James grew up and lived with his family at their Orange County plantation that would eventually come to be called Montpelier. The Madisons were a prosperous and respected family and played an important role in the local economic, political, and social aspects of the surrounding county. James Madison was prepared from a young age to succeed his father as a planter and member of the Virginia plantation aristocracy. As such, this meant learning from a young age the business of being a man of action as well as a man of leisure.

At age ten (1762), and after extensive tutoring at home, Madison went away for five years to a school in King and Queen County run by Donald Robertson. Robertson was something of a university don without a university. Highly educated and apparently a good communicator in the classroom, Madison found Robertson the perfect guide for his fast-developing mind. Here, Madison studied English, Greek, Latin, French, geography, and the various branches of mathematics. Robertson was Scottish and a graduate of the University of Edinburgh. He was, by all accounts, influenced by the philosophical movement known as the Scottish Enlightenment. This thinking, eagerly digested by young students such as Madison, would greatly impact the future of what would become the United States.

After Madison left Robertson's school, in 1767, he returned to Montpelier for more extensive tutoring by the Reverend Thomas Martin, rector of the Brick Church, the Anglican church the Madison family attended. In 1769 he entered the College of New Jersey at Princeton. Here, under the college's president, the influential John Witherspoon, Madison flourished even more than he did under Robertson (interestingly, both men were Scottish). In New Jersey he continued his studies of the classics and mathematics, and added moral philosophy, rhetoric, and science. Madison was one of the few Southern students at a Northern university. Fortunately for Madison, Witherspoon was equally (perhaps even more so) indoctrinated into the prevailing elements of the Scottish Enlightenment as had been his former teacher, Robertson.

The late 1760s at the College of New Jersey were wonderful times. Madison had as classmates—not necessarily the same class year—men such as William Bradford, Philip Freneau, and Hugh Henry Brackenridge, all of whom would go on to positions of great standing in the new country, as would Madison himself. In many ways the College prepared, or finalized his preparation, for the life that lay ahead of him, whether he knew it or not. In his chapbook biography of Madison, historian John Kaminski writes, "The College of New Jersey not only made Madison into a scholar, but prepared him to be a revolutionary and a statesman."[2]

There is something of a perception that the founding generation of leaders were all somehow swaggering, intense, physically dominating characters. This was not the case, but it makes for great storytelling. Such was certainly not the case with James Madison. Estimated at being barely five feet tall, Madison was a sickly youth and young man, and he also leaned towards hypochondria (much like John Jay). Madison suffered from intestinal problems, hemorrhoids, seizures, panic attacks, and assorted pains and maladies, both real and imagined. Madison was someone who impressed with his mind, not his physical bearing.

This frail young man returned home to Orange County after graduating from the College of New Jersey in 1772. Determined to find a career for himself, he took a turn at the usual paths of employment for a man of brilliance: religion and law. He found neither to be to his liking. Madison roamed about in his sheltered world as a planter's son and spent most of two years reading and studying numerous subjects, mainly government and law. He taught his younger (and less intellectually gifted) siblings and bided his time. He entered what would be his life's calling in 1774 when he got involved with a freedom of religion case in Culpeper County. His role was to provide moral support for the rights of the accused (who had been preaching non–Anglican tracts without appropriate permission). Madison himself was not overly religious and was not compelled by the case on sectarian grounds, but rather by the principle of freedom of worship. Like most of his contemporaries, Madison, while well versed in religion, was not a believer in the traditional sense. He did not regularly attend service, but he did spice his writings with obligatory, socially useful, religious language, giving the impression of a follower of a strict sect.

James Madison's political career began in earnest in 1774, the same year as the meeting of the First Continental Congress. In fact, his new position with the Orange County Committee of Safety was to enforce embargo guidelines of the Continental Association created by the First Continental Congress. From the beginning, Madison was associated with the reform elements of American politicians.[3] Madison cast his lot early and became committed to the colonial cause. Madison finally, at age twenty-three, had a purpose in life. A year later, in 1775, Madison was created a colonel in the Orange County militia— though he would never see active duty (just like John Jay). In the significant year of 1776, Madison was elected to statewide office in the Virginia Provincial Convention, the constituted state authority after the collapse of British rule. It was as a member of this body that Madison voted on May 15 (in the majority) to instruct Virginia's delegates to the Second Continental Congress to vote for independence.

Later in 1776, Madison first met Thomas Jefferson. When the Virginia Provincial Convention reconvened in October, in Williamsburg, after a summer adjournment, Jefferson, the celebrated author of the recently adopted Declaration of Independence, had left the Continental Congress and returned to Virginia to work on more local matters. Here, the two young scholars became quick friends and political allies.

The next year, 1777, Madison lost his bid to be a state delegate but was appointed by the General Assembly to an executive council of state, which collectively shared power with the governor. Madison would serve two years in this capacity and gain much experience about the practical workings of state government during wartime. The years 1777–1779 were not particularly good years for the American cause. The war was essentially a stalemate with a slight edge going to the British. In December 1779, Madison was elected by the Virginia General Assembly to be a representative to the Continental Congress. This would be Madison's first exposure to national government. As with his election to the executive council of state, Madison's election to the Continental Congress did not involve campaigning to the "average" voter, something he did not relish and in fact abhorred.

In many ways, James Madison was the ideal congressman. Not only was he formally educated, studying was his hobby. He was unmarried, wealthy, and lived at home with his prosperous—still very much alive and in charge—father and mother. He had known little hardship in his short life, and was not indebted to anyone. John Kaminski quotes Martha Dangerfield Bland as describing Madison at the time as "a gloomy, stiff creature. They say [he] is clever in Congress, but out of it, he has nothing engaging or even bearable in his manners—the most unsociable creature in Existence."[4] Two years later, in 1783, Eliza House Trist, daughter of Madison's landlady, commented, "He has a soul replete with gentleness, humanity and every social virtue."[5] Clearly, Madison grew during his time in Congress and became less of a social misfit.

Whatever his newfound social graces, Madison was, foremost, a legislator and a thinker. Early in his career in Congress, he was appointed to a committee to consider revisions to the Articles of Confederation. While perhaps sounding grand, the Articles were in a state of nearly constant threat or in need of revision during their lifetime. However, Madison quickly gained a reputation as being highly competent in matters of legislative development that had some impact upon agreements between the states. Already, Madison displayed the serious, deep, penetrating thought that would benefit him so well a few years hence when he attended the Constitutional Convention and immediately afterward when he wrote nearly half of *The Federalist* papers.

In Congress, Madison wrote an essay on paper money and public finance. He served on the Board of Admiralty and was part of the negotiations of the cessation of Virginia land northwest of the Ohio River to Congress. Madison also dealt with foreign affairs and drafted instructions for John Jay—American envoy to Spain—detailing American navigation rights on the Mississippi.

The Articles of Confederation were adopted, after four years, on March 1, 1781. Three weeks later, Madison was already calling for amendments to give Congress more power over states that defied Congress—especially states that refused to fulfill their financial obligations. Madison supported the efforts of superintendent of finance Robert Morris to restore public credit; and before his re-election in 1781, Madison participated in drafting instructions to American peace negotiators in Paris attempting to formally end the Revolution.

As a member of the committee to revise and realign the Articles, Madison took a course much more radical than most of his colleagues would consider. Madison sought to dramatically alter the relationship between the states and Congress, much to Congress's favor. Madison envisioned an arrangement whereby the states were much more subordinate to the Congress, rather than the situation that existed when Madison first arrived in Congress. His views on refashioning the relationship between Congress and the states would come back in vogue several years later when Madison was at the Constitutional Convention. For now though, in 1782, his concepts were too much, too soon. The War was technically not even over yet, and in fact would not be until the fall of 1783.

Due to term limits, Madison left Congress in 1784 and returned to Montpelier. He maintained his connections with colleagues during the next several years. He was at this point a well-known small man with big ideas, indeed, many ideas. He was elected to the state legislature and dutifully served there, but his real goals were to be found on the national scene. Madison spent his time in the state legislature exhibiting as much drive as he had in the Continental Congress.

The first item on his agenda was to attempt to pass a revised code of laws for the state of Virginia. These draft laws were written by Thomas Jefferson, George Wythe, and Edmund Pendelton, between 1777 and 1779, when Jefferson was no longer a member of the national Congress and working on issues of his home state. Long a priority for Jefferson, the laws were left unresolved during his time as governor of Virginia from 1779 to 1781. This was mainly due to the proximity of the actual fighting when the British invaded Virginia, forcing the state government to flee from Williamsburg to Richmond. These law code revisions sought to strengthen the power of the state, protect individual freedom, reform the penal code, and establish an education system statewide. Most importantly, Jefferson,

Wythe, and Pendleton sought to establish religious freedom and do away with an established state religion.

Madison had his supporters, and he had his foes—most spectacularly in Virginia governor Patrick Henry. In the end, Madison was able to get nearly half of Jefferson's revisions passed. Madison fought vigorously against Governor Henry, who sponsored a bill calling for an established religion in Virginia along with Richard Henry Lee. Madison wrote a "Memorial and Remonstrance Against Religious Assessments" in June 1785, which was highly praised by many legislators who ultimately voted with Madison to enact legislation that "extinguished forever the ambitions of making laws for the human mind."[6]

In 1785, Madison was elected to the American Philosophical Society. This institution, founded as America's intellectual society during the Enlightenment, was Madison's arrival as a recognized thinker and intellectual benefactor of mankind. In fact, most members elected during the eighteenth and nineteenth centuries were elected for their devotion to natural philosophy, a rather large view of what we now see as the separate disciplines of science and philosophy. Essentially, in the eighteenth century, anyone who did not accept the status quo—regardless of what aspect of life was involved—were somehow considered natural philosophers. Madison was certainly one such candidate who did not accept the status quo; whether in government, farming, astronomy, or any other subject he approached.

The National Scene Yet Again

On January 21, 1786, the Virginia Assembly adopted a resolution calling for a "general meeting of the states to consider adopting uniform commercial regulations."[7] The Assembly appointed Madison as one of eight delegates to represent Virginia. Once again, Madison was called by his state to represent its interests on the national stage. This time was different. By 1786, the United States was officially independent and functioning as a sovereign power, however weak it may have been. The United States, still not totally unified under the Articles of Confederation and commercially unable to compete with Europe, saw the situation beginning to drift out of hand. The time had arrived for the country to make some difficult decisions: Would we be thirteen independent states with a loose confederation holding us together? Would we be a sovereign nation with respect to the individual states and in our relations with foreign powers? Could the United States go forward with the knowledge that the legal system was established enough to ensure a stable, precedent setting environment for American officials and citizens to function secure in the knowledge an appropriate legal framework existed for their business endeavors? The decision to gather in September of 1786 in Annapolis, Maryland, marked a turning point in post–Revolutionary America. Enough of the leaders in and out of Congress saw the need to gather and attempt to come to some common understanding to strengthen the union of states from a commercial standpoint. Without some action, the states would face a future of uncertainty and constant inability to engage in ever more complex financial undertakings at home and more importantly abroad.

The delegates in Annapolis were too few to make any progress (only five states sent representatives). However, two of the most important young leaders were in attendance—James Madison of Virginia, and Alexander Hamilton of New York. While both recognized the importance of the task at hand in Annapolis, they realized they needed to redouble their efforts and try for an even larger gathering with even more ambitious goals. The two men agreed to help persuade the states to back a general meeting for May 1787 in Philadelphia, with the express purpose of revising the Articles of Confederation.

John Jay

John Jay is counted among those Founders who have had the title of "forgotten" bestowed upon them by history. Not only is Jay forgotten as a Founder in general, he's also forgotten as the first Chief Justice of the United States. His name, and contributions to the founding of our third co-equal branch of government, are lost among the confusion attendant to the founding and development of that least photogenic of the constitutionally mandated branches. Jay began his duties as Chief Justice in February of 1790. Like so many of the Founders, Jay is overshadowed by the achievements of one even greater than him—John Marshall, fourth Chief Justice of the United States. Marshall is seemingly forever misremembered as not only the first Chief Justice, but also (and not without reason) as the greatest justice.[8]

Of the co-authors of *The Federalist* papers, John Jay had the most extensive résumé as a politician and statesman. He was a Whig even before the Revolution began, and moved into the most radical Whig circles once the fighting started. Many of his activities prior to the authoring of several Federalist papers should have earned him the title of Founding Father, among them service in both the First and Second Continental Congresses; President of the Second Congress (1778–1779); Minister to Spain and diplomat around Europe on behalf of the struggling new country; and, perhaps most significantly, delegate to the Paris Peace Conference that formally ended the American Revolution in 1783. Yet, with all of these accomplishments, Jay is still a vaguely remembered, misty figure from history for the vast majority of Americans. That cannot be rectified here, but some element of recognition can be offered from just a brief look at a long and event-filled life.

John Jay, after John Trumbull, c. 1875 (courtesy of Independence National Historic Park).

John Jay was born the eighth child of Peter Jay and Mary Van Cortlandt on December 12, 1745, in New York City. Somewhat prophetically for a future Chief Justice, he was named after his aunt's husband, John Chambers, a justice of the Supreme Court of the colony.[9] Jay was descended from French Protestants who had escaped Louis XIV's religious persecutions and emigrated to America. Listening to vivid family stories about persecution and religious intolerance as a child left a lifelong impression on Jay; who was one of the most outwardly religious—in a traditional sense—of the Founders and keen to recognize and object to royal tyranny, whatever the motivation.

At the age of six, Jay was sent to a grammar school kept by the Reverend Stoope in New Rochelle. Even at this early age, John Jay impressed his parents by taking "to learning exceedingly well."[10] Jay stayed with the Reverend Stoope three years before returning home for private tutoring before entering college. The time young John spent with the Reverend Stoope was useful, but nowhere near as transformative as the time young James Madison spent with Donald Robertson. The Reverend Stoope was not steeped in the Scottish Enlightenment, as Robertson was.

In 1760, not yet fifteen, Jay journeyed from his home in Rye, New

York, to King's College (later Columbia) in New York City. In May 1764, Jay graduated top in his class with a Bachelor of Arts degree. He had already decided to pursue law as a career. Without delay, Jay entered the legal office of Benjamin Kissam to study law. After three years of study and practical experience, Jay was admitted to the bar in 1768. His reputation for hard work, sound reasoning, and strong principles gained Jay a lucrative business practice in short order. Jay's first big assignment came in the early 1770s when King George III appointed a commission to adjudicate the boundary dispute between New York and New Jersey. The commission appointed Jay to be the secretary. In 1774, Jay married Sarah Livingston, daughter of the future first non-royal governor of New Jersey, William Livingston.

John and Sarah Jay's honeymoon was short lived. News reached the colonies of the March 31, 1774, Boston Port Bill scheduled to go into effect in May of that year. The Port Bill closed the port of Boston as punishment in part for the Boston Tea Party. On May 16, 1774, prominent men of New York City met to discuss the turn of events in Boston and what implications this Bill could have on New York. This gathering produced a committee of fifty to work with the other colonies on a joint response to Parliament. The newly wed John Jay was appointed to this committee.

This committee drafted correspondence and communicated with their counterparts in Boston. Both committees agreed the time had arrived for all the colonies to meet together to discuss mutual concerns. Simply sending correspondence amongst colonies was too time-consuming given the seriousness and rapid escalation of the disagreements with Great Britain which were impacting every colony. Likewise, by coming together to form a joint response to Britain, the colonies would avoid the danger of being just one colony against Britain (which was Massachusetts' greatest fear). Although a Whig politically, Jay felt a meeting might be premature and would quite possibly be viewed as hostile by the King.

Nevertheless, on September 5, 1774, John Jay took his place among the delegates who gathered in Carpenter's Hall in Philadelphia for the First Continental Congress. Jay was one of the youngest delegates—if not the youngest—to be a representative of his colony. As was discussed, this Congress was not sanctioned by the King or Parliament and could be seen as riotous or even treasonous. Jay was appointed to a committee to prepare a petition and proposal to the British people, bypassing the King and Parliament to go directly to the colonist's fellow subjects. The idea was to appeal to the "average" Englishman in the hopes of winning their support in the colonists' efforts to have their ancient liberties restored; which by their view had been ignored by the King and especially Parliament.

Jay wrote the remonstrance for his committee, which was praised by another young delegate, Thomas Jefferson. The First Continental Congress adjourned after six weeks of work. During those six weeks Jay made the most of his first experience with national issues, and impressed nearly all the delegates with his energy and determination. Before adjourning, the Congress, on Jay's suggestion, instructed colonies to appoint committees of observation to monitor the non-importation embargo imposed by the colonies against British goods. It was on one of these committees too, in Virginia, that James Madison got his first extended exposure to national issues and perhaps first became aware of John Jay. The First Continental Congress adjourned calling for a second meeting to occur in May of 1775. Once again, John Jay was elected to the post of delegate. Concurrently, Jay was elected to the New York legislature. This would be the start of incredibly hectic and stressful times for Jay and his family.

Events moved quickly throughout 1775. Armed hostilities broke out between the Americans and the British at Concord, Massachusetts; George Washington was named commander-in-chief of the American forces; lesser officers were appointed; more colonies organized their defenses and struggled to enforce the embargo; feelings and actual hostilities were growing to the point of no return. Jay wrote an address to the inhabitants of Canada on behalf of Congress asking, if nothing else, for the moral support of the Canadians.

On July 6, 1775, a year before the Declaration of Independence, Congress passed another declaration that sought to justify the taking up of arms by the Americans. Once again, Jay was on this committee. Jay had an extraordinary track record in being called to important committee service. This can no doubt be attributed to his abilities, seriousness (even in someone so young), and commitment to the American cause. But it is impossible not to wonder if, because of a perceived overly eager approach to the work, that his colleagues let Jay shoulder too much of the work knowing that Jay, while having the ability, would not complain, or criticize his less productive colleagues?

The 1775 Declaration had a much different tone than the 1776 Declaration. In the 1775 version, Congress wrote, "we have not raised armies with ambitious designs of separating from Great Britain, and establishing independent states."[11] Congress sought to absolve itself from any fault, laying all blame on Great Britain for having violated America's long held liberties and sense of justice: "In our native land, in defense of the freedom that is our birthright, and which we ever enjoyed till the late violation of it—for the protection of our property, acquired solely by the honest industry of our forefathers and ourselves against the violence actually offered, we have taken up arms."¹²

Congress wanted the world, and posterity, to know that America was driven to the acts that were taking place and that threatened to escalate far beyond 1775. More to the point, Congress was appealing to a tradition in petitioning the King for redress that in 1775 was well over a century old.¹³ The right of petition was in the English Bill of Rights in 1689, drafted after the Glorious Revolution of 1688. The right surfaces in the Massachusetts Body of Liberties of 1641, and of course surfaces today in the First Amendment to the United States Constitution. The unwritten concept (*lex non scripta* as the legal historians might say), certainly dates much further back, into the mists of time.

Also in the beginning of July 1775, Jay, along with John Dickinson of Delaware, wrote a petition to the King himself. Dickinson wrote most of the petition, which again was designed to give Britain one more chance to accommodate the colonies and their grievances. Lastly, the petition was meant to absolve Congress and the colonists of fault, should the situation escalate. The month of July 1775 was, in essence, spent laying out culpability for the fast-approaching general war. Regardless of what was about to happen, America was not at fault. Finally, Jay was part of the committee to draft a petition to Ireland and Jamaica, explaining to their fellow British subjects what exactly they were doing. These two petitions boiled down to the line, "Who can censure us for repelling the attacks of such a barbarous band [the British]?"¹⁴

The ultimate act foreswearing all responsibility for what could happen occurred on July 20, when Congress called for a day of fasting and prayer. Not content with just writing and publishing petitions to explain their actions, Congress felt the need to provide an unassailable veneer of religion to strengthen their cause. The religious aspect of their actions forever sealed their fate, given the aura of respectability religion provided the cause. In fact, the Congress probably had few illusions that, by this point, there was any turning back. Their call for religious sanction for their efforts makes July 20 more about blessing the troops preparing for battle than about praying for peace.

By late 1775, it was certain that Britain and America would go separate ways (the colonies had been officially declared in rebellion in August of 1775). The British had refused to accept any of the American petitions and sought to enforce their rule by arms. For Jay, and his fellow members in Congress, the future for America seemed clear—independence.

Independence was naturally a proposition fraught with all manner of

7. The Cast

difficulties. Such a move would forever render reconciliation out of reach. Was independence what the people—as "the people" were understood in 1776—really wanted? In New York, the new convention harbored grave doubts as to whether they truly represented the wishes of the colony. Furthermore, 1776 saw the British invade New York City and occupy it as a base of operations. For New York, the time had come to make a decision.

The decision was made on July 9. When the Convention abandoned the city they reestablished the government in White Plains. Jay, having been recalled from Congress by the Convention to deal with state matters, helped to arrange the government in exile. On July 9, the first day the White Plains government met, news arrived that Congress had adopted a Declaration of Independence for the colonies. Jay, by virtue of being recalled from Philadelphia, missed the opportunity to sign the document. Instead, his committee in White Plains considered the Declaration and reported to the Convention:

> Resolved unanimously, that, the reasons assigned by the Continental Congress for declaring these United Colonies free and independent states are cogent and conclusive, and that while we lament the cruel necessity which has rendered this measure unavoidable, we approve the same, and will, at the risk of our lives and fortunes, join with the other colonies in supporting it.[15]

Jay did have the satisfaction of having his name, and his committee, recommend the Declaration to the people of New York.

Jay seems to have never suffered from second thoughts about his decision to oppose the British—or, if he did, he left no record. Indeed, Jay wrote a lengthy address to his fellow citizens in New York (it was reprinted and shared with all the states) of the righteousness of their cause. He admonished them that Britain and her king could no longer be trusted to ensure the necessity of the benefits of government and of a moral life. Jay sought to strengthen his readers' resolve in the face of multiple setbacks.

Jay's work over the past two years (1774–1776), since his arrival at the First Continental Congress, had by the end of 1776 made his name very well known among his fellow New Yorkers and put Jay on a path to what would be an extremely busy and challenging career as a Revolutionary War diplomat.

Throughout 1776, as things went from bad to worse for the colonists, Jay continued with his heavy workload with the state convention. He oversaw many of the initiatives designed to incarcerate, harass, or exile many of the Tory Loyalists in the newly proclaimed state of New York. He did this even though New York City, Staten Island and Long Island were in the hands of the British. Jay's committee was responsible for hundreds of arrests and other forms of behavior meant to intimidate Loyalists or even those who simply did not choose a side. (Jay's view of the legal protections due to Loyalists would change dramatically over the next ten years.)

Although Jay built a reputation as a strong patriot and promoter of liberty by dealing sternly with Loyalists, he apparently could be fair and understanding as well. According to his son William Jay, who compiled and published a selection of his father's correspondence in 1833, "He invariably discountenanced all inhumanity and unnecessary rigor towards the enemy, or the tories."[16] William Jay, naturally eager to cast his father in the most favorable light, relayed a story in a biography of his father to show his humility:

> On one occasion, having reason to believe that a zealous committee-man in Westchester county had exercised his power with unjustifiable severity, he complained of his conduct, and procured a vote of censure against him from the convention. Some time after, this person met him, and assured him that he was innocent of the alleged charge, and complained that he had been condemned without having an opportunity of vindicating himself. Mr. Jay, struck with the justice of this remonstrance, instantly replied, —"You are right, and I am wrong, and I ask your pardon."[17]

The astonished committeeman accepted Jay's apology (as per this bit of family lore) and felt he had met a just and honorable man.

Throughout the American War, Jay became known for his equanimity concerning Loyalists. In a letter to New York Governor George Clinton on May 6, 1780, Jay wrote that he saw a report in an English paper (which he felt must have been propaganda) concerning an act allowing for the confiscation of Loyalist property. Jay wrote, "An English paper contains what they call, but I can hardly believe to be, your confiscation act. If truly printed, New-York is disgraced by injustice too palpable to admit even of palliation."[18] Jay asked that Governor Clinton send him the truth concerning the act. Unfortunately, the English paper was all too accurate. New York, under Clinton, had passed a law allowing for the seizure of Loyalist property. Jay found the law so repugnant and unjust that he refused to purchase any property from such sales.[19]

As the War dragged on through the difficult years of the late 1770s, Jay was busy with his duties in New York and in the Continental Congress. In the spring of 1776 he wrote a draft of the New York State Constitution. Called out of town to attend his dying mother, he found on his return the draft had passed nearly as he wrote it. Jay felt that the Convention perhaps acted too quickly in passing a draft that even Jay admitted needing revising. Yet, given the pressing needs of the times America was facing, the new Constitution met the demands confronting the new state of New York. Jay wrote about the hastiness of adopting his draft: "Though the birth of the Constitution is, in my opinion, premature, I shall, nevertheless, do all in my power to nurse and keep it alive; being far from approving the Spartan law, which encouraged parents to destroy such of their children as, perhaps by some cross accident, might come into the world defective and misshapen."[20]

These were extremely strong words no doubt chosen to cause alarm. Jay was clearly using the metaphor of his draft constitution being represented as a misshapen child which thus should be destroyed—much as the law allowed of deformed children in ancient Sparta. Jay was not someone to mince words or metaphors—and clearly had given much thought to the development of constitutions—an asset that would serve him well in June 1788 in Poughkeepsie when debating the proposed American Constitution at the State Ratifying Convention.

Under the new state Constitution of New York in 1777, Jay was named the chief justice of the state Supreme Court. He was offered the governorship, but declined, saying he felt he could best serve New York by being a part of the judiciary, and not the executive branch. Although he realized this meant less pay and prestige, staying on the court allowed Jay to continue in the realm which suited his education and abilities. It was also a perfect match for someone named after a relative who served in the same capacity under the colonial regime. For over two years Jay worked at this position while no longer being a member of the Continental Congress. In late 1778, this situation ended when Jay was recalled back to Congress and made its president. Upon this distinction, he resigned as chief justice of New York.

On September 27, 1779, the Continental Congress selected their president, John Jay, to be the next minister plenipotentiary to Spain. Jay's voyage to Spain was not without incident. John and Sarah Jay left Philadelphia on the *Confederacy*, at the end of October 1779. The ship had problems just getting out of the Delaware River and into the Delaware Bay and Atlantic. Then, a fierce storm nearly sank the ship, leaving it virtually helpless in the ocean. It limped to Martinique where the Jays were immediately placed on the French ship *Aurora*. The ship was forced to change course as it neared France after being chased by a British warship and instead put in to port in Cadiz, Spain. The original idea was to have the French introduce Jay to the Spanish. Spain was not overly keen on acknowledging American independence. For Jay, American independence was an established fact, never mind the war being fought. The Spanish however, colonial masters themselves, were not so sure independence was a suitable course for colonies to pursue. They wanted proof America was ready to go its separate way; Jay could not provide proof.

Spanish officials treated Jay accordingly, he wrote "Pains were taken to prevent any conduct towards me that might savour of an admission or knowledge of American independence."[21] Once settled, Jay ran into issues with Spanish diplomats from the beginning. The Spanish king, Charles III, eventually agreed to a small loan to help the Americans, but that was about as far as he was willing to go. Overall, after more than a year in Spain, Jay had little to show for his efforts.

While in Spain, Jay began to keep a diary of sorts which he may have intended as notes for some future history of his work as an American minister. He never produced a history, and only fragments of this diary remained among Jay's papers after his death in 1829. In early parts of his notes he attempted to give the reasons for keeping a journal: "The same principles which then committed me to the disposal of my fellow-citizens demand that as I have the best opportunities of knowing, so I should transmit to posterity the memory of their political transactions with the kingdom, and thereby prevent their being by representations founded on conjecture and partial information."[22]

Ever the optimistic patriot, Jay continued: "America exhibits a new spectacle to the political world, and is rising to empire and greatness in a manner so singular as to render her steps interesting to all mankind, and especially to the people of that country."[23]

Little had occurred by 1779 that would have given Jay unqualified reason to think the Revolution was going to be a success without question. Yet, as many other writers of the period, Jay had undiluted confidence in the final outcome of America's War. Jay's optimism was evident in a letter to Silas Deane on November 1, 1780. Jay struck his familiar, upbeat tone: "The state of America I admit to be a serious matter; but I still think it will terminate well, though it may be scorched by the ordeal through which it is to pass."[24] This was not an unusual viewpoint. The colonies had a long list of writers (from many fields) who foretold a great future for the colonies. When many of these early, colonial, writers prophesized about America's future, it was as a colony of Great Britain. It was not until after relations soured between America and Great Britain that writer's, still optimistic about America's future, began to see the future as separate from Great Britain.

A major point of contention with the Spanish was navigation of the Mississippi River, which Jay had been instructed to demand for the new country. The Spanish were not interested in bargaining with what they saw as their most strategic and financially important part of their North American empire. The United States at the very least expected free navigation rights.

Word reached Jay on May 18, 1781, that Congress had voted to no longer insist on free navigation of the Mississippi below the Southern boundary of the United States (roughly about mid–Louisiana today). This of course meant access to the all-important port of New Orleans was no longer an American goal. Jay was horrified by the instruction. He had spent his entire time in Spain as minister arguing for free navigation of the entire Mississippi and thought now his position was completely undermined. Jay dutifully followed the order; but he made sure that if peace concluded with Great Britain before a treaty with Spain was signed, relinquishing navigation rights to the Mississippi by America were to be withdrawn.

For Jay, much worse was to come during the summer of 1781. He received word from Congress that he was to participate, with other American diplomats in Europe, in talks with Great Britain for peace; the talks were to be mediated by the Russian and German Emperors. On September 20, 1781, Jay wrote a powerful letter to Thomas McKean, president of the Continental Congress. Writing from St. Ildefonso in Spain, Jay did not hold back his feelings on what he was being asked to do in his new instructions: "At the commencement of the present troubles I determined to devote myself, during the continuance of them, to the service of my country, in any station in which she might think it proper to place me. This resolution, for the first time, now embarrasses me."[25]

Jay was not alone in his feelings towards Congress and their turning over of American sovereignty to the French to negotiate for them. Even members of Congress felt the majority had gone too far in handing the French authority to sue for peace on behalf of the United States.

For a variety of reasons, Jay felt this course of action to be misguided. Yet, he consented to do his duty, however odious he found it. In the final analysis, a brokered peace agreement became a moot point. The victory at Yorktown occurred less than a month after Jay's letter which he had no way of knowing was about to occur when he sat down to write his letter on September 20. Yet, less than two weeks after Jay wrote, Washington sent the first American cannon ball flying into the British camp at Yorktown, the prelude to the end of Britain's Colonial American holdings.

Amidst the fast-paced flow of events occasioned by the end of the War, Jay received a letter from Benjamin Franklin in May 1782 asking him to proceed to Paris to join in preparation for anticipated peace negotiations with England. Overall, Jay's efforts in Spain were not very productive. The

Spanish simply were too conservative to be swayed by the freedom and liberty arguments being advocated by the Americans. However, Jay did learn a great deal about diplomacy, politics, and the limits of effective engagement. His move to Paris would mark a new aspect of his career and a further enhancement of his credentials.

Paris

Both Jay and Franklin, who was already in Paris, had to contend with the fact that Congress had allowed France to lead the discussions and negotiations with England for a final peace treaty. This situation still struck Jay as paternalistic and he felt it left the United States as less than an equal power.

When Jay arrived in late June 1782, he immediately set to work with Franklin and the French ministers. Jay was convinced there would be nothing to gain by delay and willingly set about his diplomatic duties. Besides Great Britain herself, Jay, Franklin, and ultimately Henry Laurens and John Adams, had to deal with France, Holland, and Spain—all countries involved in some manner with American independence. Almost immediately, negotiations with Spain on the western boundary of the United States bogged down on the issue of the Mississippi River. The United States had three demands: 1) the establishment of the western boundary, and navigation of, the Mississippi River (again); 2) an acknowledgment of peace by England before negotiations began; and 3) access for American fishing ships to the rich fishing waters off of Newfoundland. These would be the guideposts the American diplomats would appeal to during the protracted negotiations seeking peace. It should always be remembered that the American Revolution was far from being just between England and the colonies. France, Spain, Holland, and indirectly the German mercenaries who populated George IIIs ranks, all had an interest in the outcome of the American War. Some more than others; none of America's allies were in the struggle simply out of their commitment to the colonists' cause. If that was the only criteria, America would have been very alone indeed in its struggle.

In October of 1782, John Adams joined Jay and Franklin in Paris as the three principle American negotiators. With these three in place, the United States and Great Britain signed provisional articles of peace; which meant the two sides had agreed to stop negotiating about negotiating a peace and agreeing to actually negotiate a treaty. (The fourth American commissioner arrived too late to sign the articles. Henry Laurens did however manage to insert a clause prohibiting the British from taking any slaves out of American territory—Laurens was the only Southerner among America's diplomatic team.)

Much of 1783 was spent in negotiations among the powers: United States, Great Britain, France, Holland, and Spain. The arduous debates were remarkably free of duplicitous behavior often associated with eighteenth century (or any century) diplomacy. Finally, on September 3, 1783, the ministers signed the Treaty of Paris formally ending the American War for Independence. Jay, John Adams, Benjamin Franklin, Henry Laurens, and Franklin's grandson (his secretary William Temple Franklin) were immortalized in a "group portrait" style of painting to commemorate the event. The British ministers however failed to participate in the work and the artist, Benjamin West, finished the painting only halfway, showing only the American delegation, and leaving a blank where the British ministers (David Hartley and Richard Oswald) should have been.

After the conclusion of his work in France, Jay, his health fragile, journeyed to Bath, England to take the famous waters. After a year of intense negotiations, Jay was more ill than he thought. He traveled alone for nearly two months before returning refreshed to Paris.

John and Sarah Jay returned to New York on July 24, 1784, five years after they left. Jay had left a colonist rebelling against his king and returned home one of the most respected diplomats of a free and independent country. When he stepped off the ship he was hailed as through a conquering hero—and in many ways he was. While Washington is often credited with keeping the army together through difficult times, few of his contemporaries are accorded the same adulation for their work. Men such as Jay, John Adams, Benjamin Franklin, Henry Laurens, and others, had the task of keeping the idea of America alive in a foreign, mostly underwhelmed, world. The Americans could barely afford to properly equip their ministers much less be in a position to leverage power on an international scene. Yet, these men, much like Washington, kept up appearances against all odds and saw their efforts through to the bitter end.

In that hot July of 1784 when Jay arrived in New York, he was showered with proclamations, gifts, well wishes, and finally, thanks. Still, there was little rest for the weary as Congress had appointed Jay to the office of Secretary of Foreign Affairs. Jay immediately accepted, despite his fatigue. He only had minimal contact with Congress during the remaining months of 1784, as he had to attend to his private affairs after an absence of several years.

The year 1785 dawned with the newly independent United States facing one crisis after another as we have seen. The weaknesses of the Articles of Confederation became ever more glaring without the specter of war added into the mix. The Congress could not even settle on a permanent home for themselves, much less govern a new country. The greatest asset America possessed in 1785 was potential; unlimited potential for Americans to make their way into a world with seemingly endless resources: coal, iron, timber, water, land; the list seemed to go on and on. Yet, for those charged with trying to govern this apparent free-for-all, conditions were dire. How could this potential, free of war, be kept from descending into a chaotic mad house? How could all of the suffering endured during the war be sure to have been worthwhile? As Jay wrote to Thomas Jefferson in Paris in 1786, "Our country is fertile, abounding in useful productions, and those productions in demand and bearing a good price; yet relaxation in government and extravagance in individuals create much public and private distress, and much public and private want of good faith."[26]

The next two years would prove crucial. Many of the country's brightest and most far sighted thinkers were already pondering this conundrum, including John Jay. As usual, money, and who controlled it, would play a major role in determining how events would proceed. As Secretary of Foreign Affairs, Jay became quite well versed on a matter that would come to his attention six years hence when he would be the first Chief Justice of the United States. The issue of foreign creditors seeking payment for debt incurred during the War was an issue Jay dealt with as both Secretary of Foreign Affairs and later as Chief Justice. In fact, on October 13, 1785, Jay, as Secretary of Foreign Affairs, submitted a report to Congress outlining abusers of a clause in the 1783 peace treaty requiring "that creditors on either side should meet with no lawful impediment to the recovery of the full value in sterling money of all bona fide debts heretofore contracted."[27] Jay singled out several states whose laws were directly in violation of the treaty—including his home state of New York. Jay advised Congress to declare state laws in contradiction to the national treaty invalid. Jay made his stand for the supremacy of national law over state law. In his own way, he was in part setting up one of the major debates the Constitutional Convention would grapple with less than two years hence. But, it was incidents like this one which in part forced the United States into the Convention in the first place. As William Jay, son of John Jay, wrote in 1835 concerning the episode:

> Congress, in accordance with the advice of their secretary [John Jay], called on the states to repel such of their laws as were repugnant to the treaty; but, unhappily, they had no power to enforce the call. There was no federal judicative to which the injured and oppressed foreigner could appeal for protection against the vindictive and unjust

enactments of the State Legislatures—no tribunal that could set aside, as void, a law that trampled upon the faith of treaties.²⁸

In what could be seen as a reply to Jay, George Washington wrote: "Experience has taught us, that men will not adopt, and carry into execution, measures the best calculated for their own good, without the intervention of a coercive power."²⁹

Alexander Hamilton

Of all three co-authors of *The Federalist* papers, Alexander Hamilton no doubt claimed the prize for the most obscure and humble birth. Compared to the posh beginnings of John Jay and James Madison, Alexander Hamilton was poor beyond all telling. From his birth, Hamilton had all the disadvantages from a social and financial standpoint the eighteenth century could bestow on someone. This inauspicious start began on January 11, 1755, on the island of Nevis, in the British West Indies. His parents, unmarried, were Rachel Lavien and James Hamilton (the mother from the West Indies and the father from Scotland). The family, including Alexander's older brother James, moved to St. Croix in 1765. Shortly afterward, the father, James Hamilton, abandoned his family. Three years later, his mother Rachel died from a fever, leaving Alexander and his brother—barely teenagers—to make their own way. James Hamilton apprenticed to a carpenter, while Alexander to the mercantile firm of Beckman and Cruger.

Alexander Hamilton, by Charles Willson Peale, c. 1790–1795 (courtesy of Independence National Historic Park).

Hamilton, seemingly destined to an island life as a brilliant bookkeeper, got a big break on the winds of a ferocious hurricane in 1772. This same year, by comparison, by which both his future co-authors, James Madison and John Jay, were well established in careers, or at least on the way to being established. In 1771, Madison was finishing his formal studies at the College of New Jersey and settling down to the career of an unpaid scholar in colonial Virginia, while John Jay had finished his legal studies and was embarking on a legal career that would take him to the top of his profession. Madison and Jay had probably never heard of Nevis in 1772, yet the prodigy Alexander Hamilton had just penned a short work about a devastating hurricane that would garner the attention of men of means who would finance his trip to America and his education. Hamilton made such an impression with his writing style and evocation to God that it drew the attention of several local island leaders, among them Hugh Knox, minister of the Presbyterian Church in Christiansted. The Reverend Knox led a drive to collect money to send young Hamilton to the colonies in America for an education. The Reverend Knox had two powerful and influential sponsors in the colonies for young Hamilton in William Livingston and Elias Boudinot.

Due partly to the influence of these two New Jersey notables, Hamilton entered the College of New Jersey in Princeton in 1773. He quickly transferred to New York's King's College where he met, through the Livingston family, the young John Jay, his future collaborator on *The Federalist* papers. Throughout 1774, the restless Hamilton devoured academic life. He quickly entered the rapidly escalating conflict between America and Great Britain by writing pamphlets and letters. The ambitious Hamilton, perhaps at first unsure of which side to take, quickly found his personal desires and wishes reflected in the restless colonial cause. Like many, Hamilton appeared to have been at first conflicted as to loyalties. As a good Englishman, he had a natural affinity to support the King. Yet, as a young man with obvious talent, he wanted to make his mark in the quickest way possible. He also needed to overcome his pedigree, something which would have been very difficult in highly class-conscious England. Putting aside his inherent longing for stability and a sense of place, Hamilton chose to cast his future with the colonials in the hope of rapid advancement both socially and professionally. He would not have long to wait.

In 1776, Hamilton became commander (with the rank of captain) of an artillery company and quickly dropped out of King's College without obtaining a degree. Like so many other young men, Hamilton was not alone in his desire for fame, glory, social advancement, or just plain thrill seeking, who withdrew from colleges throughout the colonies to take a stand against Great Britain. Hamilton's timing was impeccable. For in December 1776, his company, having been assigned to New Brunswick, New Jersey, was close enough to be called upon to assist in what would come to be seen as one of the seminal (symbolically and actually) moments of the war—Washington's crossing of the Delaware River to surprise the Hessians at Trenton on December 24, 1776. Through his reckless bravery, Hamilton came to the attention of his commander, George Washington.

By March 1, 1777, Hamilton was appointed an aide-de-camp to General Washington with the rank of lieutenant colonel in the Continental Army. He held that position until 1781. For a young man whom John Adams would later describe as the bastard brat of a Scotch peddler, Hamilton had clearly come a long way from the obscurity of a Caribbean island. His meteoric rise, professionally and socially, would only continue with his extremely close association with Washington. In 1778, in addition to his extensive duties for Washington, Hamilton wrote and published three anonymous letters in the *New York Journal* using the name Publius, the same name he would choose ten years later with *The Federalist* papers. The anonymous letters attacked Samuel Chase for speculating in the flour market based on information received as a member of the Continental Congress from Maryland. Chase would later be a Supreme Court Justice appointed by President Washington in 1796. (President Jefferson would later attempt to remove Chase from the Supreme Court by impeachment—Chase survived.)

After spending the 1779–1780 winter encampment with Washington at his headquarters in the Ford mansion at Morristown, New Jersey, Hamilton realized his boredom at the now routine tasks he performed for Washington. Eager to distinguish himself more, he asked Washington for a field command. While Hamilton was more than ready to leave Washington's side, Washington was not so ready to give up his trusted and extremely talented aid. This refusal by Washington was the start of tensions between the two men. While Hamilton may have felt slighted by the refusal of a command, his social prospects advanced considerably in 1780. Hamilton began a courtship with Elizabeth Schuyler, the daughter of a wealthy and prominent New Yorker named Philip Schuyler. Philip Schuyler also happened to be a general in the Continental Army, and a member of the New York Legislature. One final note during the busy year of 1780 saw Hamilton aggressively proposing changes and amendments to the Articles of Confederation to his friend James Duane. In correspondence, Hamilton laid out plans that would eventually come to light in the Constitutional Convention, *The Federalist* papers, and during his role as first Secretary of the Treasury.

During 1781, Hamilton continued to agitate for a stronger congress through the medium that was quickly becoming his signature style: the anonymous letter or essay sent through a newspaper. After resigning his position on Washington's staff in the summer of 1781, Hamilton began work on six essays that would be called "Continentalist." (See appendix 2) By the title, it was clear that the topic was more than about individual state concerns. Hamilton, writing anonymously, argued for an expansive interpretation of the Articles of Confederation in the *New York Packet* from July of 1781 through July of 1782.

Hamilton's last experience in the military occurred right in the middle of his essays when he led a New York based light infantry battalion at Yorktown which proved highly successful for Hamilton. After he formally left the Army at the end of 1781 he began the study of law and was admitted to the Bar in July of 1782—the same period he was writing the "Continentalist" essays. The very busy year of 1782 (he became a father that year as well) also saw the New York Legislature adopt a resolution drafted by Hamilton calling for a convention to revise and strengthen the Articles of Confederation. In November 1782 he traveled to Philadelphia to attend Congress and met for the first time James Madison. Together they drafted measures for increasing revenues to pay the army and other public debts.

After leaving the military at the end of 1781, Hamilton proceeded to set an almost superhuman pace in advocating for a stronger central government in the five years between 1782 and 1787, the year of the Constitutional Convention and the beginning of *The Federalist* papers project. He still dabbled in military life by being a member of the Society of the Cincinnati and by attending Washington's farewell at Fraunce's tavern on December 4, 1783. Mostly though, Hamilton spent his time on politics, writing, his legal career, and his family.

In 1784, he published two pamphlets, both under the penname of "Phocion."[30] In these essays he argued against the many state laws denying former Loyalists access to a legal remedy in American courts for damage or loss of property during the war. These state laws, Hamilton argued, were in direct contravention to the Paris Peace Treaty of 1783. This very same issue would bedevil John Jay years later when Jay, as Chief Justice, had to hear several cases that landed before the Supreme Court. For Hamilton though, this issue went straight to the heart of his efforts to strengthen the federal government.

Hamilton carried his argument to open court on June 29, 1784, in *Rutgers v. Waddington*. This case involved a female brewer in New York City who sued over damages to her facility during the British occupation of New York under the Trespass Act. Hamilton argued that the Trespass Act was in violation of the 1783 Paris Peace Treaty and a violation of the laws of nations. The court found partially in Hamilton's favor later that year and Hamilton continued to push his political agenda. (It is worth noting that John Jay, while minister to Spain, had opposed the Trespass Act himself when he first heard of its passage in 1780.) For much of 1785 Hamilton was in court defending former Loyalist's and British subjects and agents against the Trespass Act.

The year 1786 saw Hamilton move his plans for a national convention to alter the Articles of Confederation one more step further along. In September 1786 twelve delegates from five states attended the Annapolis Convention. While the turnout was poor, and little was accomplished, the delegates did agree to pursue calling a convention in Philadelphia for May 1787 to consider changes to the federal system. This one agreement was enough to buoy Hamilton's spirit as he entered the New York Assembly in January 1787, facing a hostile Governor George Clinton who opposed any strengthening of the federal government. Further souring his mood was news that while the legislature appointed Hamilton to the delegation for the Philadelphia Convention, they also appointed Robert Yates and Robert Lansing, Jr. Both men were vehemently opposed to any strengthening of the federal government as much as Governor Clinton was. Hamilton's experience was frustrating and at times humiliating given his being outnumbered at the Convention two to one by Yates and Lansing. On September 17, Hamilton, the only delegate from New York still in attendance, signed the Constitution as an achievement he took great personal pride in. Immediately after the Convention Hamilton began work on *The Federalist* papers.

Remembrance

In 1832, forty-five years after *The Federalist* papers were written, and three years after Jay's death (Madison would die in 1836, and Hamilton had been dead nearly thirty years, having died in his famous duel with Aaron Burr in 1804 in Weehawken, New Jersey), Elizabeth Hamilton asked the highly regarded Chancellor of the State of New York, James Kent (1763–1847), to write his memories of her late husband Alexander Hamilton for her. James Kent was a living monument in American law, having written *Kent's Commentaries on American Law* in the late 1820s. This digest of American Law was similar in design to William Blackstone's *Commentaries on English Law* from the 1770s which was so influential in the training of American lawyers before the days of law schools. Indeed, James Kent is often referred to as the "American Blackstone." Kent was also a staunch member of the Federalist party (long after it had died) and in his formative years was very close to Hamilton and they had a mentor/student relationship as Kent was making his mark as a lawyer and judge.

Elizabeth Hamilton's request was quite in keeping with her efforts during her fifty years as a widow to do everything she could to keep her husband's memory alive. Kent responded to Mrs. Hamilton on December 10, 1832, with a reply heavy on the importance of *The Federalist* papers:

> Dear Madam, ... I beg leave to assure you that it is sufficient that the application comes from the daughter of General Schuyler and the widow of General Hamilton, to make it command all the information within my power to impart....
>
> That immortal work *The Federalist* is the most incontestable evidence of his fervent attachment to the liberties of this country, and of his extreme solicitude for the honor and success of the republican system....
>
> Those essays, as they successively appeared, were sought after and read, with the greatest avidity and constantly increasing admiration, by all persons favorable to the adoption of the Constitution....
>
> The essays composing *The Federalist* made, at the time, a wonderful impression upon reflecting men. The necessity and importance of the union of states, the utter incompetency of the Articles of Confederation to maintain that union, their fundamental fatal defects ... were all of them topics of vast magnitude and affecting most deeply all our foreign and domestic concerns.[31]

Clearly James Kent was a proponent of the Constitution and *The Federalist* papers, but also an admirer of Alexander Hamilton. While his praise may have been effusive under the circumstance, his comments are illustrative of the veneration in which Hamilton and his contributions were held in the early years of the republic. And not just Hamilton, the Founders in general were accorded tremendous respect. Those few surviving by the 1830s were indeed living monuments. Even those representing a direct link to a Founder, such as Elizabeth Hamilton, or Dolly Madison after James' death in 1836, were revered as a living link to that by-gone, heroic era.

The 1820s though 1850s represented something of a grand period of American historical writing about the Founding and those associated with it. Scholar Jared Sparks might represent the manifestation of this period with his many publications focusing on individual members of the Founding generation. His work culminated in 1837 with the publication of his *Writings of George Washington*.[32] Even after America's second great war— the Civil War—the Founders were looked to in spirit in an effort to promote guidance and inspiration to heal the fractured nation. The American centennial in 1876 was probably the best example of this inspirational effort after the Civil War.

Chapter 8

The Federalist Papers

With the close of the Philadelphia Convention in September 1787, the future of the United States hung in the balance. If the draft Constitution failed to pass ratification in nine states, the country faced the very real prospect of splintering into factions along regional lines at best, or completely coming unglued into thirteen separate nations, at worst. This may sound alarming, but in 1787 it was not that far-fetched. The demagogues of liberty, whose oratorical skills turned that concept into a fighting word during the Revolutionary War, still held tremendous sway, despite being hobbled. Their brand of political fireworks though was painfully out of place in a new country, at peace, with so much promise, seemingly at war only with itself.

The Federalist papers have been referred to and quoted many times already in this book. Their meaning and purpose have been hinted at around the periphery and a full exposition was unnecessary until now. This chapter puts *The Federalist* papers in their proper sequential time frame and at the apex of the chronological thought process of the Founders. The seven or so years covered in detail in this book did not naturally unfold by some plan unknown to the participants to which, to paraphrase Shakespeare, they were all but actors upon a stage carrying out their individual assigned roles without any conscious awareness. Rather, these participants, these Founders, consciously engaged in their work with all the vigor they saw necessary to accomplish the task. It was a task with two objectives: separating from Great Britain, and establishing an effective, mature, government. The worst thing that could have happened would have been to win independence and lose the government. The winning of the government (in many ways a battle not unlike the Revolution—minus the destruction and death) is the topic of this chapter. *The Federalist* papers were the strategic war plan which James Madison, Alexander Hamilton, and John Jay developed to wage their conflict; the battle to determine America's future. The Constitution that emerged from Philadelphia, it will be remembered, was only a proposed document. It could just as easily have been rejected by the states, rather than approved.

Quite simply, *The Federalist* papers were written to promote the understanding of, and encourage support for, the proposed Constitution written during the summer of 1787. The primary intended audience were the undecided voters of the state of New York—a key state in the union given its size and power and a state that did not formally approve the draft Constitution when the Convention concluded its work in September 1787. Although the New York delegation left early, out of frustration, Hamilton remained and signed the final draft. He signed as Alexander Hamilton of New York, not Alexander Hamilton on behalf of New York and their delegation. As a delegation of one, he lacked standing to sign on behalf of the state. Thus, New York officially did not have a delegation approve the draft Constitution in September 1787. Hamilton acted purely on behalf of Alexander Hamilton.

It was this boldness that gave Hamilton the willingness to orchestrate *The Federalist* project. If Madison was the Father of the Constitution, Hamilton was unquestionably the Father of *The Federalist*. As we have seen, Hamilton had already been publishing essays advocating for a stronger federal government over the course of the last decade. This was Hamilton's moment to shine—even if it was anonymously.

Unlike the grand and stately physical settings associated with the Constitutional Convention and the Continental Congress (when not being chased by the British), the settings for the composition of *The Federalist* papers were humbler. Most were written in boarding rooms, some on a small boat traveling the Hudson River to Albany and back, some in private homes, and some were probably sketched out in various coffee houses or taverns over dinner. As his initial plan came together, Hamilton sought to engage at one point or other John Jay, James Madison, William Duer, and Gouverneur Morris. For a variety of reasons, Duer and Morris did not participate in the final project. The pseudonym Publius was chosen to mask the identity of the three final authors.[1] Concealing authorship of an essay, pamphlet, or book was quite common in eighteenth century America. This was especially true where political topics were discussed and especially in relation to *The Federalist* papers where two of the three authors were delegates to the Constitutional Convention and sworn to secrecy about the proceedings. Hamilton and Madison would not necessarily be discussing the Convention in their essays, but they did have an inside view of the making of the document that few could claim. Because of this, they had to proceed with caution and discretion so as not to unwittingly reveal any inside knowledge. This was probably not too difficult to accomplish for these two seasoned statesmen and scholars.

When Hamilton actually conceived the idea for *The Federalist* is not known, but probably sometime during the summer of 1787; especially after Hamilton's fellow New York delegates abandoned him in Philadelphia leaving him the sole, and powerless, representative of New York. Hamilton no doubt knew by this time that getting his home state to agree to the proposed Constitution was going to be difficult. Not only were New York's two delegates gone, and officially on record as opposing the Constitution, but New York Governor George Clinton, a powerful political force, would eventually oppose ratification. Hamilton's choice of colleagues was thought out too—George Clinton and John Jay were political enemies. In a way, Hamilton was reflecting the very real political situation in his state and determining how to get the upper hand on his rivals by writing essays in support of the Constitution which was quite in keeping with the character of Hamilton's way of dealing with his political rivals.

Once the team was assembled, the work began. The overall idea was to take the Constitution, article by article and section by section, and compare and contrast it with existing conditions, especially with the Articles of Confederation. The Articles were the primary target to defame for Publius. The sequence, workload, and schedule was somewhat random. Each writer took those aspects of the Constitution that they had a specialty in—Jay wrote on foreign affairs and general theory; Madison wrote on republican principles, human nature, and historical precedent; while Hamilton wrote on the executive, judiciary, and all other topics as necessary. In fact, all three blended elements of "the necessary" into their respective essays.

Once the date of the New York Ratifying Convention was set, the three had a deadline to look toward and a terminus to their project. In the beginning though, October 1787, the project simply needed to establish itself. To keep with tradition, this chapter will acknowledge, as Hamilton family lore places it, the beginning of *The Federalist* papers to have been aboard a packet ship, owned by Hamilton's father-in-law, plying the Hudson River between New York and Albany, with Hamilton sitting on deck (or probably below for privacy), first putting pen to paper to begin writing *Federalist* one. (See appendix 3 for a greater explanation of what putting pen to paper meant in the eighteenth century.)

With the team in place, Hamilton set the tone for the next eighty-four essays when he introduced the fragile country to the world of *The Federalist* papers on October 27, 1787, in the *Independent Journal*:

> After an unequivocal experience of the inefficiency of the subsisting federal government, you are called upon to deliberate on a new Constitution for the United States of America. The subject speaks its own importance; comprehending in its consequences nothing less than the existence of the UNION, the safety and welfare of the parts of which it is composed, the fate of an empire in many respects the most interesting in the world. It has been frequently remarked that it seems to have been reserved to the people of this country, by their conduct and example, to decide the important question, whether societies of men are really capable or not of establishing good government from reflection and choice, or whether they are forever destined to depend for their political constitutions on accident and force. If there be any truth in the remark, the crisis at which we are arrived may with propriety be regarded as the era in which that decision is to be made; and a wrong election of the part we shall act may, in this view, deserve to be considered as the general misfortune of mankind....
>
> I propose, in a series of papers, to discuss the following interesting particulars:
>
> THE UTILITY OF THE UNION TO YOUR POLITICAL PROSPERITY, THE INSUFFICIENCY OF THE PRESENT CONFEDERATION TO PRESERVE THAT UNION, THE NECESSITY OF A GOVERNMENT AT LEAST EQUALLY ENERGETIC WITH THE ONE PROPOSED, TO THE ATTAINMENT OF THIS OBJECT, THE CONFORMITY OF THE PROPOSED CONSTITUTION TO THE TRUE PRINCIPLES OF REPUBLICAN GOVERNMENT, ITS ANALOGY TO YOUR OWN STATE CONSTITUTION, and lastly, THE ADDITIONAL SECURITY WHICH ITS ADOPTION WILL AFFORD TO THE PRESERVATION OF THAT SPECIES OF GOVERNMENT, TO LIBERTY, AND TO PROPERTY [emphasis in original].[2]

Hamilton was clearly laying the groundwork for the succeeding essays in the series and lets the readers know *The Federalist* papers would be a muscular, unabashed support platform for the proposed Constitution. Whether or not Hamilton and the team knew at this point that in total they would produce eighty-five essays is unlikely. And, it is unlikely they decided how many each person would write. Early on in the process, John Jay was taken ill with a severe bout of rheumatism which dramatically reduced his ability to participate in the project. In fact, overall, Jay would only produce five essays. This of course meant Hamilton and Madison had to produce even more essays than they expected. In the end, Hamilton produced fifty-one essays; Madison twenty-six; and three disputed or credited to a Hamilton/Madison collaboration. It should be noted that this list of attribution is as of 2015; the credit for up to a dozen of the essays has always been in dispute since the nineteenth century. It could very well change again at some future date.

Of the three, John Jay was probably the most famous; yet, today, he is probably the least recognizable. Both Hamilton and Jay had political and personal animosity toward New York Governor George Clinton—who opposed the proposed Constitution and has long been suspected as being the author of the Anti-Federalist writings of "Cato"—and their collaboration makes perfectly good sense. Madison lacked the sense of a political fight within the New York system; his participation in the project can be seen as purely motivated by ensuring passage of the Constitution in the State Ratifying Convention. Surprisingly, none of the original drafts of final copies from Madison or Hamilton are extant. When or why they were destroyed (presuming they are not lying undiscovered in some dusty archives) is not known. However, a few drafts of John Jay's essays do exist.[3] Similarly, the collected correspondence of the team shows no communication among them as they put the essays together. This is not surprising given that all three were in New York City and probably communicated face-to-face or via courier when necessary. They lived within relatively close proximity in the bustling New York City of 1787–1788. Hamilton had his all-consuming law practice; Madison was a member of the Continental Congress, then meeting in New York; and Jay was serving as Secretary of Foreign Affairs and living with his wife and children in a substantial brick house. Hamilton too was married by 1787, having married Elizabeth Schuyler in 1780 and thus entering the highly influential Schuyler family network of New York.

It has already been shown how *The Federalist* papers dealt with the two overarching questions of the national debate: sovereignty and taxation. While the essays delivered a forceful defense of these two topics, the essays also deconstructed the proposed Constitution into its constituent parts for examination by Publius in detail.

The Federalist *Papers by Topic*

The eighty-five *Federalist* essays cover a range of topics all found within the proposed Constitution being considered by the State of New York for ratification that summer of 1788 (and of course the country at large). The essays were written in a formal, mostly pedantic, tone that made them difficult to understand and follow even at the time. No one, outside of the highly educated or politically astute could manage them without some assistance when first published (even today most only read them with the guidance of a teacher or professor). Those who could would likely be delegates to the New York ratifying convention in Poughkeepsie or those who could influence the delegates one way or another. In that respect the Federalist team found their intended audience. Fittingly, Hamilton began with *Federalist* one as we have seen. This essay introduced readers to the

Federalist series and spelled out in broad terms why the Constitution was necessary and why the Constitution was not a betrayal of the liberties fought for in the recently ended War for Independence. Hamilton also argued that the current Articles of Confederation were inadequate to the needs of a responsible, mature (at least in thought if not in years) government. The time, Hamilton felt, was over for demagogues; the time had arrived to govern. As Jay would write in *Federalist* two, "Nothing is more certain than the indispensible necessity of government, and it is equally undeniable, that whenever and however it is instituted, the people must cede to it some of their natural rights...."[4]

John Jay made his most consistent contribution to the project in essays two through five. Jay looked at the American scene and beheld a singularity to the American fabric that was much more strongly bound when together than if separate. Jay saw a united federal government as more capable of making better judgments for the country as a whole than any individual state ever could. Jay, with his extensive foreign-service background, looked at how other nations would see America as a country as opposed to America as a land where individual states carried more power than the federal government. The states would be constant prey to other nations looking to gain favor or advancement with one state or another. As Jay wrote in *Federalist* four: "Wisely, therefore, do they [the people of America] consider union and a good national government as necessary to put and keep them in *such a situation* as, instead of *inviting* war, will tend to repress and discourage it [emphasis in original]."[5]

Jay also warned against the tendency between individual states towards rivalry that could easily turn hostile given the various advantages and disadvantages states naturally would possess. The fear of civil war would be greatly reduced through a united federal government working for the best purposes of all the united states. Jay finished *Federalist* five with an apocalyptic view of a disunited America. Jay quoted Queen Anne from 1706 speaking about the union of England and Scotland. Somewhat prophetically, Jay saw the Northern states and Southern states as examples of regional rivalries best kept within a union of states north and south. Jay ended *Federalist* five: "Let candid men judge when, whether the division of America into any given number of independent sovereignties would tend to secure us against the hostilities and improper interference of foreign nations."[6]

After *Federalist* five Jay was taken ill and would only contribute one more essay (sixty-four) in the series.

Hamilton picked up the theme of a disunited America in numbers six through nine, painting vivid pictures of how the jealousies and greed of human nature would work to tear the cohesion of America to shreds—something he feared was already happening. As Hamilton stated in *Federalist* six: "A man must be far gone in Utopian speculations who can seriously doubt that, if these states should either be wholly disunited, or only united in partial confederacies, the subdivisions into which they might be thrown would have frequent and violent contest with each other.'"

Hamilton then looked to that favorite topic of his for promoting a union of states—the public debt. He used the fear of a debt to warn against a breakup of the union in *Federalist* seven: "The public debt of the union would be a further cause of collision between states or confederacies. The apportionment, in the first instance, and the progressive extinguishment afterwards, would be alike productive of ill humor and animosity."[8]

Finally, Hamilton began *Federalist* nine: "A firm union will be of the utmost moment to the peace and liberty of the states, as a barrier against domestic faction and insurrection."[9]

Hamilton, consciously or not, set the stage in these four essays for what is probably the most famous *Federalist* essay and surely the one most read today, Madison's number ten. Madison began his contribution to the series with a classic discussion of human nature applied to and within governments established by and for people.

Madison began *Federalist* ten: "Among the numerous advantages promised by a well-constructed Union, none deserves to be more accurately developed than its tendency to break and control the violence of faction."[10]

Madison defined a faction as: "...a number of citizens, whether amounting to a majority or minority of the whole, who are united and actuated by some common impulse of passion, or of interest, averse to the rights of other citizens, or to the permanent and aggregate interests of the community."[11]

Madison saw the causes of faction to lie deep within human nature, something that goes to our very core but yet could be controlled. Madison wrote: "The latent causes of faction are thus sown in the nature of man; and we see them everywhere brought into different degrees of activity, according to the different circumstances of civil society."[12]

Madison continued:

> A landed interest, a manufacturing interest, a mercantile interest, a moneyed interest, with many lesser interests, grow up of necessity in civilized nations, and divide them into different classes, actuated by different sentiments and views. The regulation of these various and interfering interests forms the principle task of modern legislation,

and involves the spirit of party and faction in the necessary and ordinary operations of the government.[13]

Madison admitted that human nature could not be overcome, only moderated: "The inference to which we are brought is, that the *causes* of faction cannot be removed, and that relief is only to be sought in the means of controlling its *effect* [emphasis in original]."[14]

Hamilton followed number ten with numbers eleven, twelve, and thirteen. Continuing to press the theme of union through a federal government (essentially a government based on representative democracy) over a confederacy, Hamilton added the financial ingredient to the mix beginning with *Federalist* eleven. Hamilton declared: "The importance of the Union, in a commercial light, is one of those points about which there is least room to entertain a difference of opinion, and which has, in fact, commanded the most general assent of men who have any acquaintances with the subject."[15]

He argued the need for a national tax which could be compelled, not just recommended, from the states. This would only help to strengthen the ties holding the nation together and bolster its role on the world stage as a nation, a singular entity, not a confederation of petty principalities as in much of Europe at the time.

In number fourteen Madison returned to the theme of the proper geographic size of a republic and unsurprisingly found that America was appropriately sized to a republican style of government as envisioned in the proposed Constitution. Madison also continued to promote federalism (the mixture of state and federal government each sovereign in its own sphere) and republicanism as the best types of government to protect American liberty and freedom. Hamilton wrote numbers fifteen, sixteen, and seventeen as attacks on the Articles of Confederation (and those that still supported it) as being wholly inadequate to managing a country through government. Hamilton starkly exclaimed that, "We may indeed with propriety be said to have reached almost the last stage of national humiliation."[16] He asked if America could stop foreign aggression; "We have neither troops, nor treasury, nor government."[17] Hamilton did not mince words. This was a constant theme which permeated not just *The Federalist* papers, but letters, broadsides, sermons, and no doubt hundreds of conversations the length and breadth of the country at the time. Without a unifying government, no matter how much it reminded people of Great Britain in some of its specifics, the United States would fail to truly win the peace. America had to have a written constitution; without it, American government would have been meaningless. This was the one aspect in law and government which set America apart from centuries of thought and practice, "…the theory of a written constitution was absolutely foreign to Greek and Roman thought."[18] Yet, a written constitution was precisely what the Americans were offering.

Hamilton and Madison co-authored numbers eighteen, nineteen, and twenty and discussed how federalism worked to pull the various factions of a country together in a manner the Articles of Confederation, or any other type of government, never could. *Federalist* numbers eighteen, nineteen, and twenty, show Publius at his most didactic and pedagogical. These three essays rarely mention the proposed Constitution (although the inference cannot be overlooked); instead they rely on a series of wide-ranging history lessons to make the point to their readers who would have been well aware of the lessons Publius was making in relation to the proposed Constitution. These essay-lectures also highlighted the intended audience of Publius: the educated, property owning, white male. No member of Publius' audience would have been unaware of the various ancient and contemporary historians that were referenced either. Publius traveled far back into history to draw out the lessons he felt worthy of bringing to the attention of his readers. *Federalist* eighteen covers examples from Greek and Roman history, showing how confederacies, as opposed to federal unions under a republic, are prone to destruction from within. Publius quoted Demosthenes, Plutarch, and more contemporary sources.

For *Federalist* nineteen, Publius moved to Europe proper for a historical discussion of Germany and France. Looking back from 1788 only one millennium instead of two, Publius cited Charlemagne as the founder of modern Europe. The attempts of the vast Carolingian Empire to function with central authority provided a contrasting example to the proposed Constitution which, while it sought central authority, still respected individual state realities. Amidst this comparison, Publius showed how the tendency to form confederacies led to near constant warfare; a fate no American could ever want. Finally, *Federalist* twenty saw Publius continue his historical overview of Europe and European governments with reviews of the trials and tribulations of the United Netherlands. Publius cautioned his countrymen to beware the jealousies and petty sniping that prevent public inspired programs from being implemented in these countries. Americans, Publius concluded, should be thankful "for the propitious concord which has distinguished the consultations for our political happiness."[19]

Federalist papers twenty-one and twenty-two were further attempts by Hamilton (twenty-one possibly with Madison) to break down the Articles of Confederation along with other forms of government. Hamilton reviewed commerce, trade, and the military; nearly every aspect of society which would benefit from a stronger national government providing some measure of overview designed to strengthen and promote the entire country as a whole. From the start of *Federalist* twenty-one, Publius expressed a disconcerting aspect of the current legal arrangement under the Articles, "The next most palpable defect of the subsisting Confederation, is the total want of a SANCTION to its law. The United States, as now composed, have no powers to exact obedience ... [emphasis in original]."[20] Publius continued: "If we are unwilling to impair the force of this applauded provision, we shall be obliged to conclude, that the United States afford the extraordinary spectacle of a government destitute even of the shadow of constitutional power to enforce the execution of its own laws."[21]

Publius pointed to the recent Shays' Rebellion as an extreme example which could become much more frequent if the proposed Constitution was not ratified. The necessity of having enforceable laws was carried forward with examples relating to taxation.

In *Federalist* twenty-two Publius focused on commerce as a casualty of unenforceable laws. As a consequence of lax enforcement, no foreign nation would dare enter into treaties of trade with the United States, thereby depriving the United States of markets for its products. As Publius wrote:

> No nation acquainted with the nature of our political association would be unwise enough to enter into stipulations with the United States, by which they conceded privileges of any importance to them, while they were apprised that the engagements on the part of the Union might at any moment be violated by its members, and while they found from experience that they might enjoy every advantage they devised in our markets, without granting us any return but such as their momentary convenience might suggest.[22]

Numbers twenty-three through twenty-eight showed Hamilton writing about national security and defense from foreign intrigue. As a unified, powerful nation adequately funded and with a proper national military, America would be much safer than with thirteen separate armies and navies. Hamilton also equated the strong national defense obtainable through the Constitution as helping to dispel civil unrest. A union of states required a defense of the union. Thus, in *Federalist* twenty-five, Publius argued that a common danger should "...be the objects of common councils and of a common treasury."[23] The time Publius spent in *Federalist* numbers twenty-five and twenty-six specifically examining the status of a standing army in peace time is indicative of just how contentious an issue that was in 1788.

Finally, Hamilton ended the discussion of defense by promoting the worthiness of the state militias in essay twenty-nine.

Hamilton continued his streak of authorship with taking up a major theme that this book has seen as a major force in the creation of the Constitution: taxation. In essay's thirty through thirty-six, he laid out in his rapid-fire fashion the undeniable need for a national tax system to support a national government. Hamilton was at his absolute best in these discussions of money (befitting a future secretary of the treasury) and role of money in government. Simply put, he argued no money, no government. Without revenue, government ends. The current system of recommendations and reminders as developed in the Articles of Confederation for states to pay was a joke, unworthy of any government, much less one spawned by the greatest empire at that time.

Hamilton wasted no time, opening *Federalist* thirty by declaring the federal government as proposed under the new Constitution as opposed to the Articles:

> …must embrace a provision for the support of the national civil list; for the payment of the national debts contracted, or that may be contracted; and, in general, for all those matters which will call for disbursements out of the national treasury. The conclusion is, that there must be interwoven, in the frame of the government, a general power of taxation, in one shape or another.[24]

Hamilton continued to compare and contrast the proposed Constitution with the Articles. He was quick to remind his readers that the failure of national taxation was a defect allowing foreign powers to view the United States as weak and vulnerable. Hamilton also dealt with the debate over internal and external taxation. Internal being those revenues raised from within the United States and which most opponents of the proposed Constitution saw as being the realm of individual states who would then pay a percentage forward to the federal government. External taxation was most commonly represented by the taxes paid by foreign powers in the form of duties or tariffs. These taxes, even the opponents of the proposed Constitution saw as proper for the national government to collect. Hamilton felt this silly, "who can pretend that commercial imposts [external taxes] are, or would be, alone equal to the present and future exigencies of the union."[25] From this, Hamilton made a bold prophecy: "I believe it may be regarded as a position warranted by the history of mankind, that, in the usual progress of things, the necessities of a nation, in every stage of its existence, will be found at least equal to its resources."[26]

Hamilton continued: "How is it possible that a government half supplied and always necessitous, can fulfill the purposes of its institution, can provide for the security, advance the prosperity, or support the reputation of the commonwealth? How can it ever possess either energy or stability, dignity or credit, confidence at home or respectability abroad?"[27]

Hamilton in *Federalist* thirty-one used the example of geometry and of mathematical truths to highlight the need for a national revenue. As Hamilton put it: "A government ought to contain in itself every power requisite to the full accomplishment of the objects committed to its care, and to the complete execution of the trusts for which it is responsible, free from every other control but a regard to the public good and to the sense of the people."[28]

To Hamilton, and Publius, this theorem was as incontrovertible as Euclid or Pythagoras in geometry and mathematics.

While Hamilton saw that the power necessary for taxation was self-evident, he also saw the states as in no way hindered in their need for separate revenue. Hamilton wrote in *Federalist* thirty-four:

> The convention thought the concurrent jurisdiction preferable to that subordination [of the states under the federal government]; and it is evident that it has at least the merit of reconciling an indefinite constitutional power of taxation in the federal government with an adequate and independent power in the states to provide for their own necessities.[29]

Hamilton ended *Federalist* thirty-five with his view of the importance and power of taxation:

> There is no part of the administration of government that requires extensive information and thorough knowledge of the principles of political economy, so much as the business of taxation.... There can be no doubt that in order to a judicious exercise of the power of taxation, it is necessary that the person in whose hands it is should be acquainted with the general genius, habits, and modes of thinking of the people at large, and with the resources of the country.[30]

When he finished *Federalist* thirty-six, Hamilton took a rest while James Madison re-entered the fray with an impressive run of the next twenty-two essays, beginning with *Federalist* thirty-seven.

In *Federalist* thirty-seven Madison offered a defense of the Constitutional Convention. Madison began by asking for some leeway to be given to the delegates at the Philadelphia Convention due to the bewildering array of social, political, economic, and theoretical applications they had to contend with. He attempted to obtain some sense of sympathy with what he and his fellow delegates had to deal with (without divulging his identity). It was easy to gripe about and criticize the delegates, but they had to contend with an enormous amount of emotion and raw-gut feeling in drafting the Constitution. Madison sought to show that the Convention was made up of many different ideas and perspectives, and as such, "... many allowances ought to be made for the difficulties inherent in the very nature of the undertaking referred to the convention."[31] This was the one chance Publius took to ask readers to give them the benefit of the doubt. Considering all of this, they produced a significant document capable of governing the United States not just in 1788, but in 1888, 1988, and even 2088. Madison made it clear that:

> Among the difficulties encountered by the convention, a very important one must have lain in combining the requisite stability and energy in government, with the inviolable attention due to liberty and to the republican form. Without substantially accomplishing this part of their undertaking, they would have very imperfectly fulfilled the object of their appointment....[32]

Taking as one of the truly inspired aspects of the proposed Constitution to be the organization of written law, Madison wrote: "The precise extent of the common law, and the statute law, the maritime law, the ecclesiastical law, the law of corporations, and other local laws and customs, remains still to be clearly and finally established in Great Britain, where accuracy in such subjects has been more industriously pursued than in any other part of the world."[33] Madison employed a variety of analogies in describing the state of the American government in 1788.

Madison, like Hamilton and Jay, wrote at his best and most forceful when he dealt with the topics at which he had personal expertise. For Madison, in this run of twenty-two essays, the topics included: republican and federal government theory and practice; the historical perspective of representative government over the centuries; the weakness of the Articles in relation to the needs of the nation at peace; and the practical compromise aspects of the Constitution assuring no one state or region would dominate. He expounded on the Constitution's "necessary and proper" and "supremacy" clauses—arguing that contrary to the opponents of the Constitution, the states would actually be more powerful than the national government; the three separate yet equal branches of the government; the impracticality of direct citizen participation in government decision making; the decision to count a slave as three-fifths of a person; and finally, Madison acknowledged that given human nature, some factions may indeed attempt to control a branch of government. However, he argued that the robust aspect of the American spirit would be too powerful and clever to allow this to happen. In many ways, Madison took on the role of a tutor or professor in his essays and it showed in many places how comfortable he was giving a lesson to his readers. Professor Madison struck a more pedagogical tone than Hamilton or Jay, both of whom could be combative at times—especially Hamilton.

Madison's tried and true use of history was never far out of reach in his writing; but a new angle was employed in *Federalist* thirty-eight, comparing America to a rapidly declining, sick, patient. The American patient was being fought over by a battery of doctors each seeming to have their own self-interest more at heart than that of the patient.[34] The best remedy, or medicine, as Madison explained in detail, was the proposed Constitution. Madison, in full professorial mode, repeated over and over how the compromises made were necessary at the Convention. It could have been no other way. No one could be completely happy with every aspect of the final result. Explaining the decision to create a republican system of government was given significant space to unfold in Madison's writing. For Madison, this approach to governing a large area, contrary to opinion and experience, was without question the best plan for the United States. Madison wrote: "It is evident that no other form would be reconcilable with the genius of the people of America; with the fundamental principles of the Revolution; or with that honorable determination which animates every votary of freedom...."[35]

Madison took great pains to make the distinction between types and operations of government. From his explanation he concluded that "the proposed Constitution ... is, in strictness, neither a national nor a federal Constitution, but a composition of both."[36] At times, Madison seemed to almost be pleading, the time had arrived he appeared to say. It truly was now or never. The proposed Constitution was far from perfect—even Publius acknowledged that—but it was what they had to work with. The time had come to put jealousies aside, to douse the inflammatory language, and to move on with the task at hand.

In *Federalist* forty, Madison took up a point which vexed many delegates to the Convention: whether or not they had the authority to propose a totally new system of government which would render the existing Articles of Confederation null and void. Madison immediately looked to the Annapolis Convention and found his answer. The Annapolis Convention did not call for a restructuring of the Articles, it called on a committee, or convention, to "...devise *such further provisions* as shall appear to them necessary to render the Constitution of the federal government *adequate to the exigencies of the Union* ... [emphasis in original]."[37] By this definition, approved by Congress in February 1787, the committee—soon to be the Philadelphia Convention—was given no direct instruction as to what to do with the Articles or anything new it might create; rather, it was to take account of the state of the union at such time of their meeting and propose remedies which were commensurate with the problems facing the United

States. Madison continued to deconstruct the language for specifics and nuances impacting the notion that the Convention overstepped its authority in proposing a new Constitution. Madison wrote, "The states would never have appointed a convention with so much latitude, if some *substantial* reform had not been in contemplation [emphasis in original]."[38] Thus, Madison concluded *Federalist* forty: "The sum of what has been here advanced and proved is, that the charge against the convention of exceeding their powers, except in one instance little urged by the objectors, has no foundation to support it…."[39]

Madison continued with his deconstruction of the Constitution by assuaging the concerns of states-rights advocates in his nearly closing contribution by showing that the states would maintain their necessary rights to govern on state matters just as the federal government would maintain those rights which "are indispensably necessary to accomplish the purposes of the Union."[40]

In *Federalist* forty-seven, Madison introduced in depth a name which is often associated with the Founding of the United States, Montesquieu. In fact, Madison refers to him as "the oracle."[41] Montesquieu (properly known as Charles-Louis de Secondat, Baron de La Brède et de Montesquieu), to Madison and many of the Founders, was the oracle when it came to the separation of powers between the legislature, the executive, and the judiciary. Madison wrote:

> No political truth is certainly of greater intrinsic value, or is stamped with the authority of more enlightened patrons of liberty, than that on which the objection [concentrating power in one ruler] is founded. The accumulation of all powers, legislative, executive, and judiciary, in the same hands, whether of one, a few, or many, and whether hereditary, self-appointed, or elective, may justly be pronounced the very definition of tyranny.[42]

Here is where the unwritten British Constitution was compared to the proposed American Constitution to contrast the concept of separation of power. Finally, Madison looked to the individual states for examples as well for the separation of power within a government. Separation of power however does not mean an unwillingness to work together for a common goal. The individual branches should guard their prerogatives, but not at the expense of moving the country forward. Madison deftly handled these concerns in *Federalist* forty-eight, concluding: "The conclusion which I am warranted in drawing from these observations is, that a mere demarcation on parchment of the constitutional limits of the several departments, is not a sufficient guard against those encroachments which lead to a tyrannical concentration of all the powers of government in the same hands."[43]

Madison here called for not just an informed cadre of voters to elect responsible members of the legislature and executive, but also for those elected members to be truly and honestly devoted to "active liberty," or an expanding essence of liberty, in the conduct of their affairs relative to the requirements of the federal union.[44]

Madison continued the theme of government propriety by looking to the role of the electorate (minimal as it was compared to today) to participate in their important role in acting as a check on the elected through the ballots they cast.

Beginning with *Federalist* fifty-one, Madison delved into an exhaustive discussion of checks and balances, and the composition of Congress through proportional representation, and how these safeguards would help ensure lasting liberty. Much like Hamilton's run of essays on taxation, Madison hammered on his theme through nearly ten essays; challenging already known opposition and even challenging anticipated opposition by the opponents of the proposed Constitution. Hamilton returned to work with essay fifty-nine. He addressed the issue of elections to the senate, House of Representatives, and the presidency, through to number sixty-one.

By *Federalist* sixty-two, Madison had moved into a similar discussion on the senate. Madison dissected the senate; its membership, election cycle, powers, terms, and the equal number of senators from both large and small states. Although composed differently from the House of Representatives, and with different mandated functions, Madison detailed its duties in the same methodical way. In fact, Publius as a whole, took on the role and purpose of the senate; the only time in *The Federalist* papers where each writer dealt with the same topic. Hamilton looked at the impeachment power of the senate. This power to sit as a courtroom (with the Chief Justice of the Supreme Court presiding) is a unique and solemn power; and Jay, who wrote his last essay as part of the senate discussion, looked at the senate and specifically its treaty approval powers. In number sixty-four, Jay, as a diplomat, convincingly explained why this power was not only necessary, but was properly placed with the senate. After *Federalist* sixty-three, Madison bade adieu to New York and *The Federalist* papers project and returned home to Virginia to prepare for his state's ratifying convention. This left Hamilton, the sole member of the Publius team, to complete the last twenty essays, beginning with essay sixty-five.

Beginning with *Federalist* sixty-seven, Hamilton turned his attention to the executive branch. In essays sixty-seven through seventy-seven, Hamilton laboriously looked at the presidency as created under the Constitution. Hamilton examined the power, election process, and term, along with the various theories of government authority that the Philadelphia Convention took into account in crafting the office. The eleven essays constituted the largest number of essays devoted to one topic throughout *The Federalist* papers. These essays helped to contribute to the oft repeated canard of Hamilton's wanting a monarchy, or framing the presidency in monarchical terms. This was the most difficult aspect of the proposed government according to Hamilton, who wrote: "There is hardly any part of the system which could have been attended with greater difficulty in the arrangement of it than this; and there is, perhaps, none which has been inveighed against with less candor or criticized with less judgment."[45]

For those who seemed inclined to compare the executive with a monarch, Hamilton had harsh words: "It is impossible not to bestow the imputation of deliberate imposture and deception upon the gross pretence of a similitude between a King of Great Britain and a magistrate of the character marked out for that of the President of the United States."[46]

As he did with taxation, and as Madison did with Congress, Hamilton methodically examined the second article of the proposed Constitution. Hamilton even attempted to rationalize the Electoral College mechanism, concluding in *Federalist* sixty-eight, "A small number of persons, selected by their fellow-citizens from the general mass, will be most likely to possess the information and discernment requisite to such complicated investigations [of electing a president]."[47] Hamilton's exhaustive review of the executive branch covered eleven essays, indicating the importance, and concern, of the executive branch and how much power it was to have relative to Congress and the third branch, the judiciary, the topic he would soon take up.

Starting with *Federalist* seventy-eight, Hamilton, in five quick essays, laid before his readers the concept of a national judiciary. With little to go on historically, the proposal was something of a novelty. Article three of the proposed Constitution, outlining the judiciary and Supreme Court, is the shortest of the articles dealing with the branches of the government. Hamilton saw three issues pertaining to the Supreme Court which he needed to address, "1st. The mode of appointing the judges. 2nd. The tenure by which they are to hold their places. 3rd. The partition of the judiciary authority between different courts, and their relations to each other."[48] Hamilton tried to explain the concept in government of a judiciary which was separate from and equal to the two other branches of government.

Hamilton began *Federalist* seventy-eight by acknowledging the federal judiciary was not well-known in its specifics, "…as the propriety of the institution in the abstract is not disputed; the only questions which have been raised being relative to the manner of constituting it, and to its extent."⁴⁹ In fact, aside from the Supreme Court, no other court was specifically created by the Constitution. The creation of lower federal courts was left to Congress. Hamilton went on to state, concerning the power of the judiciary:

> The judiciary, on the contrary, has no influence over either the sword or the purse; no direction either of the strength or of the wealth of the society; and can take no active resolution whatever. It may truly be said to have neither FORCE or WILL, but merely judgment; and must ultimately depend upon the aid of the executive arm even for the efficacy of its judgments [emphasis in original].⁵⁰

Hamilton was clearly trying to fend off the attacks of those who feared a powerful judiciary. Yet in Hamilton's explanation, the judiciary strangely came across as not a co-equal branch of government, but rather a subordinate younger sibling.

Hamilton touched on the tricky topic of judicial review, or the power of the court to render laws unconstitutional. This was a power Hamilton wholly agreed with and was consistent with powers already exercised in England and to an extent in some states. This concept was a real issue among those who saw the Constitution as always correct and the people's representatives as not being able to pass unconstitutional laws. Yet, as Hamilton noted, "some perplexity respecting the rights of the courts to pronounce legislative acts void … has arisen from an imagination that the doctrine would imply a superiority of the judiciary to the legislative power."⁵¹ A concern to which Hamilton replied, "There is no position which depends on clearer principles, than that every act of a delegated authority, contrary to the tenor of the commission under which it is exercised, is void."⁵²

Tenure in office, compensation, method of removal, and powers, are some of the topics Hamilton dealt with concerning the judiciary. Hamilton also looked at the levels of courts created, or called to be created, in addition to the Supreme Court, "The power of constituting inferior courts is evidently calculated to obviate the necessity of having recourse to the Supreme Court in every case of federal cognizance."⁵³

Hamilton also compared the Supreme Court, a separate branch of government, with the British House of Lords, the highest appeals court which also was part of the British legislature. Thus, Hamilton argued the American version was better situated and more independent than the dependent House of Lords. Aside from its independence as a separate, equal branch, the judiciary, as constituted in Article III, "has been carefully restricted to those causes which are manifestly proper for the cognizance of the national judicature; that in the partition of this authority a very small portion of original jurisdiction has been preserved to the Supreme Court, and the rest consigned to the subordinate tribunals...."[54]

Concern was also raised by opponents of the proposed Constitution over the creation of inferior courts by Congress. The concern was over whether these created inferior national courts would compete or be superior to state courts. Hamilton patiently explained the concept of concurrent jurisdiction, "but I hold that the state courts will be divested of no part of their primitive jurisdiction, further than may relate to an appeal; and I am even of opinion that in every case in which they are not expressly excluded by the future acts of the national legislature, they will of course take cognizance of the causes to which those acts may give birth."[55]

Further, Hamilton stated: "The courts of the (states) will of course be natural auxiliaries to the execution of the laws of the union, and an appeal from them will as naturally lie to that tribunal which is destined to unite and assimilate the principles of national justice and the rules of national decisions."[56]

Finally, Hamilton concluded his essays on the Supreme Court and the judiciary with the topic of trial by jury, a concept which was ancient even when Hamilton wrote in 1788. Opponents of the proposed Constitution had argued since it said nothing about trial by jury in civil cases, the concept must be prohibited under the new government. "The disingenuous form in which this objection is usually stated has been repeatedly adverted to and exposed, but continues to be pursued in all the conversations and writings of the opponents of the plan."[57] For comparisons, Hamilton looked at the states, and Great Britain, to determine just how trial by jury was enshrined (for civil cases), or not, yet operated within the legal system. Hamilton found "That no general rule could have been fixed upon by the convention which would have corresponded with the circumstances of all the states."[58]

In *Federalist* eighty-four, Hamilton approached those topics "which either did not fall naturally under any particular head or were forgotten in their proper places."[59] Hamilton admitted that, "the most considerable of the remaining objections is that the plan of the convention contains no bill of rights."[60] Hamilton's argument was well known. For the Federalist supporters of the proposed Constitution, their claim that the Constitution already contained protections for citizens from the federal government did not convince the Anti-Federalists. As Hamilton intoned, "...why declare that things shall not be done which there is no power to do?"[61] Many of the topics which ultimately became the Bill of Rights in 1791 were addressed by Hamilton in *Federalist* eighty-four.

Hamilton bid adieu to his readers in essay eighty-five which reflected back on the preceding essays and the topics covered. He also commented on the number of states which had already ratified the proposed Constitution—seven—leaving just two more to reach the mandated nine whereby the proposed Constitution would no longer be a proposal, but an approved, functioning government. Hamilton exhorted his fellow Americans not to give in to the fears being expressed by the opponents of the Constitution. That to survive as a nation (which is after all what they wanted) a cohesive government, established and operated under a written constitution, was necessary. This was the only way to add predictability to a range of topics whose unpredictability plagued the United States; these included commerce, trade, elections, defense, power, taxation, foreign relations, and many others which only seemed to bind the country closer in a unified government capable of speaking with one voice. The written constitution had its origin in colonial governance too, "This development of a written constitution as binding upon government had its origins in the existence in the colonies of royal charters under which colonization had taken place."[62]

Publishing

During Publius' lifetime, there were three editions of *The Federalist* papers published in book form. These included the McLean edition of 1788; the Hopkins edition of 1802; and the Gideon edition of 1819. The Hopkins and Gideon editions contained corrections approved by Hamilton and Madison respectively. Naturally, this begs the question as to what the revisions and corrections were and if they greatly altered the original newspaper printed version. This could be easily traced though by comparing the book versions with the newspaper versions. Revising the written record is nothing new, nearly the entire cast of the Founder's generation re-examined their respective writings late in life and corrected any number of mistakes or omissions to set the record straight as they saw it for posterity.

Interestingly, not all of the eighty-five essays were originally printed in the newspapers. Only essays one through seventy-seven saw publication in the New York press before coming out in book form. The last eight numbers were published in volume two of the collected essays, and subsequently published in the New York press, in June of 1788. On January 1,

1788, the publisher J. & A. McLean announced that they would publish the first thirty-six *Federalist* essays in book form. That volume appeared March 2, 1788, in New York and elsewhere. Meanwhile, *Federalist* thirty-seven through seventy-seven were published in the New York press, just as the earlier essays were. On May 28, 1788, McLean published numbers thirty-seven through seventy-seven in book form with an additional eight more essays. In essence, the work of writing the essays was finished by the end of May for Hamilton, Madison, and Jay.

The Federalist papers were widely distributed in book form during the year after their publication amongst the Founders and civilian leaders. Especially among those associated with Congress the essays were quite popular. They were initially published in a full leather version and a less expensive hard paper cover version. Charles Thomson (secretary of the Continental Congress) wrote to Maryland Congressman James McHenry on April 19, 1788, concerning the publication of *The Federalist* papers in book form. Thomson wrote of the packet he sent: "Enclosed I send you the first volume of the *Federalist* the second volume is in the press and will, it is expected be out in the course of a week or two. As soon as it is published I will forward it to you."[63]

Law

While the Constitution established a new government, it also established a new, national, written legal foundation. Unlike the unwritten English common law system, this system was for all to see and divine, not just the be-wigged judges as in England. A written code of law, fashioned under the auspices of the Constitution, was unquestionably a dramatic step forward in the Rights of Man (although it was not the first such attempt). No longer would humanity be subject to the whims of a single ruler who could dictate law. In the United States, a predictable, debatable, guide would exist. All American law would have to pass constitutional muster before going into effect. Law was, and is, a powerful unifying force in any society. Law which can be identified, traced, read, and understood, is by far the most constructive aspect of a modern state. In 1788, the United States was far ahead of other nations in this regard. This singular aspect has been the most emulated feature of the American Founding since that time.

All three co-authors of *The Federalist* can be said to have made significant contributions to this process. Certainly being authors of the essays would have been enough. But all three went on to greater careers, especially Madison and Jay. As the first Chief Justice of the Supreme Court, John Jay established the Court as the final arbiter as to what was law and what was not law during the first critical years of the Constitution's existence. Madison's career as law maker extended well into and beyond the 1790s in his role as a congressman and later as president.

Written American law did not so much begin with the Constitution as continue a process begun in England roughly a millennium prior; in a time before the Magna Carta (1215) or the Norman invasion (1066), when England was barely a cohesive kingdom. A written legal system in fact for all intents and purposes goes back into the mists of time. Some of the earliest writing known to exist deals with legal issues. Whether those laws were believed to have been imposed by a supreme being, or known to have been promulgated by a monarch, rules for living have been with us as long as we humans have been human. The Americans who created the Constitution were of course far removed in time from those ancient beginnings. The true genius of the American system was the establishment of a written set of permanent, predictable, and human, law. As Abraham Lincoln would so simply and powerfully articulate at Gettysburg in 1863, this was law of the people, by the people, and for the people. Naturally, "the people" have changed in definition over the centuries, but the groundwork for later advancements in expanding that had already been set. Even in 1787 though, "the people" included far more in the United States than just about any other country, depending on how one charted civil liberties in the eighteenth century. In fact, by the time the Americans crafted the Constitution in 1787, much of the bedrock of a legal system had already been in place for centuries, if not longer. It was that system of ancient law that the revolutionaries looked to as early as 1774, before the fighting began and the First Continental Congress was just beginning to gather enough support to convene. We have seen that both Thomas Jefferson and James Wilson published pamphlets about those ancient rights and liberties in an effort to make the revolutionaries seem less revolutionary and more conservative in the sense of wanting to return to those rights and liberties which the early Founders saw as having been taken from them. Rather than creating something new, without precedent, the American War of Independence was actually about reinstating, about returning to an ideal that had been challenged and trampled upon by the British government (mainly the Parliament) of the time.

The English common law has been referred to numerous times. The common law simply refers to those laws that had already been decided in court cases over the centuries, throughout the country (England), which were recorded in decisions and therefore established precedent. In the American system, those precedents would eventually work themselves into written law as passed by the Congress and signed by the President (for federal law). The swirling mass of written and unwritten law was referred to by historian Ellis Sandoz as: "This is to suggest that, behind and, one must suppose, through the veil of symbols, modes of discourse, legalistic and historiographic collisions, distinctions, and polemics, a living tradition of personal, social, and historical reality finds articulate embodiment."[64]

Sandoz's idea of "historiographic collisions" is an apt and wonderful metaphor for the intersection of law and life, of the present with the past, and of the general atmosphere wherein we try and determine how to live with, and, among ourselves.

This reliance on written human law in the Constitution placed it in a somewhat awkward position relative to the Declaration of Independence, which relied on "Nature's Law." Natural law too had a long history in Western thought. Natural law is often times associated with a supreme being of one sort of another and is seen as a way to provide an identity to an insular group. In the case of the Declaration of Independence, this call to "Nature's Law" allowed Jefferson to insert a rallying cry in the document which the varied groups who ultimately favored and fought for independence could look to which would be seen as the common heritage of mankind free of national encumbrances weighing down the "natural" aspects. Natural law was seen as a type of law that was inherently known or recognized by human beings. Natural law was something that we all were inheritors of by the simple fact of being born. It is written in our DNA and cannot be taken away except by tyranny, which violates the unique freedom we enjoy as humans. This concept has its adherents to this day, although certainly fewer than two centuries ago. For the Constitution, it was a much different story. The Constitution could not rely on high-spirited verbiage; it needed concrete, predictable, law and language. As Hamilton wrote in *Federalist* fifteen, from December 1, 1787, in the *Independent Journal*: "Government implies the power of making laws. It is essential to the idea of a law, that it be attended with a sanction; or, in other words, a penalty or punishment for disobedience."[65]

The English Tradition

Sir John Fortescue was a giant of English law. He was born ca. 1395, and died ca. 1480. He lived an eventful life; having survived the Wars of the Roses (1455–1487), backing the losing Lancasters over the victorious Yorks. He was pardoned after fleeing to Scotland and France, and finished his life unmolested by the victorious Yorks in England. His greatest contribution to law was a work entitled *De Laudibus Legum Angliae* (Commendation on the Laws of England), written ca. 1470. This work celebrates the brilliant achievement of written, codified law in human form. Fortescue, despite being a socially conscious Christian, wrote:

> Human laws are none other than rules by which perfect justice is manifested. But ... the Justice which the laws disclose is not the kind that is called commutative or distributive or any other sort of virtue, but is itself the Perfect Virtue that is called by the name of Legal Justice, which ... is perfect because it eliminates all vice and teaches every virtue, so that it is in itself justly called [the whole of excellence or] Virtue.... This justice, indeed, is the object of all royal administration, because without it a king judges unjustly and is unable to fight rightfully. But this justice attained and truly observed, the whole office of king is fairly discharged. Therefore, since happiness is the perfect exercise of virtues, and human justice, which is not perfectly revealed except by the law, is not merely the effect of virtue, but of all virtue, it follows that he who is in enjoyment of justice is made happy by the law.[66]

Just as the American Founders were intellectual descendants of Fortescue, Edward Coke (1552–1634), and Henry de Brackton (ca. 1210–ca. 1268; Brackton also wrote a treatise on English law, *De Legibus et Consuetudinibus Angliae* ["On the Laws and Customs of England"]), Fortescue, Coke, and Brackton were descendants of the ancient Romans and Greeks.

Law has evolved since before we could write about it. What Jefferson argued against in his common-place book—that English common law was completely separate from religious law because the Parliament did not pass those religious laws—Fortescue saw as so intimately bound as to be indistinguishable. As Ellis Sandoz wrote, "Thus, the historically *ancient* and the ontologically *higher* law—eternal, divine, natural—are woven together to compose a single harmonious texture in Fortescue's account of English law."[67] The concept of a separate religious law and separate human law is also symptomatic of the power that law has over people. Does law need or require a divine inspiration to be accepted by the larger community? This question has been around since law was first recorded. It is sufficient to say that this concept existed, and still exists, but does not add materially to the story of the Constitution, or *The Federalist*. Whatever discussions occurred outside of the final documents, the end result was that neither the Constitution nor *The Federalist* papers were over-burdened with extra-legal references to a deity. In fact, both documents fit squarely into the ethos of the period of their creation—the Enlightenment.

In his common-place books from his years as a student, Thomas

8. The Federalist *Papers*   207

Jefferson can be seen as deeply concerned about the place of religious law in secular law. In fact, in 1814, looking back to a simpler time as a student, Jefferson wrote a letter to Dr. Thomas Cooper about Christianity and the common law. Jefferson wrote: "When I was a student of the law, now half a century ago, after getting through Coke-Littleton, whose matter cannot be abridged, I was in the habit of abridging and common-placing what I read meriting it, and of sometimes mixing my own reflections on the subject."[68]

Jefferson framed the question to himself, the young law student, as "the whole case and arguments show that the question was how far the Ecclesiastical law in general should be respected in a common law court."[69] Jefferson, as he would do in his influential pamphlet of 1774, *The Rights of British North America*, looked to history to see the development of common law (or as he called it, *Lex non Scripta*). Jefferson found two centuries that the common law existed prior to the introduction of Christianity in England. He also deduced that Christianity, if it did enter the common law, had to have happened prior to Magna Carta in 1215. Jefferson concluded his letter to Dr. Cooper:

> If, therefore, from the settlement of the Saxons to the introduction of Christianity among them, that system of religion could not be a part of the common law, because they were not yet Christians, and if, having their laws from that period to the close of the common law, we are able to find among them no such act of adoption, we may safely affirm (though contradicted by all the judges and writers on earth) that Christianity neither is, nor ever was a part of the common law.[70]

It was certainly clear that this topic was something he gave a great deal of time to studying. His common-place books are filled with musings about the role of religion in society beyond a cohesive function of social identity. At the end of the day, religion is a personal belief, whereas law is a duty intended to ensure that everyone, not just certain members of a social unit believing in a unique power, have access to justice. As Jefferson put it, when comparing reason and belief (in the forms of Newtonianism and Christianity), "The truth is that Christianity and Newtonianism being reason and verity itself, ... they are protected under the wings of the common law from the dominion of other sects, but not erected into dominion over them."[71] Like a good lawyer, Jefferson strengthened his case by citing a long list of sources which point to a divergence of religious and secular law. As to why the religious law should not be seen as part of the secular law, Jefferson stated "we may say they are not because they never were made so by legislative authority."[72]

Will Durant, in his massive The Story of Civilization series, wrote in volume one, *Our Oriental Heritage*, on the foundation of law and the role of Natural Law, which was relied upon so heavily during the Revolutionary War as a rallying cry to inspire the fight. Durant ended a section on primitive law by stating, "Rights do not come to us from nature, which knows no rights except cunning and strength; they are privileges assumed to individuals by the community as advantageous to the common good. Liberty is a luxury of security; the free individual is a product and a mark of civilization."[73]

It was this civilization that so many of the Founders looked to for inspiration when putting together the government of the United States. Winning independence was one thing, winning a government, creating a government, was something altogether different. This point has already been made numerous times throughout this work, and it cannot be overstated. All of the Founders acknowledged that the British government, monarchy and all, was the greatest system existing in the mid- to late-eighteenth century. It was the freest, most liberal (in the eighteenth century use of the term) government on the earth. There were many who saw the written Constitution as creating a government, certainly in the presidency (which gets more *Federalist* essays devoted to it than any other topic), as more conservative than the British (unwritten) constitution.[74] For the Founders, the goal was to prevent the tyranny of the Parliament over the king or the Congress over the presidency. The Founders saw King George III at the mercy of Parliament and some recent scholarship places the Revolution as a revolt against that body as opposed to the tyranny of the king.[75]

The Founders as a whole would have been as familiar as Jefferson with the outlines of this history and thinking—even if not as articulate and conversant. These ideas were part and parcel of the common knowledge of late eighteenth century America. They were not unique to the Founders, they got them from a long line of thinkers dating back to at least Fortescue himself in the fifteenth century. Fortescue was however the first to expound on the properties of English versus Continental or Roman law.

This was no small distinction. The English common law was unique from the Continental (European) law. Out of the ashes of the fall of the Roman Empire came the remnants of the Roman law. This law can rightly be seen as a gift to humanity to have survived the decades of "barbarian" attacks which culminated in 476 CE when the last Western Roman Emperor (Romulus Augustus) left the throne (the Eastern Empire would limp along another one-thousand years before vanishing in 1453 at the hands of the Ottoman Turks). The legal historian John Maxcy Zane, wrote about the Roman legal influence:

The modern world is indebted to Rome for its classification, general theory, and method of applying the law. It is impossible to conceive what our legal system would be had not the Roman jurists labored for centuries upon the general principles and particular rules that gradually created the finished law of Rome. When the Western Roman Empire was overthrown by hordes of savages, who were incapable of either applying the Roman law or comprehending the situations to which it was applicable, civilization went into an eclipse that did not pass from the earth until barbarous usages became slowly absorbed into the reviving Roman law. That law came back to Europe as the written law and furnished a common law for Italy, France, and Spain and at last for Germany. Just as the ancient temples and public buildings, so the Roman law was an unfailing treasure house of legal reasoning and principles for the modern world. Modern European law and even the English law in its substance and deductive methods was built of Roman materials.[76]

The Continental law by at least 1100 was making great strides in establishing itself throughout Europe. England, by this time becoming more formally the England we recognize politically now, was charting its own legal system with the common law and some saw a need to adopt the Continental system instead. "The English prevented overwhelming infiltrations by the superior Romanesque law almost solely by their proud and patriotic insularity and by the guild solidarity of the English lawyers."[77] We can be grateful to those "proud and patriotic" lawyers of a thousand years ago who kept the common law common, and perhaps even crude, for the Americans to inherit and graft onto those elements from Roman law deemed necessary. Without the common law, our system would look much different today.

The great epicenters of English common law were (and still are) the Inns of Court, where so many Founders studied. Even those who did not study law at the Inns studied with someone, or studied the writings of someone, who did attend the Inns. While John Fortescue was indeed a name well known to American lawyers and educated non-lawyers, others included Edward Coke (1552–1634), Francis Bacon (1561–1626), Thomas Littleton (1407–1481), and John Selden (1584–1654), to name but a handful. The one name that is most prominent during this period in American history is William Blackstone. By Blackstone's time (1723–1780) more elements of the Continental law had entered England as trade expanded and more contrast fueled advances in commercial law. Blackstone produced his masterpiece, *Commentaries on the Laws of England*, between 1765 and 1769. After failing as a lawyer Blackstone sought employment as a professor of law at Oxford. Strangely, Blackstone's appointment in 1758 was the first time a chair of English law had been created at an English university. Blackstone, despite rejecting the American claim for independence, was highly influential during and after the Revolution. He "taught" generations of American lawyers. "One-thousand copies of the first edition were sold in America, and fourteen hundred subscriptions were received in advance of the first American reprint in 1771. Twenty-five hundred copies were sold in America before the Declaration of Independence."[78] Blackstone was a best-seller before that was a recognized term. His work spawned numerous American versions—James Kent wrote *Commentaries on American Law*, which imitated Blackstone's work, in 1826–1830. Noted Virginia jurist St. George Tucker published a revised version of Blackstone in the early nineteenth century attempting to make it more "American."

It is somewhat amusing to read Blackstone from the perspective of his views of Americans. Even though he held these feelings, he was still quite popular as a writer and authority here in the United States. Blackstone "considered [Americans] beyond the pale of decent human society. But what he probably disliked most about the Americans was their insistence on [no taxation]. What would happen to England if the common people insisted on [such a point]...."[79] This was exactly the same issue faced in America in the six years focused on in this book. Blackstone had many shortcomings, but his positive aspects proved strong enough to keep him on the American reading list for decades. We have seen that the issue of taxation was one of the cornerstone topics of the postwar years; leading into the Annapolis Convention and the Philadelphia Convention. Taxation was a huge concern for America, England, and every country then extant. The need for revenue would never end. What the Founders had to figure out was how to get a reluctant people (who fought a horrible war in part over taxation) to accept taxation. Hamilton did his best in *Federalist* numbers thirty through thirty-six.

CHAPTER 9

The Foundations of *The Federalist* Papers and the Philosophy of the American Founding

While *The Federalist* papers were an American creation, they were an American creation intimately in tune with English and European thought. The dominant concept of European thought during the latter eighteenth century was the period generally labeled the Enlightenment. This was no monolithic movement and it was as complex and multi-faceted as any other segment of history. It did however contain certain characteristic elements which have come down to us as being labeled as The Enlightenment. It was a period of exploration and discovery throughout Europe that tested the boundaries of human knowledge and questioned the centuries-old patterns of life; especially those patterns of religion and government. The American Enlightenment came in many shapes and sizes and was (and still is) reflected in art, literature, economics, social customs, education, and for our purposes, American law. This aspect of the American Enlightenment is most profoundly embodied in *The Federalist* papers.

The American Founders were largely steeped in this European intellectual tradition. In many ways, as much as America rebelled against Britain, and by some extension, Europe, the European thinking ended up filtering back into the American consciousness. Much like (as is often commented upon) ancient Rome conquered Greece militarily, and ancient Greece conquered Rome intellectually. Likewise "the invasion of America by Roman law and Greek political philosophy ... was in itself a major event in the history of American thought and a major contribution of the Enlightenment."[1]

While the similarities are admittedly not precise, the parallels are nevertheless relevant.

The Enlightenment (in the eighteenth century) is a term that is used repeatedly to describe the overarching intellectual approach to life and society that captured the minds of some of Europe's and America's greatest thinkers. Naturally, no one person suddenly woke up one day in the mid-eighteenth century and said, "I think it's time for some enlightenment," and sat down to write out a draft. No, in fact, the ideas for the Enlightenment had been bubbling to the surface for decades, if not centuries, in European thought. In a larger sense, the Enlightenment was not confined to the realm of theoretical thought. Indeed, the Enlightenment covered the theoretical and applied sciences as well as the humanities. This being said, we will concentrate our overview of the Enlightenment to those areas of the humanities that dealt with government and social policy—which is what impacted the American Founding generation to such a great extent. America, after gaining independence, was as near to being a blank slate as any society could be in terms of government and the creation of societal norms. It is little wonder then that the Founding generation sought out the best and the brightest of native and foreign thinkers to guide them in their new adventure in government.

The Scottish Enlightenment

One of the main tenants of the Enlightenment overall, and of the Scottish Enlightenment in particular, was the understanding known as Natural Law—a concept alluded to in the previous chapter. This idea presupposed an existing set of laws which had guided humanity since time immemorial and which were the proper and indisputable inheritance of all humankind. The foundation of the Law was often associated with some higher being, generally associated with the notion or understanding of God. The *Stanford Encyclopedia of Philosophy* identifies Natural Law with "a tradition of scientific investigation of human nature with a view to constructing an account of the principles that are morally [not necessarily in a religious sense] binding on us."[2] This understanding would ebb and flow, twist and contort, until it was put down by Thomas Jefferson as "inalienable rights" in 1776 in the Declaration of Independence; and indeed come to define a revolution built in part on an idea—an idea which cannot be proven. Still, the thinking that produced the Natural Law line of thought was profound and dedicated to researching its claims. After 1776, this idea again became focused in America through the Constitution and ultimately *The Federalist* papers, but in no way in as significant, direct, language as Jefferson used.

The early studies of Natural Law at the beginning of the Scottish Enlightenment (ca.1710) abound with an understanding that God was the source and promulgator of Natural Law as relates to the connection between man and society, between the citizen and the state. On one level, this was not much of a change. The individual was always portrayed as an element in the political makeup which included the monarch as the earthly representative of God and each individual had a duty to see the monarch's vision as inspired by God. The Enlightenment focus slightly refashioned this approach. The monarch was now less seen as the only leader anointed by God in the state. All citizens in this new approach were anointed through Natural Law to have rights (and duties) that devolved directly to them; more importantly, not even the monarch could violate these Laws. This argument was in part laid out in the Declaration, and appears in a secular fashion in the Constitution, and most certainly in the Bill of Rights. In fact, it can be easily argued that the genius of the American experiment is the removal of the foundation of God from the realm of Natural Law thought. No longer, under the 1787 Constitution (there is no reference to God in the Constitution; God is referenced, as "Nature's God"—just like in the Declaration of Independence—only a handful of times in the eighty-five *Federalist* essays were Natural Rights were found as emanating from God; rather, from 1788 onward, we were a nation of human law. Turning to the *Stanford Encyclopedia of Philosophy* again we find this summary: "These precepts, concerning duties to God, to self and to others, are the fundamental precepts of natural law, and though the precept that God is to be worshipped is prior to and more evident than the precept that one should live sociably with men, the requirement that we cultivate sociability is a foundation of the well-lived life."[3]

The distilled Enlightenment that reached America by mid-century had the luxury of being free of the religious debates that encumbered it in Europe (including Scotland). Like many aspects which migrated from Europe to America, the Enlightenment by 1775 had undergone decades of re-working and re-purposing which left it ready for use in the fractious American cause.

Founders such as James Madison, although very young, were completely in tune with the broader aspects of Enlightenment thought. In Madison's case, he was most fully exposed to this while at the College of New Jersey, headed by John Witherspoon during the time. Witherspoon was from Scotland, and an academic and a Churchman. Witherspoon was a noted moderate in religious affairs and saw the Enlightenment in human terms. Madison's contributions as a Founder, however, were in the realms of Congress. In 1783, when the Congress asked him to recommend books for the federal legislature to consult, Madison, already known for his academic abilities, put together a list that was lopsided with Scottish authors who contributed to the Enlightenment.[4] Madison, like Hamilton and Jay, his Federalist co-authors, had both the ability and the opportunity to acquire access and understanding of the best the eighteenth century had to offer students out to make a mark on the world through their future leadership.

In his article on Madison and the Scottish Philosophers, historian Roy Branson notes four thinkers whose work closely aligned with Madison's: David Hume, Adam Smith, John Millar, and Adam Ferguson. No Founder, including Madison, adopted without reserve the philosophy of any particular European thinker. Rather, the Founders adapted those elements of a particular thinker's thought that fit the American model. Madison, like many other Founders, adapted, as needed, the variety of qualities that suited the American experience he encountered. In their efforts to complete the break from the "Old World," most American thinkers were well aware that a political and military break from Britain was one thing; an intellectual break was quite another—and one was not possible without the other. The Scottish Enlightenment provided a veritable smorgasbord of prepackaged ideas ready for transplanting in the new United States.

> The issues Scots debated in the course of addressing their agenda were intellectually momentous, including social organicism versus contactualism, government intervention versus laissez faire, free will versus determinism, Christianity versus skepticism, ethical sentimentalism versus ethical rationalism. The Scots spread a rich intellectual table from which the Americans could pick and choose and feast.[5]

This of course is not to say the Americans transposed these ideas en masse. That effort would have been pointless. America needed a functioning government quickly. American thinkers could not take the centuries of development the Scottish and English thinkers had to come to their existing state of conditions which confronted them in the 1780s.

The American thinkers who structured the American Enlightenment were not wholly original thinkers—very few thinkers are. Neither the Declaration of Independence nor the Constitution (nor even *The Federalist* papers for that matter), were systematic expositions of philosophy which had never been heard of before. Likewise, they were neither simply appropriated language of more formal philosophers. Rather, the American experience in philosophy writ large was to adapt and package it into a useable American derivative; this would be something that was similar to what William James would refer to as pragmatism one hundred years later (and his contemporary legal colleagues would term Legal Positivism). The American thinkers of the Founding were less interested in grand theories than grand practicalities. These practicalities would include compromising at the Constitutional Convention and elsewhere, taking chances, realizing it was better to try something and risk failure than try nothing and accept certain failure. It is this atmosphere that allows us today to realize just how radical some American thinkers were—they were able to put in place a system which, far from being static and immutable, was energetic and changeable.

This accelerated schedule also fit nicely in the predicament the Americans found themselves in after achieving independence—namely, the nearly open, untouched, canvas upon which to craft a government. All options, short of monarchy, seemed potential candidates for adoption and adaptation.

The American Enlightenment

As in Europe, the Enlightenment in America took many forms in response to the range of thinkers who sought to adapt its principles. Most adaptations died a quick death, as most high-end ideas do, when faced with reality. Those ideas that took are in part what we celebrate today as our legacy. As historian Herbert Schneider has written concerning the American Enlightenment, "…there was no period in our history when the public interests of the people were so intimately linked to philosophical issues."[6] Schneider continued, noting, "seldom since the days of classical Greece has philosophy enjoyed greater opportunity to exercise public responsibility."[7]

In addition to the written Constitution, for our purposes, the second idea (although it was actually ideas) which took from that age of the American Founding was the idea of law. As was stated early on in this book, the heroes would be the ideas, and the thinkers who breathed life into those thoughts. Those thinkers, human to the core of their being, sought answers to goals that vexed their intellectual ancestors for centuries. For the American thinkers, "there was a reliance on the power and reach of the human mind, and a belief that … reasoning deductively from secure principles to secure conclusions, men might expand their knowledge indefinitely without the need of supernatural aid."⁸ Those ideas, encapsulated in the idea of law, were the greatest legacy of the American Enlightenment.

The law was the most tangible aspect of how the Enlightenment left its mark on America. To be sure, there was also nearly a millennium of development in the Anglo world from which the Americans would draw. Yet, it was the period of the 1780s, the period of the high-Enlightenment, which coincided so closely with the rapid creation and development of American law. The law was anything but static or unchanging. In fact, the law was written and adapted to promote the expansion of the American settlement and economy. Especially during the nineteenth century, the concepts set in place at the end of the eighteenth truly blossomed. As legal historian Edward White has written: "In these ways, in the first six decades of the nineteenth century, law played a significant part in the mass movement of both settler populations and commercial traffic into newly acquired western territories by supporting ventures in transportation and helping to create and to protect the corporate entities participating in those ventures."⁹

Some could certainly argue that American law set up an unfair advantage for the exploitation of America's resources. (That is a discussion for another day.) The significance for us is that American law adapted to uniquely American circumstances without losing sight of its ancient past while ensuring its future.

Way Back: The Magna Carta

This chapter cannot end without a brief look at the second most famous legal document in the world: Magna Carta. As many no doubt know, these two documents, Magna Carta and the Constitution, share a space at the National Archives building in Washington, D.C., on permanent exhibit.

The English Magna Carta of 1215 (2015 being the eight hundredth anniversary), "signed" by King John and a host of worthy knights (it must be remembered that "Magna Carta was first and foremost a peace treaty"), established one of the earliest written versions of law that can be said to be, however loosely, a lineal ancestor of the United States Constitution.¹⁰ Having acknowledged a familial relation, the relationship between the two documents should not be overstressed. While the Magna Carta did limit the power of the monarch, and outlined a series of duties for the knights, it was not a system of government like the Constitution. The Magna Carta had virtually nothing to do with "the people," as the Constitution was all

9. The Foundations of The Federalist Papers

about "the people," as that concept was understood in eighteenth-century North America. The Magna Carta represented an aspiration for greater clarity between those wielding governmental authority and those on the receiving end. Again, it must be understood that when discussing "rights," or "the people," those concepts need to be from the perspective of the time in which those documents were created.

The charter has not had an easy life, as Nicholas Vincent points out: "the charter as a whole was already treated as an archaic relic as long ago as 1300, when it was for the last time granted a full reissue by a king of England.... By then, it had already become more a totemic monument to past struggles than something tailored to current political circumstances."[11]

In fact, "within nine weeks of its issue, it was to all intents and purposes redundant"; yet, "the guardians of Henry III [King John having died in October 1216] now reissued the great charter of June 1215, reissuing it at Bristol in November 1216, no longer as an assault upon royal privilege but as a manifesto of future good government."[12]

Perhaps one of the most succinct definitions of what the Magna Carta means today came in the 1950s from Winston Churchill in his *History of the English Speaking Peoples*.[13] Churchill came close to a more modern definition, which holds "the desire for direct contact with the past remains a potent modern equivalent to the medieval seeking out of relics and saints' bones as a means of accessing the sacred or charismatic."[14] Churchill was cautioning anyone who would unduly draw comparison between two related, yet separate, documents. Historian Nicholas Vincent, summarizes Magna Carta thus:

> As is well known, Britain has no written constitution. Yet just as historians of America or France have fetishized pieces of paper or parchment ... for the history of England there are at least three or four documentary relics that all students might be expected to name. The 1086 Domesday Book would be one, the Great Reform Act of 1832 another. A third might be the 1689 Bill of Rights. At their head, looming over all others, would stand ... Magna Carta.[15]

The earliest attempts to organize English law date even earlier than Magna Carta and no doubt some attempts have been lost to time. Ranulf de Glanville, King Henry II's chief legal officer in the 1170s and 1180s, wrote "English laws are unwritten [as] it is utterly impossible for the laws and rules of the realm to be reduced to writing."[16] "One reason was that there was no representative machinery and no possibility of any representative machinery, beyond the Lords and Commons, that could make a constitution."[17]

Even earlier written codices of law before Magna Carta included

Alfred the Great and the Anglo-Saxon codes. The Avalon Project of Law at Yale Law School sums up early English law: "but English law, from its first to its latest phase, has never possessed an authoritative, constructive, systematic, or approximately exhaustive statement, such as was attempted by the great compilers of the civil and canon laws...."[18]

The frieze that decorates the courtroom at the Supreme Court building in Washington, D.C., contains images of "law givers" dating back to antiquity. While in a large sense this depiction is arguably accurate, rigorous scrutiny could easily dismiss many of the supposed lineal connections continually drawn between the Constitution and the ancient past. The Constitution, *The Federalist* papers, like Thomas Jefferson said about his Declaration of Independence, were an "expression of the American mind."[19]

American law has a long and distinguished pedigree. From this sketch on the American Enlightenment and law we can see that the two concepts were intimately linked in a way highly beneficial to the development of the United States.

The idea of the perfectibility of man, an Enlightenment concept, played out in its most visible form during the American Revolution and the Founding era. Ideas flowed like a fast moving river where it was hard for anything to take hold. Those ideas which did were fortunate and hardy given the odds against them. It was these ideas which not only challenged, but changed contemporary attitudes and patterns of life. The American Revolution: "was a period of radical changes in men's ways of thinking about religion and science as well as a period of political upheaval and of new directions in political theory. The thought of the men of the revolutionary period was hostile to traditional institutions, whether political or religious."[20]

This faith the American Founders had, and how they put that faith into practice, did not go unnoticed in Europe. The Americans gave European Enlightenment thinkers hope "that man had some capacity for self-improvement and self-government, that progress might be a reality instead of a fantasy, and that reason and humanity might become governing rather than merely critical principles."[21]

The final word on *The Federalist* papers and the American Enlightenment, and the Founding Era, in this book will be from a Jewish refugee from Nazi Germany. Peter Gay, the eminent historian who studied the Enlightenment period for nearly his entire academic career, wrote of *The Federalist* papers (and it can easily be attributed to the entire Founding Era):

9. The Foundations of The Federalist Papers

The three authors of *The Federalist* papers ... sound all the great themes of the Enlightenment, if often by implication only: the dialectical movement away from Christianity to modernity; the pessimistic though wholly secular appraisal of human nature coupled with an optimistic confidence in institutional arrangements; the pragmatic reading of history as an aid to political sociology; the humane philosophy underlying their plea for the proposed constitution; the commitment to the critical method and the eloquent advocacy of practicality.[22]

Conclusion

By the time Madison returned to Virginia in March 1788, his involvement in the production of the *Federalist* essays had ceased. He had a burst of creative energy in January and February of 1788, where he wrote "a series of twenty-two essays which appeared in less than six weeks [numbers thirty-seven through fifty-eight]."[1] During that time, the essays, while enjoying gathering attention in New York, had limited appeal outside of the state. Even though they were intended for New York state, Publius harbored hopes their impact would be felt in other states where ratification was strongly contested. Publius clearly meant the essays to be seen as a whole, in their entirety, rather than as a series of disjointed essays. In most studies, *The Federalist* is referred to as one complete writing, such as a novel or narrative history covering one topic. This is true inasmuch as the essays all take the Constitution as their topic. But, *The Federalist* papers are still a collection of separate essays linked thematically yet capable of standing (mostly) alone, singularly, by themselves. So, *The Federalist* papers are both singular and plural, individual and collective.

The most difficult aspect of understanding the Revolutionary period is trying to parse out the meaning of liberty or freedom. What did that mean to the colonists? The centuries-old concept of English liberty was not well known to the "average" American. Yet, it sounded good and the Founders knew they had a rallying cry for the war. Was it different when discussing the individual versus the state or national government? Crucially, did it mean liberty and freedom for the individual sovereign states as opposed to the national government? What if the talk and language about freedom was about *state* sovereignty and not *national* sovereignty? How many actually felt it meant liberty from all government? The Articles of Confederation (section VI) seem fairly determined to have the power of a national government:

No State, without the consent of the United States in Congress assembled, shall send any embassy to, or receive any embassy from, or enter into any conference, agreement, alliance or treaty with any King, Prince or State;

No two or more States shall enter into any treaty, confederation or alliance whatever between them, without the consent of the United States in Congress assembled [did the Mount Vernon Compact violate this?]...No State shall lay any imposts or duties, which may interfere with any stipulations in treaties, entered into by the United States in Congress assembled.... No vessel of war shall be kept up in time of peace by any State ... nor shall any body of forces be kept up by any State in time of peace, except such number only, as in the judgment of the United States in Congress assembled, shall be deemed requisite to garrison the forts necessary for the defense of such State; but every State shall always keep up a well-regulated and disciplined militia, sufficiently armed and accoutered [preview of the second amendment?]...

No State shall engage in any war without the consent of the United States in Congress assembled, unless such State be actually invaded by enemies ... nor shall any State grant commissions to any ships or vessels of war, nor letters of marque or reprisal, except it be after a declaration of war by the United States in Congress assembled....[2]

It is abundantly clear the Continental Congress saw American liberty and freedom through the prism of Congressional power. It was this power, focused from the morass of war and centuries of debate, which led to the Constitution and ultimately *The Federalist* papers.

This goes back to language of John Adams in the First Continental Congress. His biggest accomplishment, he wrote to his wife Abigail, was to secure the support of the other colonies in their (Massachusetts) argument with Britain. To Adams, this was a national contest, not just a state contest. Historian Akil Reed Amar has written in an opposite tone, "The obvious answer was that both before and after ratifying the Articles, the people of each state—and not the people of America as a whole—were sovereign."[3] John Maxcy Zane seemed to support Adams when he wrote, "using a new word, the formula of the claim of secular government was summed up in the statement that each national government is sovereign, that is to say, independent of all outside control.... All lawyers accepted the conception of the Roman law that sovereignty existed in the body of the people and this popular power was supposed to be the supreme power in the state."[4] There is no one right or wrong answer (although some could be more right or more wrong) and the debate will occupy historians (and increasingly, politicians) who look to create what cannot be—the definitive history of the whole Founding Era, which culminated in 1789 and the beginning of the new federal government.

APPENDIX 1

Closing Communication of the Annapolis Convention, September 1786

Mr Dickinson was unanimously elected Chairman.[1]

The Commissioners produced their credentials from their respective States; which were read.

After a full communication of sentiments, and deliberate consideration of what would be proper to be done by the Commissioners now assembled; it was unanimously agreed: that a Committee be appointed to prepare a draft of a Report to be made to the States having Commissioners attending at this meeting-adjourned until Wednesday morning.

WEDNESDAY SEPTEMBER 13th 1786

Met agreeable to adjournment.

The Committee, appointed for that purpose, reported the draft of the report; which being read, the meeting proceeded to the consideration thereof, and after some time spent therein, adjourned until tomorrow morning.

THURSDAY SEPTEMBER 14th 1786

Met agreeable to adjournment.

The meeting resumed the consideration of the draft of the report, and after some time spent therein, and amendments made, the same was unanimously agreed to, and is as follows, to wit.

To the Honorable, the Legislatures of Virginia, Delaware, Pennsylvania, New Jersey, and New York—

The Commissioners from the said States, respectively assembled at Annapolis, humbly beg leave to report....

That there are important defects in the system of the Federal Government is acknowledged by the Acts of all those States, which have concurred in the present meeting; that the defects, upon a closer examination, may be found greater and more numerous, than even these acts imply, is at least so far probable, from the embarrassments which characterize the present state of our national affairs, foreign and domestic, as may reasonably be supposed to merit a deliberate and candid discussion, in some mode, which will unite the sentiments and councils of all the States. In the choice of the mode, your commissioners are of opinion, that a Convention of Deputies from the different States, for the special and sole purpose of entering into this investigation, and digesting a plan for supplying such defects as may be discovered to exist, will be entitled to a preference from considerations, which will occur, without being particularized.

Your Commissioners decline an enumeration of those national circumstances on which their opinion respecting the propriety of a future Convention, with more enlarged powers, is founded; as it would be an useless intrusion of facts and observations, most of which have been frequently the subject of public discussion, and none of which can have escaped the penetration of those to whom they would in this instance be addressed. They are however of a nature so serious, as, in the view of your Commissioners to render the situation of the United States delicate and critical, calling for an exertion of the united virtue and wisdom of all the members of the Confederacy.

Under this impression, Your Commissioners, with the most respectful deference, beg leave to suggest their unanimous conviction, that it may essentially tend to advance the interests of the union, if the States, by whom they have been respectively delegated, would themselves concur, and use their endeavors to procure the concurrence of the other States, in the appointment of Commissioners, to meet at Philadelphia on the second Monday in May next, to take into consideration the situation of the United States, to devise such further provisions as shall appear to them necessary to render the constitution of the Federal Government adequate to the exigencies of the Union; and to report such an Act for that purpose to the United States in Congress assembled, as when agreed to, by them, and afterwards confirmed by the Legislatures of every State, will effectually provide for the same.

Though your Commissioners could not with propriety address these observations and sentiments to any but the States they have the honor to represent, they have nevertheless concluded from motives of respect, to transmit copies of this report to the United States in Congress assembled, and to the executives of the other States.

By order of the Commissioners.
Dated at Annapolis
September 14th, 1786

APPENDIX 2

The Continentalist Number 1, July 1781

by Alexander Hamilton

It would be the extreme of vanity in us not to be sensible, that we began this revolution with very vague and confined notions of the practical business of government. To the greater part of us it was a novelty: Of those, who under the former constitution had had opportunities of acquiring experience, a large proportion adhered to the opposite side, and the remainder can only be supposed to have possessed ideas adapted to the narrow coloneal sphere, in which they had been accustomed to move, not of that enlarged kind suited to the government of an INDEPENDENT NATION.

There were no doubt exceptions to these observations—men in all respects qualified for conducting the public affairs, with skill and advantage; but their number was small; they were not always brought forward in our councils; and when they were, their influence was too commonly borne down by the prevailing torrent of ignorance and prejudice.

On a retrospect however, of our transactions, under the disadvantages with which we commenced, it is perhaps more to be wondered at, that we have done so well, than that we have not done better. There are indeed some traits in our conduct, as conspicuous for sound policy, as others for magnanimity. But, on the other hand, it must also be confessed, there have been many false steps, many chimerical projects and utopian speculations, in the management of our civil as well as of our military affairs. A part of these were the natural effects of the spirit of the times dictated by our situation. An extreme jealousy of power is the attendant on all popular revolutions, and has seldom been without its evils. It is to this source we are to trace many of the fatal mistakes, which have so deeply endangered the common cause; particularly that defect, which will be the object of these remarks, A WANT OF POWER IN CONGRESS.

The present Congress, respectable for abilities and integrity, by experience convinced of the necessity of a change, are preparing several important articles to be submitted to the respective states, for augmenting the powers of the Confederation. But though there is hardly at this time a man of information in America, who will not acknowledge, as a general proposition, that in its present form, it is unequal, either to a vigorous prosecution of the war, or to the preservation of the union in peace; yet when the principle comes to be applied to practice, there seems not to be the same agreement in the modes of remedying the defect; and it is to be feared, from a disposition which appeared in some of the states on a late occasion, that the salutary intentions of Congress may meet with more delay and opposition, than the critical posture of the states will justify.

It will be attempted to show in a course of papers what ought to be done, and the mischiefs of a contrary policy.

In the first stages of the controversy it was excusable to err. Good intentions, rather than great skill, were to have been expected from us. But we have now had sufficient time for reflection and experience, as ample as unfortunate, to rectify our errors. To persist in them, becomes disgraceful and even criminal, and belies that character of good sense and a quick discernment of our interests, which, in spite of our mistakes, we have been hitherto allowed. It will prove, that our sagacity is limited to interests of inferior moment; and that we are incapable of those enlightened and liberal views, necessary to make us a great and a flourishing people.

History is full of examples, where in contests for liberty, a jealousy of power has either defeated the attempts to recover or preserve it in the first instance, or has afterwards subverted it by clogging government with too great precautions for its felicity, or by leaving too wide a door for sedition and popular licentiousness. In a government framed for durable liberty, not less regard must be paid to giving the magistrate a proper degree of authority, to make and execute the laws with rigour, than to guarding against encroachments upon the rights of the community. As too much power leads to despotism, too little leads to anarchy, and both eventually to the ruin of the people. These are maxims well known, but never sufficiently attended to, in adjusting the frames of governments. Some momentary interest or passion is sure to give a wrong bias, and pervert the most favorable opportunities.

No friend to order or to rational liberty, can read without pain and disgust the history of the commonwealth of Greece. Generally speaking, they were a constant scene of the alternate tyranny of one part of the people over the other, or of a few usurping demagogues over the whole. Most of them had been originally governed by kings, whose despotism (the natural disease of monarchy) had obliged their subjects to murder, expel, depose, or reduce them to a nominal existence, and institute popular governments. In these governments, that of Sparta excepted, the jealousy of power hindered the people from trusting out of their own hands a competent authority, to maintain the repose and stability of the commonwealth; whence originated the frequent revolutions and civil broils with which they were distracted. This, and the want of a solid federal union to restrain the ambition and rivalship of the different cities, after a rapid succession of bloody wars, ended in their total loss of liberty and subjugation to foreign powers.

In comparison of our governments with those of the ancient republics, we must, without hesitation, give the preference to our own; because, every power with us is exercised by representation, not in tumultuary assemblies of the collective body of the people, where the art or impudence of the ORATOR or TRIBUNE, rather than the utility or justice of the measure could seldom fail to govern. Yet whatever may be the advantage on our side, in such a comparison, men who estimate the value of institutions, not from prejudices of the moment, but from experience and reason, must be persuaded, that the same JEALOUSY of POWER has prevented our reaping all the advantages, from the examples of other nations, which we ought to have done, and has rendered our constitutions in many respects feeble and imperfect.

Perhaps the evil is not very great in respect to our constitutions; for notwithstanding their imperfections, they may, for some time, be made to operate in such a manner, as to answer the purposes of the common defense and the maintenance of order; and they seem to have, in themselves, and in the progress of society among us, the seeds of improvement.

But this is not the case with respect to the FEDERAL GOVERNMENT; if it is too weak at first, it will continually grow weaker. The ambition and local interests of the respective members, will be constantly undermining and usurping upon its prerogatives, till it comes to a dissolution; if a partial combination of some of the more powerful ones does not bring it to a more SPEEDY and VIOLENT END [emphasis in original].[1]

APPENDIX 3

Putting Pen to Paper: How *The Federalist* Papers Physically Came to Be Written

How does one write about writing? The act of writing, putting pen to paper, producing words, crafting thoughts through grammar, punctuation, and language, is today something of a lost art form. So then, how to make that process engaging and appealing to the "modern" reader? Especially a reader who may only "write" with a keyboard, be it a virtual one projected onto a hard surface, or a physical one attached to a computer, tablet, or phone? Yet, even for those familiar with the scratch of a pen on paper, how does one make the story of a particular written work compelling even to read without some recourse to tangents and diversions employed to jazz or juice up the narrative? What were the actual physical processes Hamilton, Madison, and Jay employed to create the essays we know today as *The Federalist* papers? The patterns and methods of writing were not much different than we would use today. What we would however find striking would be the paper, ink, and pens used by Publius to compose *The Federalist* papers. This appendix will present a description of how one set about writing in 1787 and what it took to create meaning from seemingly random strokes of ink placed on a page of paper.

Once Hamilton had the outlines of his plan in place, and his co-authors on board, the actual business of literally putting pen to paper began. What did this entail? What kind of paper, ink, and pens, were the authors using? A reference to Hamilton's purchasing of virtual mountains of paper, ink, pens, and accessories, has already been made. But this can also be applied to Madison and Jay, and nearly every literate household in the country, if not for the large amounts, at least the similar items. What exactly though was the paper, ink, and pen used by the authors? One answer is, quite simply, that information does not exist. What does exist though is enough information to make an educated outline of the process of actually writing the essays before they went to the printer—which is a process with its own story as well.

The predominate type of paper being used in eighteenth century America was handmade laid paper. "The paper made in the colonial period was always 'laid' paper. It was only in 1757 that Baskerville perfected in England the process of making "wove" paper…."[1] This paper was made from linen rags, beaten, with water added, which was then placed in a mold. The mold, usually of a standard size, had four wooden sides enclosing a screen mesh covering one complete side, much like a common window screen today. This would be dipped into a vat containing the rag pulp, allowed to dry enough to remove the newly formed sheet, and then the sheet would be stacked with others to be pressed dry before being hung to fully air dry.

As has already been speculated, the essays were probably written in a variety of settings—everything from Hamilton's study at his home, his office, and probably even that boat on the Hudson River. Madison too probably wrote at his boarding house room and Jay no doubt wrote at his home and possibly office. There is every reason to believe as well that taverns or coffee-houses would also have provided a suitable place to think and write. Each of the authors likely had a portable writing desk and probably kept note size paper at the ready for when an idea struck them. The well-stocked eighteenth century desk, portable or full-size, contained quill pens, a pen knife, ink, inkpot, paper, sealing wax candles, and maybe sand or pounce for drying the ink by absorbing the excess ink left on the paper after writing.

Ink

We give even less thought to ink today than we do paper. Ink and pens are disposable, and barely given a second thought by most people. (Ballpoint pens, so ubiquitous today, were not perfected until the 1950s.) In the eighteenth century, the predominate type of ink—some sources insist the only type—was iron gall ink. This ink type dated back at least to Roman times and the main recipes changed only slightly over the centuries. The basic recipe of iron gall ink was, and is, tannin, vitriol, gum Arabic, and water. While these basic ingredients will yield a fine ink, other additives can be used to create certain specific qualities. Tannin is gathered from tree gall, which is found in the area where a leaf meets a branch. The gall is a growth the tree creates to protect itself from the agitation of various insects (the wasp being the primary insect which, when a larva, is protected within this shell created by the tree it produced to protect itself).

> … gall is excrescence produced when the commonly called gall wasp punctures the bark of an oak tree and deposits an egg. When the larva develops, the tree produces the gall which serves not only as a house but as food for this insect. If the larva dies or leaves at a certain stage, the tree discontinues the production of tannic and gallic acids within the gall. This gall is of greatest value to the ink-maker when it contains the maximum amounts of those two acids.[2]

Gall can come from many trees, but comes primarily from oak. The Aleppo oak is particularly prized, as are Chinese and Japanese oaks. The Aleppo gall "was recognized and recommended in most ink formula's as being best for [making ink] … they [the galls] were about the size of nutmeg and were imported from Syria or other parts of Asia Minor."[3] The acid content in Aleppo gall was considered of the highest quality. (Acid content was something to be concerned with; high acid kept ink black while low acid turned ink brown. Too much acid would cause ink to eat through paper; much like modern tree pulp paper, high in acid, causes modern mass-produced paper to become brittle and break after only a few years.) The harvested gall—Aleppo or otherwise—was dried and ground into a powder and mixed with vitriol (sulfate of iron). This iron salt is used to produce the color of iron gall ink. The intensity of the iron sulfate, and whether anything else was added, can easily impact the final product. Finally, gum Arabic was added to promote viscosity, to keep the ink from being too thick or too thin. Again, the amount of gum Arabic varied, as per the needs of the purchaser of the ink. A late sixteenth century English recipe for iron gall ink states:

> Take an ounce of beaten gall, three or four ounces of gum Arabic, put them together in a pot with rain water, and when the gum is almost consumed, drain it through a cloth, and put into it almost half a cup of vitriol beaten to powder.[4]

This is just one of many such recipes to survive. According to the Iron Gall Ink website:

> Hundreds of recipes for iron gall ink have been published over the centuries. The sheer variety and number of these recipes testify to the widespread use of iron gall ink and its primary importance to our literary and artistic traditions. Artists and scribes, domestics and entrepreneurs each concocted their own formula to suit their particular needs.[5]

It is hard to imagine Hamilton, Madison, or Jay, using anything but pre-made dry ink which probably required little preparation beyond adding water, or buying it already mixed in liquid form. Even colonial printers had to rely on ink (different from writing ink but the same general recipe). "It is probable that the normal practice of the colonial printer in the maintenance of his ink supply was to import the ready-mixed product from English manufacturers."[6]

Mixing ink was always tricky. It required patience, judgment, and temperament. "Doubtless the mixing of ink in their own shops was an economy in cash expenditure for the American printer and a means of occupying the spare time of apprentices, but whether moved by these or other considerations it is clear enough that ink-making continued to be one of the practices of the colonial printing shop throughout the eighteenth century. It is not certain when the making of printing ink for sale became a specialty in American manufacturing...."[7]

The pen employed by Publius was a quill (from a large bird) which had been split into two nibs and sharpened at the end with a pen knife. This splitting into nibs would allow the ink to gather, in a small, manageable amount, and flow onto the paper. Some steel nibs were in existence at this time as were pencils. However, it is nearly certain that the quill pen was the instrument of choice in composing *The Federalist* papers. Having a manageable amount of ink on the pen, and an ink of the correct viscosity, was absolutely necessary to prevent blotting and ungainly attempts at writing or drawing. There was at the time a real art to writing.

In a study published in the American Archivist journal in 1948, William J. Barrow wrote concerning the goal of putting pen to paper:

> If compounded with the proper amount of gum Arabic, the iron gall inks flow easily from a quill pen, penetrating the fibers of the paper to form a black insoluble compound. Writing in

these inks is quite difficult to bleach or remove from paper without leaving some evidence of alteration, qualities highly valued in an ink and often mentioned in the formula as being the principal reason for their use.[8]

The goal of Publius, and any writer, was to produce a manuscript where the ink on the paper was stable—it would not run or smear, turn colors, or worse, fade. One component in this goal was the ink. The other component was paper.

Paper

Paper is a sheet consisting of overlapping vegetable fibers that bond together to form a compact mat. Its origin can be traced to China ... to ca. 105 CE. Paper remained exclusive to the Middle East and East Asia until around 1151, when there is evidence of its being made in Spain during the Moorish occupation. Slowly, the craft spread across Europe, from Italy in 1276 to France in 1348, Germany in 1390, and eventually into England by 1495.[9]

Eighteenth century paper was not the mass produced paper we use today. Eighteenth century (and earlier) paper was manufactured with products of much higher quality than we are used to. Specifically, prior to the Industrial Revolution in approximately 1830, paper was produced with rags. Linen rags, from discarded clothing, unused pieces from the tailor, and any other source of discarded rags provided the raw material for the papermaker to ply his trade. This paper was inherently strong and took ink well, especially if sized (coated) with gelatin to increase the ability to affix the ink more permanently to the paper.

Like ink, like food, the best paper had just a handful of ingredients. And like any good recipe, there were many ways to mix those ingredients which involved much trial and error over the centuries to perfect. Early on, it was not uncommon for foreign substances (hair, insects) to find their way into paper by falling into the vat of pulp. The great historian of papermaking, Dard Hunter, put early American and European papermaking efforts in to perspective:

> The tone of the old paper was never entirely uniform, and owing to the absence of chemicals in the manufacture, the grades of paper differed strikingly in color. The best paper was of a creamy tint, while the poorer grades, made from old and discolored materials, were a light coffee tone, and at times even a dark gray. The bleaching of linen and cotton rags for papermaking was not in general use until the early nineteenth century, and all paper made before that time assumed the tone of the material from which it was made; the water used in the early mills also had considerable influence upon the shade or tint of the paper. In the winter time, especially, it was difficult to clarify the water for use in the paper mills. This muddy appearance is noticeable in many of the early American-made papers.[10]

Whether Publius was aware of all of this or not, crafting the paper necessary to write the eighty-five essays was not as simple as they may have commonly thought.

Just about every type of vegetable fiber can be used—or has been tried—to make paper. Of course the quality of the paper varied considerably depending on the fibers used. Some were naturally better than others. In the Middle East and East Asia craftsmen used unprocessed, raw material; in Europe pre-processed materials began to be used. These included textile leftovers, worn and discarded rags, and even rope. This had to be reduced to a pulp before it could be put in to a mold to make a sheet of paper. Many times the beaten material would have additives mixed into the pulp to adjust the acidity or create a more pleasing color. As with all recipes, papermakers had to guard against over-emphasizing one part of the process over another. As an example, over-beating of the rag to pulp material could damage the fibers resulting in a weak sheet of paper. As with anything handmade, slight imperfections would always occur.

The papermaker was essentially a separate craftsman from the printer, who would create pages of books or newspapers, or hymnals, or whatever job they were contracted to do. Naturally, some paper was sold in shops to individual purchasers. Much like today, it depended on the end purpose to determine how the paper was marketed and bought by the consumer. For Publius, this meant buying paper outright in a shop for personal use; but it also meant the printer purchasing paper in bulk for the printing of *The Federalist* papers. In essence, *The Federalist* provides an excellent micro-economic unit on one aspect of the production/marketing/consumption perspective relating to paper. Of course, this dynamic could be applied to ink as well, although the ink trade was not as specialized as papermaking. Many printers made their own ink (and printers ink was different from writing ink), but they still had to acquire the raw ingredients from a supplier. This supplier would probably have been involved with more than just ink, unlike the papermaker. In the process of creating *The Federalist* papers—both as written manuscript and in book form—the most specialized trade was that of papermaker. That of printer was not far behind.

> As public printer of New York, of Massachusetts, or of South Carolina, or of any other colony, he handled the business of a separate political division, of a commonwealth proud of its entity, proud of its comparative independence of Parliament or of any restraint upon its actions save the will of the sovereign and their legality in the opinion of the attorney general of the realm. The English provincial printer, his counterpart in most other respects, knew no such relationship.[11]

One American who knew quite a bit about the paper trade was Benjamin Franklin. This polymath, an American's American, spent his early career as a printer, as most know. While he is justly famous and well-known for the output of his printing press, his understanding of the business aspect (which made him wealthy) was just as profound. As a buyer and seller of paper and ink in large quantities, he was uniquely qualified to be seen as an expert on the entire process spanning several specialized trades. In an address (someone else probably read it for him) to the American Philosophical Society (which he helped to found in 1743) in 1788, Franklin listed the steps of papermaking:

> A number of small sheets are to be made separately; these are to be couched, one by one, between blankets; when a heap is formed it must be put under a stronger press, to force out the water; then the blankets are to be taken away, one by one, and the sheets hung up to dry; when dry they are to be again pressed, or if to be sized, they must be dipped into size made of warm water, in which glue and alum are dissolved [this would facilitate the ink adhering to the paper]; they must be pressed again to force out the superfluous size; they must be hung up a second time to dry, which if the air happens to be damp requires some days; they must be taken down, laid together, and again pressed; they must be pasted together at their edges; the whole must be glazed by labor, with a flint.[12]

Franklin was America's best known papermaker, having even created his own watermark. Franklin took great pride in introducing printing to areas where it did not exist in the colonies:

> The earliest [paper]mill in the South was that which the printer William Parks, with aid and advice from Franklin, established at Williamsburg, Virginia, about the year 1743. Franklin, indeed, was deeply interested in the papermaking industry. In the later years of the century he told the French traveler, Brissot de Warville, that alone he had established or helped establish no fewer than eighteen paper mills. His account books show him to have been a large and, presumably, a successful dealer in papers of all sorts—printing paper, writing paper, and the coarser papers for wrapping—and a dealer on an equal scale in linen rages, the raw material of paper manufacture.[13]

Franklin had a vast knowledge of papermaking, not just in America and Europe, but in the Far East as well. In one sense, Franklin was fortunate. The printing world was not a rapidly changing world. It was static in approach and execution:

> In the English colonies, as elsewhere throughout the world in the seventeenth and eighteenth centuries, the actual equipment of the printing-houses was very little different in its mechanical features from that used by the European typographers of the closing years of the fifteenth century. It might even be said that in all essential principles the equipment of the colonial American printer was even less elaborate than that with which Gutenberg of Mainz initiated the art of typography, for this printer of the seventeenth and eighteenth centuries had long ago given up the practice of casting his own type....[14]

Paper was invented in the Far East, in the first or second century CE. It would take nearly a thousand years before papermaking skills arrived in Europe via Spain. England would not see papermaking until nearly the beginning of the sixteenth century. The first papermaking in North America (South America was producing paper over one- hundred years before North America) did not occur until 1690, in Pennsylvania. Until that time, and well into the eighteenth century, paper was imported from England. In fact, the Navigation Acts of Charles II made this law. In the decades leading up to the Revolutionary War, the printer, bookbinder, papermaker, and bookseller faced many challenges. With their trade toggling between acceptance and scorn by Britain, the ultimate attack on the entire paper trade was one of the first acts of the Parliament against America—the Stamp Act. This Act not only caused outrage, it put tremendous pressure on America's nascent paper and book industry to make greater efforts. Colonial legislatures saw the need to strengthen this craft domestically. "The war suspended the transatlantic trade in books and most other commodities. Printers struggled to survive, and membership in the trade was marked by high turnover."[15]

By the time the new Constitution went into effect, the implications for printing and publishing (and thus for paper and ink and all the accessories) were indeed bright. Overall, "the country as a whole was able to count fourteen colleges within its borders, claiming an enrollment among them of 1200 students ... the total periodical publication of the nation numbered 103 titles, of which eight were daily newspapers, seven were magazines, and the remainder were weekly or semi-weekly newspapers."[16]

These were all highly encouraging signs for the book industry. The world into which *The Federalist* papers were released was fast becoming one of great potential for the new country and a fast-growing industry.

The world of book printing, binding, and publishing which greeted *The Federalist* papers when they were first published in book form in 1788 was a complicated one:

> The private employment of the press in those communities would have been insufficient in amount to keep their printers alive, and it was only as the commercial life of the country slowly developed that the government work became merely an incidental source of income to a printer who might be engaged in the publication of a newspaper, an annual almanac, legal manuals, business guides, separately printed advertisements, sermons, and finally, original and reprinted works of literary character.[17]

The recently independent United States was still dependent on England and Europe for specialized titles. But, with political independence came the natural desire for complete economic independence in a wide range of crafts, including book printing and binding:

> But in the smaller towns like Annapolis, Williamsburg, and Baltimore, where existing conditions made the division of labor uneconomical, the printer had perforce to become also the binder. Inadequate patronage was not the only reason for linking the two crafts; we must not forget the nature of the printer's role in the community. He frequently ran the general store, was postmaster, and sometimes held town office, as well as being printer and publisher. In the turn of events he mastered whatever came to hand, and in the case of binding, so closely allied to his main purpose, it was many years before he discontinued this activity. He overcame the lack of skilled binders by employing one or two printers familiar with the processes of folding, gathering, sewing, lacing, covering, and decorating.[18]

While most states had moved beyond having official printers as was the case in the early years of colonial printing, printers in the United States faced a competitive, often cutthroat business environment. Most printers took on multiple jobs at once to keep the press running, "Colonial printers made a living by combining printing and bookselling and by emphasizing jobbing printing and government printing over work on their own account."[19] And this of course meant that it needed large quantities of paper, ink, and associated supplies. More and more, these raw business essentials were manufactured in the United States.

By the time *The Federalist* papers were published in 1788, the publisher knew that a market existed for the books. America, by 1788, had moved beyond being a place where only the affluent had substantial numbers of volumes. Still, while literacy rates grew throughout the nineteenth century, book ownership, while increasing, was still mainly the domain of the wealthier Americans. For most Americans, almanacs, bibles, and a few other titles constituted their entire collection.

Chapter Notes

Preface

1. *The Selected Papers of John Jay Digital Edition,* Elizabeth M. Nuxoll, editor. Charlottesville: University of Virginia Press, Rotunda, 2014–. http://rotunda.upress.virginia.edu/founders/JNJY-01-03-02-0163 [accessed 17 Mar 2015]. Main Series, Volume 3 (1782–1784).
2. Friedenwald, Herbert. "The Continental Congress." *The Pennsylvania Magazine of History and Biography* 19, no. 2 (1895), 200.
3. *The Papers of Thomas Jefferson Digital Edition,* ed. Barbara B. Oberg and J. Jefferson Looney. Charlottesville: University of Virginia Press, Rotunda, 2008–2015. http://rotunda.upress.virginia.edu/founders/TSJN-01-14-02-0062 [accessed 09 Feb 2015]. Main Series, Volume 14 (8 October 1788–26 March 1789).

Chapter 1

1. Martha Washington letter to Burrell Bassett, Morristown National Historical Park, Lloyd W. Smith Rare Book and Archival Collection.
2. John Rhodehamel, ed., *The American Revolution, Writings from the War of Independence* (New York: Literary Classics of the United States, 2001), 615.
3. *Ibid.*, 615.
4. *Ibid.*, 616.
5. By Andrew O'Shaughnessy. The prize is given every year and is co-funded by Mount Vernon, Washington College, and the Gilder-Lehrman Institute.
6. Rhodehamel, ed., *The American Revolution,* 631.
7. *Ibid.*, 663.
8. *Ibid.*, 647. Washington further communicated to Schuyler that he knew the mutineers had no intention of desertion. British intelligence confirmed this, reporting, "they [the mutineers] have shown no intention of coming to us, but on the contrary declared that should the British interfere, they would take up arms to oppose them as readily as ever." *Ibid.*, 646.
9. The author is well aware of the concept of military discipline. However, the American War of Independence was at base a war of rebellion, now ostensibly punishing rebellion. For a man of "justice," Washington certainly knew his actions were more than what was called for. No doubt, the soldiers who killed the officers at the start of the mutiny should have faced justice, but we don't know that they did. Were they part of the "few" whom Washington wished dealt with? Perhaps Washington saw the need to act quickly. This was no doubt a wise move, of course. But, the fact still remains, he hastily sent quite possibly innocent men to their deaths.
10. Edmund C. Burnett, ed., *Letters of Members of the Continental Congress* Volume 5 (Washington, D.C.: The Carnegie Institution of Washington, 1921), 515.
11. Chauncey Worthington Ford, ed., *Journals of the Continental Congress 1774–1789* Volume XIX (Washington, D.C.: U.S. Government Printing Office, 1904), 79.
12. The piece, while clever, served no real purpose. It began: "In the name of Devil Amen. We the Congress of America in Congress assembled, being weak in body, low in credit, and poor in estate, but rich, high, and

strong, in expectation; that by our hellish faithful behavior on earth, we shall be advanced to the highest esteem and favour of Satan in his kingdom, do, make, publish, and declare, this our Last Will and Testament...." It is hardly necessary to go on to get the feel for the satire. Rhodehamel, ed., *American Revolution*, 664.

13. Burnett, ed., *Letters*, Volume 5, 552.
14. *Ibid.*, 520.
15. *Ibid.*, 551.
16. *Ibid.*, 529–531.
17. Philip B. Kurland, and Ralph Lerner, ed., *The Founders' Constitution* Volume 1 (Chicago: University of Chicago Press, 1987), 155.
18. *Ibid.*
19. *Ibid.*, 157.
20. Burke Davis, *The Campaign That Won America: The Story of Yorktown* (N.p.: Eastern Acorn Press, 1979), 218.
21. Dr. James Thatcher made a similar comparison in his journal at the time. Quoted in Stephen Brumwell, *George Washington: Gentleman Warrior* (New York: Quercus, 2012), 396. Dr. Thatcher's journal is also the main source for Washington firing the first ceremonial American cannon shot. Joseph Plumb Martin also mentions that Washington dug the first ceremonial (presumably American) trench. George F. Sheer, ed. *Private Yankee Doodle; Being a Narrative of Some of the Adventures, Dangers and Sufferings of a Revolutionary Soldier* (N.p.: Eastern Acorn Press, 1979), 232. Cannibalism at the Jamestown settlement was discovered in 2013 and reported in many outlets. http://www.smithsonianmag.com/history-archaeology/Starving-Settlers-in-Jamestown-Colony-Resorted-to-Eating-A-Child-205472161.html (visited 11–22-13).
22. Rhodehamel, ed., *The American Revolution*, 702.
23. Burnett, ed., *Letters*, Volume 5, 574.
24. *Ibid.*, 574.
25. Davis, *The Campaign That Won America*, 134.
26. Burnett, *Letters*, Volume 6, 206–207.
27. *Ibid.*, 207.
28. *Ibid.*, 209. In a separate letter, President Thomas McKean wrote to Thomas Rodney of Delaware that de Grasse had twenty-eight ships of the line, two forty-four gun ships and two frigates of thirty-two guns each. He also had a cutter of eighteen guns with 4,000 troops. *Ibid.*, 210.
29. *Ibid.*, 225–226.
30. *Ibid.*, 227.
31. John C. Fitzpatrick, ed, *The Writings of George Washington from the Original Manuscript Sources 1745–1799* Volume 23 (Washington, D.C.: United States Government Printing Office, 1937), 137.
32. Andrew Jackson O'Shaughnessy, *The Men Who Lost America, British Leadership, the American Revolution, and the Fate of Empire* (New Haven, CT: Yale University Press, 2013), 280.
33. Rhodehamel, ed., *The American Revolution*, 721.
34. *Ibid.*
35. *Ibid.*, 723–724.
36. *Ibid.*, 724.
37. Contrary to popular opinion or belief, there is no contemporary record of the British playing the tune "The World Turned Upside Down" during the surrender ceremony.
38. Rhodehamel, ed., *The American Revolution*, 725.
39. *Ibid.*, 744.
40. Burnett, ed., *Letters*, Volume 6, 247.
41. *Ibid.*
42. *Ibid.*, 519.
43. *Ibid.*, 249, in footnote.
44. *Ibid.*, 252.
45. Congress knew the dire situation. Without a victory, America would be at a crossroads. The Virginia delegation wrote to Governor Nelson on October 9: "It is impossible to expect, that France, engaged as she is in expanse, should maintain the American war out of her own treasury. Her advances for America have been generous, but not sufficient to overcome the necessity of the exertions of the different states." Burnett, *Letters*, Volume 6, 235.
46. O'Shaughnessy, *The Men Who Lost America*, 281.
47. Richard B. Morris, *The Peacemakers, The Great Powers and American Independence* (New York: Harper & Row, 1965), 252.
48. *Ibid.*, 192, in footnote.
49. "Reviewing the diplomatic history of the period of the American Revolution we perceive that bitter international rivalries of the eighteenth century had built up such a situation, grievous but not abnormal for Europe, that once the American insurrection broke out it precipitated a combination of factors and set in motion a train of events that engulfed the whole world in war." Samuel Flagg Bemis, *The Diplomacy of the American*

Revolution (Bloomington: Indiana University Press, 1965), 255.

50. John Richard Alden, *The American Revolution, 1775–1783* (New York: Harper Torchbooks, 1962), 249.

51. *Ibid.*, 250.

52. The hazards of communications were summed up by Richard Morris: "Letters sent through the regular mails were opened up in the post office; no systematic schedule of ship sailings existed; before a reply to a letter was received some five to six months on an average had elapsed." Morris, *The Peacemakers*, 439.

53. Burnett, *Letters*, Volume 6, 362.

54. Bemis, *The Diplomacy of the American Revolution*, 215.

55. Max Farrand, *The Fathers of the Constitution, A Chronicle of the Establishment of the Union* (New Haven, CT: Yale University Press, 1921), 57–58.

56. Henry Laurens had a particularly interesting story. The Journals of the Continental Congress from March 1781 record:

> That Mr. Lurens who was formerly President of Congress came into that body long after the Independence of these States was solemnly declared and being in a high character in their service, and taken upon the high seas, instead of being treated as a Prisoner of War, was sent to the Tower of London, put into close confinement, and by the tenor of his commitment is pretended to be considered as a traitorous subject of the King of Great Britain [Ford, *Journals*, Volume XIX, 227].

57. Burnett, *Letters*, Volume 6, 118.

58. Morris, *The Peacemakers*, 440.

59. *Ibid.*, 439.

60. *The Selected Papers of John Jay Digital Edition*, Elizabeth M. Nuxoll, editor. Charlottesville: University of Virginia Press, Rotunda, 2014–. http://rotunda.upress.virginia.edu/founders/JNJY-01-03-02-0011 [accessed 27 Feb 2015]. Main Series, Volume 3 (1782–1784).

61. Morristown National Historical Park, Lloyd W. Smith Archival and Rare Book Collection, MORR 10987.

62. *The Selected Papers of John Jay Digital Edition*, Elizabeth M. Nuxoll, editor. Charlottesville: University of Virginia Press, Rotunda, 2014–. http://rotunda.upress.virginia.edu/founders/JNJY-01-03-02-0092 [accessed 27 Feb 2015]. Main Series, Volume 3 (1782–1784).

63. Rhodehamel, ed., *The American Revolution*, 790.

64. *The Adams Papers Digital Edition*, ed. C. James Taylor. Charlottesville: University of Virginia Press, Rotunda, 2008–2015. http://rotunda.upress.virginia.edu/founders/ADMS-06-14-02-0009 [accessed 27 Feb 2015]. Papers of John Adams, Volume 14, October 1782–May 1783.

65. *The Selected Papers of John Jay Digital Edition*, Elizabeth M. Nuxoll, editor. Charlottesville: University of Virginia Press, Rotunda, 2014–. http://rotunda.upress.virginia.edu/founders/JNJY-01-03-02-0071 [accessed 27 Feb 2015]. Main Series, Volume 3 (1782–1784).

66. This appears in the Journals of the Continental Congress on April 11, 1783, due to the transit time from Europe to America. Ford, *Journals*, Volume XXIV, 238.

67. Farrand, *The Fathers of the Constitution*, 56.

68. Burnett, *Letters*, Volume 6, 431.

69. *Ibid.*, 562.

70. *Ibid.*, 442.

71. This is the day Congress approved the November 30, 1783 Preliminaries. Ford, *Journals*, Volume XXIV, 241. On May 23, 1783, Congress moved forward with disbanding the Continental Army. *Ibid.*, 358.

Chapter 2

1. Max Farrand, *The Fathers of the Constitution: A Chronicle of the Establishment of the Union* (New Haven, CT: Yale University Press, 1921), 84.

2. The Mayflower Compact is undoubtedly one of shortest issuances on governing ever created. It reads:

> IN THE NAME OF GOD, AMEN. We, whose names are underwritten, the Loyal Subjects of our dread Sovereign Lord King James, by the Grace of God, of Great Britain, France, and Ireland, King, Defender of the Faith, &c. Having undertaken for the Glory of God, and Advancement of the Christian Faith, and the Honour of our King and Country, a Voyage to plant the first Colony in the northern Parts of Virginia; Do by these Presents, solemnly and mutually, in the Presence of God and one another, covenant and combine ourselves together into a civil Body Politick, for our better Ordering and Preservation, and Further-

ance of the Ends aforesaid: And by Virtue hereof do enact, constitute, and frame, such just and equal Laws, Ordinances, Acts, Constitutions, and Officers, from time to time, as shall be thought most meet and convenient for the general Good of the Colony; unto which we promise all due Submission and Obedience. IN WITNESS whereof we have hereunto subscribed our names at Cape-Cod the eleventh of November, in the Reign of our Sovereign Lord King James, of England, France, and Ireland, the eighteenth, and of Scotland the fifty-fourth, Anno Domini; 1620 [http://avalon.law.yale.edu/17th_century/mayflower.asp (accessed 15 Sept 2015)].

3. The greatest single slogan from that period which every school child learns today—"no taxation without representation"—is indeed even on license plates in Washington, D.C.

4. Womersley, David, ed. *Liberty and American Experience in the Eighteenth Century* (Indianapolis: Liberty Fund, 2006), 140.

5. Womersley, ed., *Liberty and American Experience*, 140.

6. *Ibid.*, 141.

7. Joseph Galloway, *Historical and Political Reflections on the Rise and Progress of the American Rebellion* (London: G. Wilkie, 1780), 77.

8. Charles E. Peterson, "Carpenter's Hall," *Transactions of the American Philosophical Society* 43, no. 1 (1953), 96.

9. Edmund C. Burnett, *Letters of Members of the Continental Congress* Volume 1 (Washington, D.C.: The Carnegie Institution of Washington, 1921), 6.

10. *Ibid.*, 101.

11. Merrill Jensen, "The Idea of a National Government During the American Revolution," *Political Science Quarterly* 58, no. 3 (Sept., 1943), 359.

12. Edmund C. Burnett, *The Continental Congress* (New York: W.W. Norton and Company, 1964), 19.

13. *Ibid.*, 1.

14. *Ibid.*

15. Karen Northrop Barzilay, "Fifty Gentlemen Total Strangers: A Portrait of the First Continental Congress" (PhD diss., The College of William and Mary, 2009), 160.

16. *Ibid.*, 178.

17. *Ibid.*, 209.

18. Burnett, *Letters*, Volume I, 4.

19. *Ibid.*, 11.

20. *Ibid.*, 2.

21. *Ibid.*, 31.

22. *Ibid.*, 61.

23. Barzilay, "Fifty Gentlemen Total Strangers," 157.

24. *Ibid.*, 158.

25. *Ibid.*, 4.

26. *Ibid.*, 5.

27. John Maxcy Zane, *The Story of Law* (Indianapolis: The Liberty Fund, 1998), 341.

28. Ford, *Journals*, Volume I, 63–67.

29. Worthington Chauncey Ford, *Journals of the Continental Congress 1774–1789* Volume 1 (Washington, D.C.: U.S. Government Printing Office, 1904), 13.

30. *Ibid.*, 43.

31. *Ibid.*, 44.

32. *Ibid.*, 45. Galloway would actually write a book after he emigrated to England called *Historical and Political Reflections on the Rise and Progress of the American Rebellion*.

33. Burnett, *The Continental Congress*, 21.

34. Ford, *Journals*, Volume I, 48.

35. Burnett, *The Continental Congress*, 50.

36. *Ibid.*, 61.

37. The number of committees over the fifteen years of the Congress' lifespan varies considerably. The First Continental Congress had the lowest number of official committees, establishing nine in their two-month meeting in 1774. The Second Continental Congress had by far the largest number of committees, peaking at four-hundred and fifty-five in 1783, the year of the Yorktown surrender and of the mutiny of the Pennsylvania Line. 1774 also marked the year for the lowest average number of committees a member was assigned to, one. By contrast, 1783 forms the year of the highest number of committee assignments, twenty-five. Rick K. Wilson, Calvin Jillson, "Leadership patterns in the Continental Congress: 1774–1789." *Legislative Studies Quarterly* 14, no. 1 (Feb., 1989), 22–23.

38. Burnett, *Letters*, Volume I, 12.

39. *Ibid.*, 12.

40. *Ibid.*, 15.

41. *Ibid.*, 49.

42. Burnett, *Letters*, Volume I, 34.

43. *Ibid.*, 54. See also Galloway, *Historical and Political Reflections*, 66.

44. Burnett, *Letters*, Volume I, 65.

45. *Ibid.*

46. *Ibid.*, 122.

47. Burnett, *Letters*, Volume I, 83.

48. Charles F. Mullett, "Coke and the

American Revolution." *Economica* no. 38 (Nov. 1932), 457.
49. *Ibid.*
50. Bernard Bailyn, *The Ideological Origins of the American Revolution* (Cambridge: Harvard University Press, 1992), 35.
51. Arthur Berriedale Keith, *An Introduction to British Constitutional Law* (Oxford: Oxford University Press, 1931), 22. See also Anthony M. Lewis, "Jefferson's Summary View as a Chart of Political Union." *The William and Mary Quarterly* 5, no. 1 (Jan. 1948), 37.
52. This section was adapted from Jude M. Pfister, "Constitutional Development in the United States Supreme Court during the 1790s." DLitt diss., Drew University, 2007, 14–15.
53. Bailyn, *The Ideological Origins*, 1.
54. John V. Jezierski, "Parliament or People: James Wilson and Blackstone on the Nature and Location of Sovereignty." *Journal of the History of Ideas* Vol. 32, No. 1 (Jan.–Mar., 1971), 101.
55. Joseph L. Blau, *Men and Movements in American Philosophy* (New York: Prentice-Hall, 1953), 37–38.
56. *Ibid.* See also Jesse S. Reeves, "The Influence of the Law of Nature Upon International Law in the United States," *The American Journal of International Law* 3, no. 3 (July 1909), 552–53.
57. Jezierski, "Parliament or People," 101. See also Lewis, "Jefferson's Summary View as a Chart of Political Union," 41–42, for a discussion of Richard Bland and Benjamin Franklin's similar approach to the foundation of law and its importance for constitutional development.
58. Trevor Colbourn, *The Lamp of Experience—Whig History and the Intellectual Origins of the American Revolution* (Indianapolis: Liberty Fund, 1998), 116. See also Bailyn, *The Ideological Origins*, 80–82.
59. Jezierski, "Parliament or People," 99.
60. *Ibid.*, 98.
61. Joseph Ellis, *American Sphinx—The Character of Thomas Jefferson* (New York: Knopf, 1997), 30.
62. *Ibid.*, 30. See also Lewis, "Jefferson's Summary," 38. Both Ellis and Lewis approach the British/American conflict as essentially a constitutional argument eventually played out on the battlefield. This experience with constitutionalism would provide much of the debate by 1787.

63. Ellis, *American Sphinx*, 30. See also A.C. McLaughlin, review of *The American Revolution: A Constitutional* Interpretation, by Charles Howard McIlwain, *The American Political Science Review* 18, no. 1 (Feb. 1924), 181.
64. Mullett, "Coke and the American Revolution," 471.
65. Dumas Malone, *Jefferson the Virginian* (Boston: Little, Brown, 1948), 182. For a discussion of John Adams' work *Novanglus* and how Adams approached the constitutional question during the revolution, see C. Bradley Thompson, ed., *The Revolutionary Writings of John Adams* (Indianapolis: Liberty Fund, 2000), and Colbourn, *The Lamp of Experience*, 114.
66. Mullett, "Coke and the American Revolution," 470.
67. Jezierski, "Parliament or People," 104.
68. *Ibid.* See Jezierski for further discussion on Wilson's legal argument and how he employed Blackstone's reasoning to support his claim.
69. Morton J. Horwitz, *The Transformation of American Law 1780–1860* (Cambridge: Harvard University Press, 1977), 4.
70. *Ibid.* See also Roy N. Lokken, "The Concept of Democracy in Colonial Political Thought," *The William and Mary Quarterly*, 3d ser., 16, no. 4 (October 1959), 575–577, for a discussion on how the various colonies reflected the British political system prior to the Revolution.
71. Horowitz, *The Transformation of American Law*, 8.
72. Bryan Garner, ed., *Black's Law Dictionary* (St. Paul, MN: West Group, 1999), 270. The common law is most easily defined as "the body of law derived from judicial decisions, rather than from statues of constitution."
73. This section was adapted from Pfister, "Constitutional Development," 15–21.
74. Burnett, *Letters,* Volume I, 44.
75. Andrew O'Shaughnessy, *The Men Who Lost America, British Leadership, the American Revolution, and the Fate of Empire* (New Haven, CT: Yale University Press, 2013), 58.
76. *Ibid.*, 59.
77. Ian Harris, "Edmund Burke," *The Stanford Encyclopedia of Philosophy* (Spring 2012 Edition), Edward N. Zalta (ed.), URL = http://plato.stanford.edu/archives/spr2012/entries/burke/ [accessed 16 Sept 2015].
78. Alden, *The American Revolution*, 62.

79. Jillson and Wilson, "A Social Change Model of Politics," 5.
80. Richard B. Morris, "The Confederation Period and the American Historian," *The William and Mary Quarterly* 13, no. 2 (Apr., 1956), 139.

Chapter 3

1. Edmund C. Burnett, *Letters of Members of the Continental Congress* Volume 1 (Washington, DC: The Carnegie Institution of Washington, 1921), 89–90.
2. *Ibid.*, 90.
3. *Ibid.*, 95.
4. *Ibid.*, 98.
5. *Ibid.*, 98–100.
6. *Ibid.*, 102.
7. John Rhodehamel, ed., *The American Revolution: Writings from the War of Independence* (New York: Literary Classics of the United States, 2001), 593.
8. Herbert Friedenwald, "The Continental Congress," *The Pennsylvania Magazine of History and Biography* 19, no. 2 (1895), 197.
9. Frank Harmon Garver, "The Transition from the Continental Congress to the Congress of the Confederation," *Pacific Historical Review* 1, no. 2 (Jun., 1932), 223.
10. The resolution read:

> Resolved, That every member of this Congress considers himself under the ties of virtue, honour, and love of his country, not to divulge, directly or indirectly, any matter or thing agitated or debated in Congress, before the same shall have been determined, without leave of the Congress; nor any matter or thing determined in Congress, which a majority of the Congress shall order to be kept secret. And that if any member shall violate this agreement, he shall be expelled from this Congress, and deemed an enemy to the liberties of America, and liable to be treated as such; and that every member signify his consent to this agreement by signing the same [*Documents Illustrative of the Formation of the Union of the American States.* Washington, D.C.: U.S. Government Printing Office, 1927. House Document No. 398. Selected, Arranged and Indexed by Charles C. Tansill. Avalon Law].

11. *Ibid.*, Volume 6, 196.
12. Every colony had representatives who, for whatever reason, did not serve. Some of the names were quite prominent figures. Naturally, some of these men no doubt had excellent reasons. Still, the fact remains they did not serve as elected and this caused great disruption to the business of the Continental Congress.
13. Friedenwald, "The Continental Congress," 201.
14. Burnett, ed., *Letters*, Volume 6, 227.
15. There are numerous letters where members of Congress discuss the genuine hardship of serving. One representative example is by Abraham Clark writing to James Caldwell. On October 3, less than two weeks before the Yorktown victory, Clark writes, "I must therefore remind you that it is well known attendance in Congress hath long been a painful service to me, and I feel a strong desire to be free from it…. The present situation of our public affairs requires the assistance of such as have a thorough knowledge in the business before Congress." Burnett, *Letters*, Volume 6, 233.
16. *Ibid.*, 236.
17. *Ibid.*, 245.
18. John Maxcy Zane, *The Story of Law* (Indianapolis: The Liberty Fund, 1998), 341.
19. Michael Lienesch, "Historical Theory and Political Reform: Two Perspectives on Confederation Politics," *The Review of Politics* 45, no., 1 (Jan., 1983), 96.
20. *Ibid.*, 101.
21. Merrill Jensen, "The Idea of a National Government During the American Revolution," *Political Science Quarterly* 58, no. 3 (Sept., 1943), 120.
22. *Ibid.*, 121.
23. Max Farrand, *The Fathers of the Constitution: A Chronicle of the Establishment of the Union* (New Haven, CT: Yale University Press, 1921), 229. See also Merrill Jensen, "The Articles of Confederation: A Re-Interpretation," *Pacific Historical Review* 6, no. 2 (Jun., 1937), 121.
24. William Jay, *The Life of John Jay* Vol. 1 (Chestnut Hill: Elibron Classics Reprint—Adamant Media Corp., 2005), 70.
25. Jensen, *The Articles of Confederation*, 121.
26. Robert Wright, *One Nation Debt*, 69.
27. Jensen, *The Articles of Confederation*, 130.
28. John Adams autobiography, part 1, "John Adams," through 1776, sheet 18 of 53 [electronic edition]. *Adams Family Papers: An Electronic Archive.* Massachusetts Historical Society. http://www.masshist.org/digitaladams/.

29. Worthington Chauncey Ford, *Journals of the Continental Congress 1774–1789* Volume V (Washington, D.C.: U.S. Government Printing Office, 1904), 433.
30. John Richard Alden, *The American Revolution, 1775–1783* (New York: Harper Torchbooks, 1962), 179.
31. Stephen Smith, *Taxation: A Very Short Introduction* (Oxford: Oxford University Press, 2015), 3.
32. Farrand, *The Fathers of the Constitution*, 88.
33. *Ibid.*, 87.
34. The Avalon Project, Yale Law School. http://avalon.law.yale.edu/18th_century/fed31.asp. Accessed March 19, 2015.
35. Darren Staloff, *Hamilton, Adams, Jefferson: The Politics of Enlightenment and The American Founding* (New York: Hill and Wang, 2005), 75.
36. *Ibid.*, 54.
37. Ford, *Journals*, Volume V, 546.
38. *Ibid.*, 555.
39. Jensen, "The Idea of a National Government," 372.
40. Ford, *Journals*, Volume IX, 933.
41. Burnett, *Letters*, Volume 2, 552.
42. *The Documentary History of the Ratification of the Constitution Digital Edition*, ed. John P. Kaminski, Gaspare J. Saladino, Richard Leffler, Charles H. Schoenleber and Margaret A. Hogan. Charlottesville: University of Virginia Press, 2009. http://rotunda.upress.virginia.edu/founders/RNCN-01-01-02-0003-0012 [accessed 16 Mar 2015]. Constitutional Documents and Records, 1776–1787, Volume I: Constitutional Documents and Records, 1776–1787.
43. *The Documentary History of the Ratification of the Constitution Digital Edition*, ed. John P. Kaminski, Gaspare J. Saladino, Richard Leffler, Charles H. Schoenleber and Margaret A. Hogan. Charlottesville: University of Virginia Press, 2009. http://rotunda.upress.virginia.edu/founders/RNCN-01-01-02-0003-0002-0001 [accessed 16 Mar 2015]. Constitutional Documents and Records, 1776–1787, Volume I: Constitutional Documents and Records, 1776–1787.
44. *Ibid.*, 562.
45. *Ibid.*, 562.
46. *Ibid.*, 562n.
47. *Ibid.*, 564.

Chapter 4

1. Ben Baack, "Forging a Nation State: The Continental Congress and the Financing of the War of American Independence," *The Economic History Review* New Series, 54, no. 4 (Nov., 2001), 648.
2. Arthur Lee was a fascinating character. He was a member of prominent Lee family but spent some years in England after graduating from medical school and law school at the University of Edinburgh. He was practicing law when the Revolution began and stayed on in England as a diplomat there and in Europe. He was also very likely an American spy in England and France and famously had a falling out with Benjamin Franklin in 1778 over the French alliance.
3. Edmund C. Burnett, *Letters of the Members of the Continental Congress* Volume 7 (Washington, D.C.: The Carnegie Institution of Washington, 1921), 28.
4. *Ibid.*, 31.
5. *Ibid.*
6. Robert E. Wright, *One Nation Under Debt: Hamilton, Jefferson, and the History of What We Owe* (New York: McGraw Hill, 2008), 67.
7. Baack, "Forging a Nation State," 650.
8. Burnett, *Letters*, Volume 7, 57.
9. *Ibid.* Jones was another American lawyer educated at the Inns of Court—Middle Temple. Jones was a Jeffersonian in his politics which created some friction with his friend George Washington.
10. *Ibid.*, 99.
11. *Ibid.*, 147.
12. Worthington Chauncey Ford, *Journals of the Continental Congress 1774–1789* Volume XXIV (Washington, D.C.: Government Printing Office, 1904), 257.
13. Wright, *One Nation Under Debt*, 68.
14. Udo Hielscher, *Financing the American Revolution: The American Revolution and the Origins of Wall Street in Contemporary Financial Documents* (New York: Museum of American Financial History, 2003), 43.
15. *Ibid.*
16. *Ibid.*
17. Philip B. Kurland, and Ralph Lerner, ed., *The Founders' Constitution* Volume 1 (Chicago: University of Chicago Press, 1987), 153.
18. Hielscher, *Financing the American Revolution*, 43.
19. Wright, *One Nation Under Debt*, 68.

20. Hielscher, *Financing the American Revolution*, 43.
21. Burnett, *Letters*, Volume 8, 354–355. King was referring to the report showing how far revenue payments were off from revenue requests.
22. Ford, *Journals*, Volume XXX, 72.
23. Burnett, *Letters,* Volume 8, 355.
24. Date Mawson Rowland, "The Mount Vernon Convention; G. Mason, Alexander Henderson, Daniel of St. Thomas Jenifer, T. Stone and Samuel Chase," *The Pennsylvania Magazine of History and Biography* 11, no. 4 (Jan. 1888), 410.
25. Section VI of the Articles of Confederation states: "No two or more States shall enter into any treaty, confederation or alliance whatever between them, without the consent of the United States in Congress assembled, specifying accurately the purposes for which the same is to be entered into, and how long it shall continue."
26. Washington had extensive land holdings in the west and naturally wanted to benefit from them. His interest in making the west more accessible via water was a passion of his. A letter from Marylander Thomas Stone attests to this:

> It gives me much pleasure to know that our Act for opening the Navigation of Potomac arrived in time to be adopted by the Assembly of Virginia. If the scheme is properly executed I have the most sanguine expectation that it will fully succeed to the wishes of those who are anxious to promote the welfare of these States and to form a strong chain of connection between the Western and Atlantic governments. Mr. Jenifer[,] Johnson[,] Chase and myself are appointed Commissioners to Settle the Jurisdiction and Navigation of the Bay & the Rivers Potomac and Pocomoke…; the Commissioners of Virginia. We have also instructions to make application to Pennsylvania for leave to clear a road from Potomac to the Western Waters—Our Assembly propose the meeting of the Commissioners to be on the 21st of March at Alexandria, if agreeable to the Commissioners of Virginia. I have no doubt but the subjects of our mission will be settled to mutual satisfaction and it will add much to the satisfaction I shall feel in discharging this trust that I shall have an Opportunity of paying my respects to You at Mount Vernon; which I have long wished

to do, but in truth the necessary attention to professional and public business have kept me so closely employed that I have never had a time when I could gratify my inclination without neglecting some duty which I was particularly bound to perform. I hope nevertheless that you will do me the justice to believe that I warmly participate in the high regard and esteem in which you are held by all the friends of this Country and that I am sir with Sentiments of very sincere Attachment….

27. from *The Papers of George Washington Digital Edition,* ed. Theodore J. Crackel. Charlottesville: University of Virginia Press, Rotunda, 2008. http://rotunda.upress.virginia.edu/founders/GEWN-04-02-02-0214 [accessed 06 Apr 2015]. Confederation Series (1 January 1784–23 September 1788), Volume 2 (18 July 1784–18 May 1785). John C. Fitzpatrick, ed., *The Writings of George Washington from the Original Manuscript Sources 1745–1799* Volume 27 (Washington, D.C.: United States Government Printing Office, 1938), 374.
28. Rowland, "The Mount Vernon Convention," 413.
29. *Ibid.*
30. *Ibid.*, 415.
31. *Ibid.*, 424. This letter is listed as not found in modern collections of Madison's papers. Miss Rowland presumably saw it in 1888 for this article.
32. *Ibid.*, 423.
33. *Ibid.*, 424.
34. Edmund C. Burnett, *The Continental Congress* (New York: W.W. Norton, 1964), 665.
35. Burnett, *Letters,* Volume 8, 359.
36. *Ibid.*, 360.
37. *Ibid.*, 361.
38. *Ibid.*, 374.
39. *Ibid.*, 389.
40. *Ibid.*, 390.
41. *Ibid.*, 416.
42. *Ibid.*, 430.
43. *Ibid.*, 460.
44. *The Papers of James Madison Digital Edition,* J. C. A. Stagg, editor. Charlottesville: University of Virginia Press, Rotunda, 2010. http://rotunda.upress.virginia.edu/founders/JSMN-01-08-02-0268 [accessed 05 Apr 2015]. Congressional Series, Volume 8 (10 March 1784–28 March 1786).
45. Commissioners who signed the final report on the Annapolis Convention in-

cluded, from New York: Egbert Benson and Alexander Hamilton; New Jersey: Abraham Clark, William Houston, and J. Schureman; Pennsylvania: Tench Coxe; Delaware: John Dickinson (chairman), Richard Bassett, and George Read; Virginia: Edmund Randolph, James Madison, and St. George Tucker.

46. Max Farrand, *The Framing of the Constitution of the United States* (New Haven, CT: Yale University Press, 1913), 10.

47. *The Documentary History of the Ratification of the Constitution Digital Edition*, ed. John P. Kaminshi, Gaspare J. Saladino, Richard Leffler, Charles H. Schoenleber and Margaret A. Hogan. Charlottesville: University of Virginia Press, 2009. http://rotunda.upress.virginia.edu/founders/RNCN-01-01-02-0016-0001 [accessed 29 Jul 2014]. Constitutional Documents and Records, 1776–1787, Volume 1: Constitutional Documents and Records, 1776–1787.

48. Ford, *Journals*, Volume XXXI, 679–680.

49. *Ibid.*, Volume XXXII, 74.

50. Burnett, *Letters*, Volume 8, 468–469.

51. *Ibid.*, 475.

52. *Ibid.*, 504.

53. *The Papers of James Madison Digital Edition*, J. C. A. Stagg, editor. Charlottesville: University of Virginia Press, Rotunda, 2010. http://rotunda.upress.virginia.edu/founders/JSMN-01-09-02-0001 [accessed 04 Apr 2015]. Congressional Series, Volume 9 (9 April 1786–24 May 1787 and supplement 1781–1784).

54. *The Papers of Alexander Hamilton Digital Edition*, ed. Harold C. Syrett. Charlottesville: University of Virginia Press, Rotunda, 2011. http://rotunda.upress.virginia.edu/founders/ARHN-01-02-02-0838 [accessed 05 Apr 2015]. Volume II: 1779–1781.

55. *The Papers of Alexander Hamilton Digital Edition*, ed. Harold C. Syrett. Charlottesville: University of Virginia Press, Rotunda, 2011. http://rotunda.upress.virginia.edu/founders/ARHN-01-02-02-0838 [accessed 05 Apr 2015]. Volume II: 1779–1781.

56. *The Papers of Alexander Hamilton Digital Edition*, ed. Harold C. Syrett. Charlottesville: University of Virginia Press, Rotunda, 2011. http://rotunda.upress.virginia.edu/founders/ARHN-01-02-02-0838 [accessed 05 Apr 2015]. Volume II: 1779–1781.

57. *The Papers of Alexander Hamilton Digital Edition*, ed. Harold C. Syrett. Charlottesville: University of Virginia Press, Rotunda, 2011. http://rotunda.upress.virginia.edu/founders/ARHN-01-03-02-0553 [accessed 04 Apr 2015]. Volume III: 1782–1786.

58. *The Papers of Alexander Hamilton Digital Edition*, ed. Harold C. Syrett. Charlottesville: University of Virginia Press, Rotunda, 2011. http://rotunda.upress.virginia.edu/founders/ARHN-01-04-02-0086 [accessed 04 Apr 2015]. Volume IV: 1787–May 1788.

59. Akhil Reed Amar, *America's Constitution: A Biography* (New York: Random House, 2005), 27.

60. *Ibid.*

61. Catherine Drinker Bowen, *Miracle at Philadelphia: The Story of the Constitutional Convention May to September 1787* (Boston: Little, Brown and Company, 1986), 9.

62. Farrand, *The Framing of the Constitution*, 8.

Chapter 5

1. Philip B. Kurland, and Ralph Lerner, ed. *The Founders' Constitution* Volume 1 (Chicago: University of Chicago Press, 1987), 165.

2. Section VIII of the Articles of Confederation states:

> All charges of war, and all other expenses that shall be incurred for the common defense or general welfare, and allowed by the United States in Congress assembled, shall be defrayed out of a common treasury, which shall be supplied by the several States in proportion to the value of all land within each State, granted or surveyed for any person, as such land and the buildings and improvements thereon shall be estimated according to such mode as the United States in Congress assembled, shall from time to time direct and appoint.
>
> The taxes for paying that proportion shall be laid and levied by the authority and direction of the legislatures of the several States within the time agreed upon by the United States in Congress assembled.

This loosely worded section left it to the states to provide funding to the general treasury, which as we have seen did not happen.

3. Max Farrand, *The Fathers of the Constitution: A Chronicle of the Establishment of the Union* (New Haven, CT: Yale University Press, 1921), 91.

4. *Ibid.*, 91–92.

5. Rachel R. Parker, "Shays' Rebellion:

An Episode in American State-Making," *Sociological Perspectives* 34, no. 1 (Spring, 1991), 99–100.

6. Edmund C. Burnett, *Letters of Members of the Continental Congress* (Washington, D.C.: The Carnegie Institution of Washington, 1921), 517.

7. Morristown National Historical Park, Lloyd W. Smith Archival and Rare Book Collection, box 86, folder 28.

8. Parker, "Shays' Rebellion," 100.

9. Morristown NHP, Lloyd W. Smith Archival and Rare Book Collection, box 86, folder 12.

10. Morristown NHP, Lloyd W. Smith Archival and Rare Book Collection, box 86, folder 30.

11. Henry Longfellow's poem was written at the urging of his second wife Fanny Appleton Longfellow after they had visited the arsenal in 1843. She wrote that "I urged H to write a peace poem." The first three stanzas are:

This is the Arsenal. From floor to ceiling,
Like a huge organ, rise the burnished arms;
But from their silent pipes no anthem pealing
Startles the villages with strange alarms.
Ah! what a sound will rise, how wild and dreary,
When the death-angel touches those swift keys!
What loud lament and dismal Miserere
Will mingle with their awful symphonies!
I hear even now the infinite fierce chorus,
The cries of agony, the endless groan,
Which, through the ages that have gone before us,
In long reverberations reach our own.

From the Springfield Armory NHS website http://www.nps.gov/spar/learn/historyculture/arsenal-at-springfield.htm (accessed 4-16-15).

12. Worthington Chauncey Ford, *Journals of the Continental Congress 1774–1789* Volume XXXI (Washington, D.C.: U.S. Government Printing Office, 1904), 457.

13. *Ibid.*, 675.

14. *Ibid.*, 698.

15. *Ibid.*, 699.

16. Edmund C. Burnett, *Letters of Members of the Continental Congress* Volume 8 (Washington, D.C.: The Carnegie Institution of Washington, 1921), 516.

17. Morristown NHP, Lloyd W. Smith Archival and Rare Book Collection, box 86, folder 10.

18. Morristown NHP, Lloyd W. Smith Archival and Rare Book Collection, box 86, folder 25.

19. Bernard Bailyn, ed., *The Debate on the Constitution* Volume 1 (New York: Literary Classics of the United States, 1993), 212.

20. *Ibid.*, 739.

21. *Ibid.*, 752.

22. *Ibid.*, 875.

23. *Ibid.*

24. *Ibid.*, 887.

25. Morristown National Historical Park, Lloyd W. Smith Archival and Rare Book Collection, box 87, folder 10.

26. Morristown NHP, Lloyd W. Smith Archival and Rare Book Collection, box 87, folder 1, 8, and 9.

27. Morristown NHP, Lloyd W. Smith Archival and Rare Book Collection, box 87, folder 4. Shepard enlisted a German doctor to hand deliver the letter as he felt a German would not be suspicious in the area.

28. Morristown NHP, Lloyd W. Smith Archival and Rare Book Collection, box 87, folder 2.

29. Morristown NHP, Lloyd W. Smith Archival and Rare Book Collection, box 87, folder 21.

30. This was actually a direct violation of Section IV of the Articles of Confederation which stated: "If any person guilty of, or charged with, treason, felony, or other high misdemeanor in any State, shall flee from justice, and be found in any of the United States, he shall, upon demand of the Governor or executive power of the State from which he fled, be delivered up and removed to the State having jurisdiction of his offense." From Avalon Law.

31. Morristown NHP, Lloyd W. Smith Archival and Rare Book Collection, box 87, folder 29.

32. Morris, Witness, pg. 169.

33. *The Papers of Thomas Jefferson Digital Edition*, ed. Barbara B. Oberg and J. Jefferson Looney. Charlottesville: University of Virginia Press, Rotunda, 2008–2015. http://rotunda.upress.virginia.edu/founders/TSJN-01-11-02-0095 [accessed 13 Apr 2015]. Main Series, Volume 11 (1 January–6 August 1787). The context of the quote reads:

The mass of mankind under that enjoys a precious degree of liberty and happiness. It has its evils too: the principal of which is the turbulence to which it is subject. But weigh this against the oppressions of monarchy, and it becomes nothing.... Even this evil is productive of good. It prevents the degeneracy of government, and nourishes a general attention to the public affairs. I hold it that a little rebellion now and then is a good thing, and as necessary in the political world as storms in the physical. Unsuccessful rebellions indeed generally establish the encroachments on the rights of the people which have produced them. An observation of this truth should render honest republican governors so mild in their punishment of rebellions, as not to discourage them too much. It is a medicine necessary for the sound health of government.

34. Merrill D. Peterson, ed. *Thomas Jefferson: Writings* (New York: Literary Classics of the United States, 1984), 911.
35. Jonathan Smith, "The Depression of 1785 and Daniel Shays' Rebellion," *The William and Mary Quarterly* 5, no. 1 (Jan., 1948), 78.
36. *Ibid.*
37. Thomas J. Humphrey, Review of "Shays's Rebellion: The American Revolution's Final Battle," *The Journal of American History* 90, no. 2 (Sep., 2003), 625.
38. Smith, "The Depression of 1785 and Daniel Shays' Rebellion," 80.
39. *Ibid.*, 91.
40. *Ibid.*, 230.
41. *Ibid.*, 241.
42. *Ibid.*, 313.
43. *Ibid.*, 482.
44. *The Federalist 1787–88* (Norwalk, CT: The Easton Press, 1979), 161–162.
45. Bailyn, *The Debate on the Constitution* Volume 1, 216.
46. Burnett, *Letters*, Volume 8, 544.
47. Burnett, *Letters*, Volume 8, 559.
48. *The Adams Papers Digital Edition*, ed. C. James Taylor. Charlottesville: University of Virginia Press, Rotunda, 2008–2015. http://rotunda.upress.virginia.edu/founders/ADMS-04-08-02-0041 [accessed 13 Apr 2015]. Adams Family Correspondence, Volume 8, March 1787–December 1789.
49. *The Adams Papers Digital Edition*, ed. C. James Taylor. Charlottesville: University of Virginia Press, Rotunda, 2008–2015. http://rotunda.upress.virginia.edu/founders/ADMS-04-08-02-0002 [accessed 13 Apr 2015]. Adams Family Correspondence, Volume 8, March 1787–December 1789.
50. *The Papers of James Madison Digital Edition*, J. C. A. Stagg, editor. Charlottesville: University of Virginia Press, Rotunda, 2010. http://rotunda.upress.virginia.edu/founders/JSMN-01-09-02-0070 [accessed 19 Sep 2015]. Congressional Series, Volume 9 (9 April 1786–24 May 1787 and supplement 1781–1784).
51. *Ibid.*
52. Richard B. Morris, "The Confederation Period and the American Historian," *The William and Mary Quarterly* 13, no. 2 (Apr., 1956), 141.
53. Washington was no stranger to the "doom and gloom" type of correspondence which this period abounded in. It was only natural; the outcome of the War for Independence was never a foregone conclusion, and with so much riding on its outcome, naturally created some highly dramatic missives. In a September 12, 1780 letter to Louis XVI, Washington all but predicted the American collapse:

> The situation of America at this time is critical—the government without finances—its paper credit sunk, and no expedients it can adopt capable of retrieving it—the resources of the country much diminished, by a five years' war, in which it has made efforts beyond its ability—Clinton [British General] with an army of ten thousand regular troops, aided by a considerable body of militia, whom, from motives of fear and attachment he has engaged to take arms, in possession of one of our capital towns, and a large part of the State to which it belongs—the Savages desolating the other frontier—a fleet superior to that of our allies, not only to protect him against any attempt of ours, but to facilitate those he may project against us—Lord Cornwallis with seven or eight thousand men in complete possession of two states, Georgia and South Carolina—a third, North Carolina, by recent misfortunes at his mercy, his force daily increasing by an accession of adherents, whom his successes naturally procure him in a country inhabited in great part, by emigrants from England and Scotland, who have not been long enough transplanted to exchange their ancient habits and attachments, in favor of their new residence [from a facsimile in the Lloyd W. Smith archival collection, Morristown National Historical Park].

54. From George Washington to La Luzerne, 1 August 1786," Founders Online, National Archives. (http://founders.archives.gov/documents/Washington/04-04-02-0175 [last update: 2015-06-29]). Source: *The Papers of George Washington*, Confederation Series, vol. 4, *2 April 1786–31 January 1787*, ed. W.W. Abbot (Charlottesville: University Press of Virginia, 1995), pp. 185–187.

Chapter 6

1. Edmund C. Burnett, *Letters of Members of the Continental Congress* Volume 8 (Washington, D.C.: The Carnegie Institution of Washington, 1921), 572.
2. Burnett, *Letters*, Volume 8, 206.
3. *Ibid.*, 207.
4. *Ibid.*, 218.
5. William Blount, writing to Joseph Clay on June 11, 1787, observed, "The members of the Convention observe such inviolable secrecy that it is altogether unknown out of doors what they are doing." Burnett, *Letters*, Volume 8, 608.
6. *Ibid.*, 611.
7. *Ibid.*, 615.
8. Worthington Chauncey Ford, *Journals of the Continental Congress 1774–1789* Volume XXXII (Washington, D.C.: U.S. Government Printing Office, 1904), 71–72.
9. Philip B. Kurland, and Ralph Lerner, eds., *The Founders' Constitution* Volume 1 (Chicago: University of Chicago Press, 1987), 189.
10. *Ibid.*, 189.
11. Burnett, *Letters*, Volume 8, 610.
12. *The Federalist 1787–88* (Norwalk, CT: The Easton Press, 1979), 259.
13. *Ibid.*, 260.
14. Kurland and Lerner, eds., *The Founders' Constitution* Volume I, 171.
15. *Ibid.*
16. *Ibid.*
17. *Ibid.*
18. *Ibid.*
19. Burnett, *Letters*, Volume 8, 572.
20. Max Farrand, "The Federal Constitution and the Defects of The Confederation," *The American Political Science Review* 2, no. 4 (Nov., 1908), 541.
21. As quoted in Farrand, "The Federal Constitution and the Defects," 541.
22. *The Federalist 1787–88* (Norwalk: The Easton Press, 1979), 262–263.
23. *Ibid.*, 311.
24. Farrand, "The Federal Constitution and the Defects," 543.
25. Edward G. White, *American Legal History: A Very Short Introduction* (Oxford: Oxford University Press, 2014), 113.
26. Kelly and Harbison, pg. 36.
27. Kelly and Harbison, pg. 44.
28. Ford, *Journals*, Volume XXXIII, 502.
29. Ford, *Journals*, Volume XXXIII, 502.
30. Bailyn, ed., *The Debate on the Constitution* Volume 1, 15.
31. *Ibid.*, 180.
32. *Ibid.*, 181.
33. *Ibid.*, 180.
34. *Ibid.*, 225.
35. Edmund C. Burnett, *Letters of Members of the Continental Congress* Volume 8 (Washington, D.C.: The Carnegie Institution of Washington, 1921), 647.
36. *Ibid.*, 650.
37. *Ibid.*, 662.
38. *Ibid.*, 654.
39. *Ibid.*, 664.
40. *Ibid.*, 690.
41. *Ibid.*, 700.
42. *Ibid.*, 710.
43. Section VI of the Articles of Confederation states:

> No State, without the consent of the United States in Congress assembled, shall send any embassy to, or receive any embassy from, or enter into any conference, agreement, alliance or treaty with any King, Prince or State; nor shall any person holding any office of profit or trust under the United States, or any of them, accept any present, emolument, office or title of any kind whatever from any King, Prince or foreign State; nor shall the United States in Congress assembled, or any of them, grant any title of nobility.

44. Burnett, *Letters*, Volume 8, 218.
45. John Fiske, *The Critical Period of American History, 1783–1789* (Boston: Houghton, Mifflin and Company, 1899), 90.
46. *The Federalist 1787–88* (Norwalk: The Easton Press, 1979), 53.
47. *Ibid.*, 92.
48. *Ibid.*
49. *Ibid.*, 127.
50. *Ibid.*, 143.
51. *Ibid.*, 434.
52. *Ibid.*, 502.
53. Morristown NHP, Lloyd W. Smith Archival and Rare Book Collection, MORR 3330.

54. Colleen A. Sheehan, and Gary L. McDowell, eds., *Friends of the Constitution: Writings of the "Other" Federalists 1787–1788* (Indianapolis: Liberty Fund, 1998), 1.
55. *Ibid.*, 3.
56. *Ibid.*, 69.
57. *Ibid.*, 110.
58. Bernard Bailyn, ed., *The Debate on the Constitution* Volume 1 (New York: Literary Classics of the United States, 1993), 106.
59. *Ibid.*, 118–119.
60. Kurland and Lerner, eds., *The Founders' Constitution* Volume I, 158.
61. *Ibid.*, 159.
62. *Ibid.*, 161.
63. *Ibid.*, 170.
64. *Ibid.*, 165.
65. *Ibid.*, 166.
66. *Ibid.*
67. *Ibid.*, 67–68.
68. *Ibid.*, 148–149.
69. *Ibid.*, 502.
70. *Ibid.*, 622.
71. *Ibid.*, 623–624.
72. Farrand, "The Federal Constitution and and the Defects," 543.

Chapter 7

1. Ron Chernow, *Alexander Hamilton* (New York: The Penguin Press, 2004), 250.
2. John P. Kaminske, *James Madison, Champion of Liberty and Justice* (Madison, WI: Parallel Press, 2006), 17.
3. The Continental Association was formed by the first Congress to enforce the trade embargo. It was not advocating for independence.
4. Kaminski, *James Madison*, 25–26.
5. *Ibid.*, 26.
6. Jack N. Rakove, ed., *James Madison: Writings* (New York: Literary Classics of the United States, 1999), 896.
7. Rakoe, *James Madison, Writings*, 896.
8. The Chief Justices who served prior to Marshall are: 1st—John Jay; 2nd—John Rutledge; and 3rd—Oliver Ellsworth.
9. William Jay, ed., *The Life of John Jay, With Selections from His Correspondence and Miscellaneous Papers* (Facsimile) (New York: J. & J. Harper, 1833), 10.
10. *Ibid.*, 11.
11. *Ibid.*, 35.
12. *Ibid.*
13. William Murchison, *The Cost of Liberty: The Life of John Dickinson* (Wilmington, DE: Intercollegiate Studies Institute, 2013), 96.
14. Jay, *The Life of John Jay*, 38.
15. *Ibid.*, 45.
16. *Ibid.*, 57.
17. *Ibid.*
18. *Ibid.*, 112.
19. *Ibid.*, 113.
20. *Ibid.*, 69–70.
21. *Ibid.*, 107.
22. *Ibid.*, 96.
23. *Ibid.*
24. *Ibid.*, 118.
25. *Ibid.*, 121.
26. *Ibid.*, 252.
27. *Ibid.*, 239.
28. *Ibid.*, 241.
29. *Ibid.*, 247. Two other letters are indicative of the atmosphere of the time among the elite. In a letter to George Washington, dated March 16, 1786, Jay wrote:
   Experience has pointed out errors in our national government which call for correction, and which threaten to blast the fruit we expected from our tree of liberty. An opinion begins to prevail that a general Convention for revising the articles of confederation would be expedient. Whether the people are yet ripe for such a measure, or whether the system proposed to be attained by it is only to be expected from calamity and commotion, is difficult to ascertain. I think we are in a delicate situation, and a variety of considerations and circumstances give me uneasiness [*ibid.*, 242–243].
Later that summer, Washington responded to Jay on August 15, from Mount Vernon:
   Your sentiments, that our affairs are drawing rapidly to a crisis, accord with my own. What the event will be is also beyond the reach of my foresight. We have errors to correct. *We have, probably, had too good an opinion of human nature in forming our confederation.* Experience has taught us, that men will not adopt, and carry into execution, measures the best calculated for their own good, without the intervention of a coercive power. I do not conceive we can exist long as a nation, without having lodged somewhere a power which will pervade the whole Union, in as energetic a manner as the authority of the different State governments extends over the several States [emphasis in original, *ibid.*, 247].
Jay wrote to Thomas Jefferson in Paris on August 18, 1786:

I have long thought, and become daily more convinced, that the construction of our federal government is fundamentally wrong. To vest legislative, judicial, and executive powers in one and the same body of men, and that, too, in a body daily changing its members, can never be wise. In my opinion those three great departments of sovereignty should be for ever separated, and so distributed as to serve as checks on each other. But these are subjects that have long been familiar to you, and on which you are too well informed not to anticipate every thing that I might say on them [*ibid.*, 250].

30. Phocion was an Athenian statesmen and general who ruled from 322–318 BCE.

31. William Kent, ed., *Memoirs and Letters of James Kent, LL.D* (facsimile) (Boston: Little, Brown, and Company, 1898), 300–303.

32. This story was the topic of *America Writes Its History*. by Jude Pfister, and published by McFarland in 2014.

Chapter 8

1. Publius Valerius Publicola was a founder of the Roman republic in ca. 509 BCE. Hamilton had used this name before in essays and was clearly impressed with the imagery of the founder of the Roman republic as a guide for the founder of the American republic.

2. *The Federalist 1787–88* (Norwalk, CT: The Easton Press, 1979), 1–5.

3. Richard B. Morris, *The Peacemakers: The Great Powers and American Independence* (New York: Harper & Row, Publishers, 1965), 5.

4. *The Federalist 1787–88* (Norwalk, CT: The Easton Press, 1979), 6.
5. *Ibid.*, 19.
6. *Ibid.*, 26.
7. *Ibid.*, 27.
8. *Ibid.*, 38.
9. *Ibid.*, 48.
10. *Ibid.*, 54.
11. *Ibid.*, 55.
12. *Ibid.*, 56.
13. *Ibid.*, 57.
14. *Ibid.*, 58.
15. *Ibid.*, 63.
16. *Ibid.*, 90.
17. *Ibid.*, 91.
18. John Maxcy Zane, *The Story of Law* (Indianapolis: The Liberty Fund, 1998), 338–339.

19. *The Federalist 1787–88* (Norwalk, CT: The Easton Press, 1979), 127.
20. *Ibid.*, 128.
21. *Ibid.*, 129.
22. *Ibid.*, 135.
23. *Ibid.*, 157.
24. *Ibid.*, 187.
25. *Ibid.*, 190.
26. *Ibid.*
27. *Ibid.*, 191.
28. *Ibid.*, 195.
29. *Ibid.*, 215.
30. *Ibid.*, 222.
31. *Ibid.*, 233.
32. *Ibid.*
33. *Ibid.*, 236.
34. *Ibid.*, 244.
35. *Ibid.*, 250.
36. *Ibid.*, 257.
37. As quoted in *Ibid.*, 528.
38. *Ibid.*, 261.
39. *Ibid.*, 266.
40. *Ibid.*, 320.
41. *Ibid.*, 322.
42. *Ibid.*
43. *Ibid.*, 335.
44. A term coined by Supreme Court Associate Justice Stephen Breyer and used as the title of his 2005 book.
45. *The Federalist 1787–88* (Norwalk, CT: The Easton Press, 1979), 450.
46. *Ibid.*, 451.
47. *Ibid.*, 456.
48. *Ibid.*, 519.
49. *Ibid.*
50. *Ibid.*, 520.
51. *Ibid.*, 522.
52. *Ibid.*
53. *Ibid.*, 545.
54. *Ibid.*, 550.
55. *Ibid.*, 553.
56. *Ibid.*, 554.
57. *Ibid.*, 556.
58. *Ibid.*, 564.
59. *Ibid.*, 572.
60. *Ibid.*
61. *Ibid.*, 576.
62. Zane, *The Story of Law*, 336.
63. *Ibid.*, 722.
64. Ellis Sandoz, ed., *The Roots of Liberty: Magna Carta, Ancient Constitution, and the Anglo-American Tradition of Rule of Law* (Indianapolis: The Liberty Fund, 1993), 4–5.
65. *The Federalist 1787–88* (Norwalk: The Easton Press, 1979), 94.

66. As quoted in Sandoz, *The Roots of Liberty*, 8.
67. *Ibid.*, 10.
68. Merrill D. Peterson, ed., *Thomas Jefferson: Writings* (New York: Literary Classics of the United States, 1984), 1321.
69. *Ibid.*, 1323.
70. *Ibid.*, 1325.
71. *Ibid.*, 1326.
72. *Ibid.*, 1329.
73. Will Durant, *Our Oriental Heritage* (Norwalk, CT: The Easton Press, 1992), 29.
74. Rene Wormser and Eric Nelson, among others.
75. See Eric Nelson, *The Royalist Revolution: Monarchy and The American Founding* (Cambridge: Harvard University Press, 2014).
76. Zane, *The Story of Law*, 148.
77. Rene A. Wormser, *The Story of Law and the Men Who Mad It—From the Earliest Times to the Present* (New York: Simon and Schuster, 1962), 268.
78. *Ibid.*, 294.
79. *Ibid.*

Chapter 9

1. Herbert W. Schneider, *A History of American Philosophy* (New York: Columbia University Press, 1963), 39.
2. http://plato.stanford.edu/entries/scottish-18th (accessed 11/12/13). It should be pointed out the morals in this sense does not *necessarily* denote a religious meaning. Morals are in this sense more of a community standard of behavior accepted in a general way and passed down through generations with modifications as necessary. The foundation of those morals is another issue.
3. http://plato.stanford.edu/entries/scottish-18th (accessed 11/12/13).
4. Roy Branson, "James Madison and the Scottish Enlightenment," *Journal of the History of Ideas* 40, no. 2 (Apr.-Jun., 1979), 236.
5. Daniel Walker Howe, "Why the Scottish Enlightenment was useful to the Framers of the American Constitution," *Comparative Studies in Society and History* 31, no. 3 (Jul., 1989), 580.
6. Schneider, *A History of American Philosophy*, 29.
7. *Ibid.*
8. Joseph L. Blau, *Men and Movements in American Philosophy* (New York: Prentice-Hall, 1953), 37.
9. Edward G. White, *American Legal History: A Very Short Introduction* (Oxford: Oxford University Press, 2014), 54.
10. Nicholas Vincent, *Magna Carta: A Very Short Introduction* (Oxford: Oxford University Press, 2012) 71.
11. *Ibid.*, 4.
12. *Ibid.*, 81–82.
13. Winston Churchill, in his *A History of the English Speaking Peoples*, sees the Magna Carta in a very reasonable light. For Churchill, the charter's essence was in the establishment of the rule of law, however unrelated to today that thirteenth century concept was. Churchill wrote:

Magna Carta had such authority that, if the king broke his promises, the Charter gave the council of twenty-five barons the right to go to war with the monarch. The term Magna Carta, at the time, was more a reference to its size than its then constitutional significance; this Great Charter was larger than the very much shorter Forest Charter of 1217. From the mid-fourteenth century Magna Carta was a benchmark in law making. The seventeenth-century authors of the Grand Remonstrance and Petition of Right believed they were following its sound constitutional footsteps. By the twentieth century there was a school that believed the document was nothing to do with common man and all to do with baronial interests. The true meaning of Magna Carta may be what it has come to signify [*A History of the English Speaking Peoples*, One-volume abridgement (New York, Skyhorse Publishing, 2011), 107].

14. Vincent, *Magna Carta: A Very Short Introduction*, 102.
15. *Ibid.*, 1.
16. *Ibid.*, 15–16.
17. John Maxcy Zane, *The Story of Law* (Indianapolis: The Liberty Fund, 1998), 337.
18. Yale Law School The Avalon Project, http://avalon.law.yale.edu/medieval/saxlaw.asp accessed 6-26-15.
19. Merrill D. Peterson, ed., *Thomas Jefferson: Writings* (New York: Literary Classics of the United States, 1984), 1501.
20. Blau, *Men and Movements*, 73.
21. Peter Gay, *The Enlightenment: An Interpretation, The Science of Freedom* (New York: W.W. Norton & Company, 1969), 555.
22. *Ibid.*, 563.

Conclusion

1. Ralph Ketcham, *James Madison, A Biography* (Charlottesville: University of Virginia Press, 1990), 240.
2. Yale Law School, The Avalon Project http://avalon.law.yale.edu/18th_century/artconf.asp accessed 3-29-15.
3. Akil Reed Amar, *America's Constitution, A Biography* (New York: Random House, 2005), 26.
4. John Maxcy Zane, *The Story of Law* (Indianapolis: The Liberty Fund, 1998), 340.

Appendix 1

1. Yale Law School, The Avalon Project http://avalon.law.yale.edu/18th_century/annapoli.asp accessed 9-21-15.

Appendix 2

1. http://founders.archives.gov/documents/Hamilton/01-02-02-1179 accessed 3-29-15.

Appendix 3

1. Hellmut Haupt-Lehmann, and Lawrence C. Wroth, *The Book in America: A History of the Making and Selling of Books in the United States* (New York: R. R. Bowker, 1964), 23.
2. William J. Barrow, "Black Writing Ink of the Colonial Period," *The American Archivist* 11, no. 4 (Oct., 1948), 294.
3. *Ibid.*
4. The Iron Gall Ink Website http://irongallink.org/igi_index8a92.html accessed 04 June 2015.
5. *Ibid.*
6. Haupt, *The Book in America*, 21.
7. *Ibid.*, 22.
8. Barrow, "Black Writing Ink," 292.
9. Michael F. Suarez and H. R. Woudhuysen, eds. *The Oxford Companion to the Book* Volume 1 (Oxford: Oxford University Press, 2010), 79.
10. Dard Hunter, *Papermaking: The History and Technique of an Ancient Craft* (New York: Dover Publications, 1978), 224–225.
11. Haupt, *The Book in America*, 17.
12. As quoted in Hunter, *Papermaking*, in footnote, 235.
13. Haupt, *The Book in America*, 22–23.
14. Haupt, *The Book in America*, 18.
15. Suarez and Woudhuysen, eds., *The Oxford Companion to the Book*, Volume 1, 428.
16. Haupt, *The Book in America*, 65.
17. Haupt, *The Book in America*, 17.
18. Haupt, *The Book in America*, 24.
19. Suarez and Woudjuysen, eds., *The Oxford Companion to the Book*, Volume 1, 427.

Bibliography

Books

Adair, Douglass. *Fame and the Founding Fathers*. Indianapolis: Liberty Fund, 1998.
Alden, John Richard. *The American Revolution, 1775–1783*. New York: Harper Torchbooks, 1962.
Amar, Akhil Reed. *America's Constitution: A Biography*. New York: Random House, 2005.
Ambrose, Douglas, and Robert W. T. Martin, eds. *The Many Faces of Alexander Hamilton: The Life and Legacy of America's Most Elusive Founding Father*. New York: New York University Press, 2007.
Bailyn, Bernard. *The Ideological Origins of the American Revolution*. Cambridge: Harvard University Press, 1992.
_____, ed. *The Debate on the Constitution*. New York: Literary Classics of the United States, 1993.
Barzilay, Karen Northrop. "Fifty Gentlemen Total Strangers: A Portrait of the First Continental Congress." PhD diss., The College of William and Mary, 2009.
Basbanes, Nicholas A. *On Paper: The Everything of Its Two-Thousand-Year History*. New York: Vintage Books, 2014.
Bemis, Samuel Flagg. *The Diplomacy of the American Revolution*. Bloomington: Indiana University Press, 1965.
Blau, Joseph L. *Men and Movements in American Philosophy*. New York: Prentice-Hall, 1953.
Boorstin, Daniel J. *The Americans: The Colonial Experience*. New York: Vintage Books, 1958.
_____. *The Lost World of Thomas Jefferson*. Chicago: University of Chicago Press, 1981.
_____. *The Mysterious Science of the Law*. Chicago: University of Chicago Press, 1996.
Bowen, Catherine Drinker. *Miracle at Philadelphia: The Story of the Constitutional Convention May to September 1787*. Boston: Little, Brown, 1986.
Brumwell, Stephen. *George Washington, Gentleman Warrior*. New York: Quercus, 2012.
Burnett, Edmund C. *The Continental Congress*. New York: W.W. Norton and Company, 1964.
_____. *Letters of Members of the Continental Congress*. Washington, D.C.: The Carnegie Institution of Washington, 1921.
Chernow, Ron. *Alexander Hamilton*. New York: The Penguin Press, 2004.
Churchill, Winston. *A History of the English Speaking Peoples*. One-volume abridgment. Edited by Christopher Lee. New York: Skyhorse Publishing, 2011.
Colbourn, Trevor. *The Lamp of Experience: Whig History and the Intellectual Origins of the American Revolution*. Indianapolis: Liberty Fund, 1998.

Davis, Burke. *The Campaign That Won America: The Story of Yorktown.* N.p.: Eastern Acorn Press, 1979.
Durant, Will. *Our Oriental Heritage.* Norwalk, CT: The Easton Press, 1992.
Ellis, Joseph. *American Sphinx—The Character of Thomas Jefferson.* New York: Knopf, 1997.
Farrand, Max. *The Fathers of the Constitution: A Chronicle of the Establishment of the Union.* New Haven, CT: Yale University Press, 1921.
_____. *The Framing of the Constitution of the United States.* New Haven, CT: Yale University Press, 1913.
Fiske, John. *The Critical Period of American History, 1783–1789.* Boston: Houghton Mifflin, 1899.
Fitzpatrick, John C., ed. *The Writings of George Washington from the Original Manuscript Sources 1745–1799.* Washington, D.C.: United States Government Printing Office, 1938.
Flower, Milton E. *John Dickinson, Conservative Revolutionary.* Charlottesville: Friends of the John Dickinson Mansion, 1983.
Ford, Worthington Chauncey. *Journals of the Continental Congress 1774–1789.* Washington, D.C.: U.S. Government Printing Office, 1904.
Freeman, Joanne B., ed. *Alexander Hamilton: Writings.* New York: Literary Classics of the United States, 2001.
Galloway, Joseph. *Historical and Political Reflections on the Rise and Progress of the American Rebellion.* London: G. Wilkie, 1780.
Garner, Bryan, ed. *Black's Law Dictionary.* St. Paul, MN: West Group, 1999.
Gay, Peter. *The Enlightenment: An Interpretation, The Science of Freedom.* New York: W.W. Norton & Company, 1969.
Haupt-Lehmann, Hellmut, and Lawrence C. Wroth. *The Book in America: A History of the Making and Selling of Books in the United States.* New York: R.R. Bowker, 1964.
Hielscher, Udo. *Financing the American Revolution: The American Revolution and the Origins of Wall Street in Contemporary Financial Documents.* New York: Museum of American Financial History, 2003.
Holton, Woody. *Unruly Americans and the Origins of the Constitution.* New York: Hill and Wang, 2007.
Horwitz, Morton J. *The Transformation of American Law 1780–1860.* Cambridge: Harvard University Press, 1977.
Hunter, Dard. *Papermaking: The History and Technique of an Ancient Craft.* New York: Dover Publications, 1978.
Jay, William, ed. *The Life of John Jay, With Selections from His Correspondence and Miscellaneous Papers.* Facsimile. New York: J. & J. Harper, 1833.
Jensen, Merrill. *The New Nation: A History of the United States During the Confederation, 1781–1789.* New York: Vintage Books, 1950.
Kaminske, John P. *James Madison: Champion of Liberty and Justice.* Madison, WI: Parallel Press, 2006.
Keith, Arthur Berriedale. *An Introduction to British Constitutional Law.* Oxford: Oxford University Press, 1931.
Kelly, Alfred, and Winfred A. Harbison. *The American Constitution: Its Origins and Development.* New York: W.W. Norton & Company, 1976.
Kent, William, ed. *Memoirs and Letters of James Kent, LL.D.* Facsimile. Boston: Little, Brown, 1898.
Ketcham, Ralph. *James Madison: A Biography.* Charlottesville: University of Virginia Press, 1990.
Kurland, Philip B., and Ralph Lerner, eds. *The Founders' Constitution.* Chicago: University of Chicago Press, 1987.

LeMay, J.A. Leo, ed. *Benjamin Franklin: Writings*. New York: Literary Classics of the United States, 1987.
Malone, Dumas. *Jefferson the Virginian*. Boston: Little, Brown, 1948.
McDonald, Forrest. *Alexander Hamilton: A Biography*. New York, W.W. Norton & Company, 1982.
Morris, Richard B. *The Peacemakers: The Great Powers and American Independence*. New York: Harper & Row, 1965.
_____. *Witness at the Creation: Hamilton, Madison, Jay, and the Constitution*. New York: Henry Holt, 1985.
Murchison, William. *The Cost of Liberty: The Life of John Dickinson*. Wilmington, DE: Intercollegiate Studies Institute, 2013.
Nye, Russel Blaine. *The Cultural Life of the New Nation, 1776–1830*. New York: Harper Torchbooks, 1960.
O'Shaughnessy, Andrew Jackson. *The Men Who Lost America: British Leadership, the American Revolution, and the Fate of Empire*. New Haven, CT: Yale University Press, 2013.
Peterson, Merrill D., ed. *Thomas Jefferson: Writings*. New York: Literary Classics of the United States, 1984.
Pfister, Jude M. "Constitutional Development in the United States Supreme Court during the 1790s." DLitt diss., Drew University, 2007.
Pound, Roscoe. *The Formative Era of American Law*. Boston: Little, Brown, 1938.
Rakove, Jack N., ed. *James Madison: Writings*. New York: Literary Classics of the United States, 1999.
Rhodehamel, John, ed. *The American Revolution: Writings from the War of Independence*. New York: Literary Classics of the United States, 2001.
Richard, Carl J. *The Founders and the Classics: Greece, Rome, and the American Enlightenment*. Cambridge: Harvard University Press, 1994.
Sandoz, Ellis, ed. *The Roots of Liberty: Magna Carta, Ancient Constitution, and the Anglo-American Tradition of Rule of Law*. Indianapolis: The Liberty Fund, 1993.
Schneider, Herbert W. *A History of American Philosophy*. New York: Columbia University Press, 1963.
Sheehan, Collen A., and Gary L. McDowell, eds. *Friends of the Constitution: Writings of the "Other" Federalists, 1787–1788*. Indianapolis: Liberty Fund, 1998.
Sheer, George F. ed. *Private Yankee Doodle; Being a Narrative of Some of the Adventures, Dangers and Sufferings of a Revolutionary Soldier*. N.p.: Eastern Acorn Press, 1979.
Smith, Stephen. *Taxation: A Very Short Introduction*. Oxford: Oxford University Press, 2015.
Staloff, Darren. *Hamilton, Adams, Jefferson: The Politics of Enlightenment and the American Founding*. New York: Hill and Wang, 2005.
Stille, Charles J. *Major-General Anthony Wayne and the Pennsylvania Line in the Continental Army*. Philadelphia: J.B. Lippincott Company, 1893.
Suarez, Michael F., and H.R. Woudhuysen, eds. *The Oxford Companion to the Book*. Oxford: Oxford University Press, 2010.
Szatmary, David P. *Shays' Rebellion: The Making of an Agrarian Insurrection*. Amherst: The University of Massachusetts Press, 1980.
Thompson, C. Bradley, ed. *The Revolutionary Writings of John Adams*. Indianapolis: Liberty Fund, 2000.
Vincent, Nicholas. *Magna Carta: A Very Short Introduction*. Oxford: Oxford University Press, 2012.
Von Holst, H. *The Constitutional and political History of the United States, Vol. 1*. Chicago: Callaghan and Company, 1889.
White, G. Edward. *American Legal History: A Very Short Introduction*. Oxford: Oxford University Press, 2014.

Womersley, David, ed. *Liberty and American Experience in the Eighteenth Century*. Indianapolis: Liberty Fund, 2006.

Wormser, Rene A. *The Story of Law and the Men Who Mad It—From the Earliest Times to the Present*. New York: Simon & Schuster, 1962.

Wright, Robert E., and David J. Cowen. *Financial Founding Fathers: The Men Who Made America Rich*. Chicago: The University of Chicago Press, 2006.

Wright, Robert E. *One Nation Under Debt: Hamilton, Jefferson, and the History of What We Owe*. New York: McGraw-Hill, 2008.

Zane, John Maxcy. *The Story of Law*. Indianapolis: The Liberty Fund, 1998.

Websites

Adams Family Papers: An Electronic Archive. Massachusetts Historical Society. http://www.masshist.org/digitaladams/ [accessed 04 February 2016].

The American Archivist Website. http://americanarchivist.org/doi/pdf/10.17723/aarc.11.4.903256p5lp2g3354 [accessed 04 June 2015].

The Avalon Project, Yale Law School. http://avalon.law.yale.edu/18th_century/fed31.asp [accessed March 19, 2015]. http://avalon.law.yale.edu/17th_century/mayflower.asp [accessed 15 Sept 2015].

Constitutional Documents and Records, 1776–1787, Volume 1: Constitutional Documents and Records, 1776–1787 [accessed 29 Jul 2014].

Founders Online, National Archives. (http://founders.archives.gov/documents/Washington/04-04-02-0175 [last update: 2015-06-29]). Source: *The Papers of George Washington*, Confederation Series, vol. 4, *2 April 1786–31 January 1787*, ed. W. W. Abbot. Charlottesville: University Press of Virginia, 1995, pp. 185–187 [accessed 01 July 2015].

Harris, Ian, "Edmund Burke," *The Stanford Encyclopedia of Philosophy* (Spring 2012 Edition), Edward N. Zalta, ed., URL = http://plato.stanford.edu/archives/spr2012/entries/burke/ [accessed 16 Sept 2015].

The Iron Gall Ink Website. http://irongallink.org/igi_index8a92.html [accessed 04 June 2015].

Kaminski, John P., Gaspare J. Saladino, Richard Leffler, Charles H. Schoenleber and Margaret A. Hogan, eds. *The Documentary History of the Ratification of the Constitution Digital Edition*. Charlottesville: University of Virginia Press, 2009. http://rotunda.upress.virginia.edu/founders/RNCN-01-01-02-0003-0012 [accessed 16 Mar 2015].

Nuxoll, Elizabeth M. ed. *The Selected Papers of John Jay Digital Edition*. Elizabeth M. Nuxoll, editor. Charlottesville: University of Virginia Press, 2014–. http://rotunda.upress.virginia.edu/founders/JNJY-01-03-02-0163 [accessed 17 Mar 2015].

Oberg, Barbara B., and J. Jefferson Looney, eds. *The Papers of Thomas Jefferson Digital Edition*. Charlottesville: University of Virginia Press, Rotunda, 2008–2015. http://rotunda.upress.virginia.edu/founders/TSJN-01-14-02-0062 [accessed 09 Feb 2015].

Smithsonian Magazine. http://www.smithsonianmag.com/history-archaeology/Starving-Settlers-in-Jamestown-Colony-Resorted-to-Eating-A-Child-205472161.html [visited 11-22-13].

Springfield Armory National Historic Site. http://www.nps.gov/spar/learn/historyculture/arsenal-at-springfield.htm [accessed 4-16-15].

Taylor, C. James, ed. *The Adams Papers Digital Edition*. Charlottesville: University of Virginia Press, Rotunda, 2008–2015. http://rotunda.upress.virginia.edu/founders/ADMS-06-14-02-0009 [accessed 27 Feb 2015].

Zalta, Edward N., Uri Nodelman, Colin Allen, eds. *Stanford Encyclopedia of Philosophy*. http://plato.stanford.edu/entries/scottish-18th [accessed 11/12/13].

Articles

Adair, Douglass. "The Authorship of the Disputed Federalist Papers." *The William and Mary Quarterly* Third Series, 1, no. 2 (Apr. 1944), 97–122.

———. "The Authorship of the Disputed Federalist Papers: Part II." *The William and Mary Quarterly* Third Series, 1, no. 3 (July 1944), 235–264.

———. "That Politics May be Reduced to a Science." *Huntington Library Quarterly* 20, no. 4, (Aug. 1957), 343–360.

Adams, Randolph G. "A View of Cornwallis's Surrender at Yorktown." *The American Historical Review* 37, no. 1 (Oct. 1931), 25–49.

Baack, Ben. "Forging a Nation State: The Continental Congress and the Financing of the War of American Independence." *The Economic History Review* New Series, 54, no. 4 (Nov. 2001), 639–656.

Barrow, William J. "Black Writing Ink of the Colonial Period." *The American Archivist* 11, no. 4 (Oct., 1948), 291–307.

Branson, Roy. "James Madison and the Scottish Enlightenment." *Journal of the History of Ideas* 40, no. 2 (Apr.-June 1979), 235–250.

Brown, E. Francis. "Shays's Rebellion." *The American Historical Review* 36, no. 4 (July 1931), 776–778.

Duncan, Christopher M. "Men of a Different Faith: The Anti-Federalist Ideal in Early American Political Thought." *Polity* 26, no. 3 (Spring, 1994), 387–415.

Erler, Edward J. "The Problem of the Public Good in 'The Federalist.'" *Polity* 13, no. 4 (summer, 1981), 649–667.

Farrand, Max. "The Federal Constitution and the Defects of the Confederation." *The American Political Science Review* 2, no. 4 (Nov. 1908), 532–544.

Ford, Paul Leicester, and Edward Gaylord Bourne. "The Authorship of the Federalist." *The American Historical Review* 2, no. 4 (July 1897), 675–687.

Friedenwald, Herbert. "The Continental Congress." *The Pennsylvania Magazine of History and Biography* 19, no. 2 (1895), 197–207.

Frisch, Morton J. Review of "The Federalist." *The Journal of Southern History* 27, no. 3 (Aug. 1961), 403–405.

Garver, Frank Harmon. "The Transition from the Continental Congress to the Congress of the Confederation." *Pacific Historical Review* 1, no. 2 (June 1932), 221–234.

Goodwin, Mary R.M. "Writing Equipment in the Eighteenth Century." Colonial Williamsburg, Inc., 1964.

Holton, Woody. Review of "Shays's Rebellion: The American Revolution's Final Battle." *The William and Mary Quarterly* 60, no. 3 (July 2003), 689–693.

Howe, Daniel Walker. "Why the Scottish Enlightenment was Useful to the Framers of the American Constitution." *Comparative Studies in Society and History* 31, no. 3 (July 1989), 572–587.

———. "The Political Psychology of The Federalist." *The William and Mary Quarterly* Third Series 44, no. 3, The Constitution of the United States (July 1987), 485–509.

Humphrey, Thomas J. Review of "Shays's Rebellion: The American Revolution's Final Battle." *The Journal of American History* 90, no. 2 (Sep. 2003), 625.

Israel, Jonathan. "Enlightenment! Which Enlightenment?" *Journal of the History of Ideas* 67, no. 3 (July 2006), 523–545.

Jensen, Merrill. "The Idea of a National Government During the American Revolution." *Political Science Quarterly* 58, no. 3 (Sept. 1943), 356–379.

———. "The Articles of Confederation: A Re-Interpretation." *Pacific Historical Review* 6, no. 2 (June 1937), 120–142.

Jezierski, John V. "Parliament or People: James Wilson and Blackstone on the Nature

and Location of Sovereignty." *Journal of the History of Ideas* Vol. 32, No. 1 (Jan.-Mar. 1971), 95–106.
Jillson, Calvin C., and Rick K. Wilson. "A Social Choice Model of Politics: Insights into the Demise of the U. S. Continental Congress." *Legislative Studies Quarterly* 12, no. 1 (Feb. 1987), 5–32.
Kaplan, Lawrence S. Review of "The Perils of Peace: America's Struggle for Survival after Yorktown." *The Journal of American History* 95, no. 1 (June 2008), 189–190.
Larson, Harold. "Alexander Hamilton: The Fact and Fiction of His Early Years." *The William and Mary Quarterly* Third Series, vol. 9, no. 2 (Apr. 1952), 139–141.
Lewis, Anthony M. "Jefferson's Summary View as a Chart of Political Union." *The William and Mary Quarterly* 5, no. 1 (Jan. 1948), 34–51.
Lienesch, Michael. "Historical Theory and Political Reform: Two Perspectives on Confederation Politics." *The Review of Politics* 45, no. 1 (Jan. 1983), 94–115.
Lokken, Roy N. "The Concept of Democracy in Colonial Political Thought." *The William and Mary Quarterly* 3d ser., 16, no. 4 (October 1959), 568–580.
Manzer, Robert A. "A Science of Politics: Hume, The Federalist, and the Politics of Constitutional Attachment." *Journal of Political Science* 45, no. 3 (July 2001), 508–518.
Mason, Alpheus Thomas. "The Federalist—A Split Personality." *The American Historical Review* 57, no. 3 (Apr. 1952), 625–643.
McLaughlin, A.C. Review of *The American Revolution: A Constitutional Interpretation*, by Charles Howard McIlwain. *The American Political Science Review* 18, no. 1 (Feb. 1924), 181.
Morris, Richard B. "The Confederation Period and the American Historian." *The William and Mary Quarterly* 13, no. 2 (Apr. 1956), 139–156.
Mullett, Charles F. "Coke and the American Revolution." *Economica* no. 38 (Nov. 1932), 457.
Parker, Rachel R. "Shays' Rebellion: An Episode in American State-Making." *Sociological Perspectives* 34, no. 1 (Spring, 1991), 95–116.
Peden, William. "Some Notes Concerning Thomas Jefferson's Libraries." *The William and Mary Quarterly* 1, no. 3 (July 1944), 265–272.
Peterson, Charles E. "Carpenter's Hall." *Transactions of the American Philosophical Society* 43, no. 1 (1953), 96–128.
Reeves, Jesse S. "The Influence of the Law of Nature Upon International Law in the United States." *The American Journal of International Law* 3, no. 3 (July 1909), 547–561.
Rowland, Date Mason. "The Mount Vernon Convention; G. Mason, Alexander Henderson, Daniel of St. Thomas Jenifer, T. Stone and Samuel Chase." *The Pennsylvania Magazine of History and Biography* 11, no. 4 (Jan. 1888), 410–425.
Schneider, Herbert W. "The Enlightenment in Thomas Jefferson." *Ethics* 53, no. 4 (July 1943), 246–254.
Smith, Jonathan. "The Depression of 1785 and Daniel Shays' Rebellion." *The William and Mary Quarterly* 5, no. 1 (Jan. 1948), 77–94.
Weaver, David R. "Leadership, Locke, and the Federalist." *American Journal of Political Science* 41, no. 2 (Apr., 1997), 420–446.
Werner, John M. "David Hume and America." *Journal of the History of Ideas* 33, no. 3 Festschrift for Philip P. Wiener (July–Sep. 1972), 439–456.
Wilson, Francis G. "The Federalist on Public Opinion." *The Public Opinion Quarterly* 6, no. 4 (Winter 1942), 563–575.
Wilson, Rick K., and Calvin Jillson. "Leadership patterns in the Continental Congress: 1774–1789." *Legislative Studies Quarterly* 14, no. 1 (Feb. 1989), 5–37.

Index

Adams, John (1735–1826): American ambassador to Britain 91–92, 151–152; delegate to the First Continental Congress 44, 48, 49, 56–57; Treaty of Paris 29–31, 34; view of sovereignty 147
Adams, Samuel (1722–1803): ardent radical 40, 55, 104; fear of national power 151; Shays' Rebellion 116–117
American Enlightenment 211, 214–216
Annapolis Convention 97–100
Arnold, Benedict (1741–1801) 69
Articles of Association 51, 57
Articles of Confederation 75–84; compared to *Federalist* papers 185, 188, 190–191, 193, 196; problems with the Articles and their revision 107, 125, 127; replaced by Constitution 130–132; written by John Dickinson 69

Blackstone, William (1723–1780) 60, 103, 181, 209
Bowdoin, James (1726–1790) 99, 108–110, 113, 121, 125–126
Burke, Edmund (1729–1797) 63

Carleton, Guy Sir (1724–1808) 29
Carpenter's Hall 43–46
classical literature, and reliance on by the Founders 73–74, 101, 158, 191, 205, 211
Clinton, George (New York governor [1739–1812]) 119, 170, 181, 185–186
Clinton, Henry (British commander [1730–1795]) 10, 16–17, 25
Constitution: debates about proposed Constitution 139–143; English 40, 53–54, 61; 1787 Convention 127–139; United States 3
Continental Congress: attendance 71–73; First Congress 38–39, 51–58; Second Congress 66–83

Declaration of Rights 51, 52–57
Denny, Ebenezer (1761–1822) 24–25
Dickinson, John (1732–1808): Annapolis Convention 99; Articles of Confederation 68, 75, 77–78; Pennsylvania Farmer nickname 67; Stamp Act Congress 43; supports new Constitution 149

Federalist papers 183–210; publishing the papers 202–203
Franklin, Benjamin (1706–1790) 58, 78; paper making 232; Paris Peace Treaty 29, 31, 173
Franklin, William (royal governor of New Jersey [1730–1813]) 50–51, 53, 54

Galloway, Joseph (1731–1803) 53–55, 56
George III, King of Great Britain (1738–1820) 27–29, 166
Grasse, François-Joseph-Paul, Comte de (French admiral [1723–1788]): Yorktown campaign 14, 16–17, 20, 22–23

Hamilton, Alexander (1757–1804): Annapolis Convention 95–98; compared to James Madison 98, 100–102; Continentalist writings 225; *Federalist* papers 183–210; life 177–182; military 20; Shays' Rebellion 119–120
Henry, Patrick (1736–1799) 40, 56–57, 126, 142, 150

ink 229–231

Jay, John (1745–1829) 4; *Federalist* papers 183–210; life 164–177; Paris Peace Treaty 29–35; Shays' Rebellion 106
Jefferson, Thomas (1743–1826): author of *Summary View* 54, 59–61, 67, 68, 101, 133;

257

law 206–207; Northwest Ordinance 134; Shays' Rebellion 113, 116

Kent, James (1763–1847): remembers Hamilton 181–182
King, Rufus (1755–1827) 91, 96, 99, 124, 126, 144

Lafayette, Marie-Joseph..., Marquis de (1757–1834): at Williamsburg 16–18, 20
law, concept of 34, 55, 58–64, 70–71, 137, 183–210, 212–216

Madison, James (1751–1826): Annapolis Convention 95–98; compared to Hamilton 98, 100–102; Constitutional Convention 127–132, 142–143, 153; *Federalist* papers 183–210; life 157–164; revenue issue 88–89, 150–151; Shays' Rebellion 116, 121; thought 214
Magna Carta 204, 207, 215–217

New Jersey Plan 128, 130, 131
North (of Kirtling), Frederick North, Lord (British prime minister [1732–1792]) 28, 29, 36, 63
Northwest Ordinance 134, 137, 143

Oswald, Richard (1705–1784) 29, 34, 35, 175

paper 231–234
Paris Peace Treaty of 1783: 12, 28–37
Pennsylvania Line mutiny 7–12

Randolph, Edmund (1753–1813) 25, 37, 75, 88, 93, 111, 121, 128, 138
Rochambeau, Jean-Baptiste..., Comte de (French general [1725–1807]) 13, 15–18
Rockingham, Charles..., 2nd Marquess of (British prime minister [1730–1782]) 14, 29–30, 34

Scottish Enlightenment 159, 212–215
Shays' Rebellion 106–123
Shelburne, William, 2nd Earl of (British prime minister [1737–1805]) 29, 34, 36
sovereignty: concept 75, 76, 81, 145–150; *Federalist* papers 103–104, 183–210
Springfield Armory 111, 113, 114

taxation: concept 40, 44, 58, 63, 64, 78, 80, 88–93, 103; *Federalist* papers 183–210

Virginia Plan 128, 129, 130, 131

Washington, George (1732–1799): Alexandria and Mount Vernon Compact 93–95; Constitutional Convention 126, 129; military in 1780 7, 8, 9; Yorktown campaign 13–16, 18, 20, 22, 23
Wilson, James (1742–1798) 60–62, 152
Witherspoon, John (1723–1794) 9, 31, 159, 213, 214

Yorktown campaign 13–28